"Madison County Cookbook"

D0102500

First Edition
First Printing - July, 1994
Second Printing - August, 1994
Third Printing - September, 1994
Fourth Printing - November, 1994
Fifth Printing - January, 1995
Sixth Printing - March, 1995
Seventh Printing - May, 1995
Eighth Printing - June, 1995
Ninth Printing - July, 1995

BRENNAN PRINTING
100 Main St. • Deep River, Iowa 52222
1-800-3740 • (515) 595-2000

Madison County Cookbook
from
Madison County, Iowa

Madison County Cookbook is a taste of cooking from the 'heart' of the Heartland-- Madison County, Iowa. Madison County is also the birthplace of John Wayne and the home of the picturesque covered bridges, the locale for the popular *Bridges of Madison County* by Robert Waller.

Madison County Cookbook is an effort spearheaded by the members of St. Joseph's Parish and friends in Madison County, offering a unique look at a small community where the simple values of faith, family, and friends have not been forgotten. Madison County Cookbook was written to celebrate food, families, friends, and festivals. Here you will find recipes that are family favorites reflective of the heartland, an amalgam of different nationalities which have been passed down from one generation to another and evoke warm and happy memories when served to family and special guests. Over five hundred different recipes are featured, often with a story behind them. Many are old fashioned down-home country recipes starting from scratch; others come from ethnic backgrounds. A wide spectrum is included: applesauce cake to marinade for pork chops, meatless main dishes, decadent desserts, homemade breads....... many of them used in family festivals and on holidays.

1

Providing a bonus and stimulating interest, a patchwork of anecdotes, stories, traditions, and family activities is interspersed through the book. These add distinctive charm. Some recall memories of family and church traditions; others tell stories of historical interest or of happenings in the county. They are delightful and as you read them, they are likely to evoke family memories and traditions of your own. There are also pictures of historic sites in Madison County.

Madison County Cookbook from Madison County is a resource for those who are 'in charge of celebrations' and are looking for ways to enhance the celebration of life. It is a 'must' to be added to the cooking bookshelf for anyone who wishes to have a taste and feel for the county that so attracted Robert Kincaid.

Dedication

We dedicate this cookbook to Fr. Frank Palmer in appreciation for his support in this endeavor and for his commitment to building community and handing down tradition.

2

Thank You . . .

We thank everyone who contributed recipes, stories, anecdotes, and time to this project. We also thank everyone who gave us permission to reprint articles, especially Ted Gorman publisher of the Winterset *Madisonian.*

A special thank you to Georgia Waller for contributing her family's favorite recipe for sour cream raisin pie. Georgia is the wife of Robert Waller. A letter from her is on the following page and her recipe is found on page 353 of this cookbook. This sour cream raisin pie is mentioned in Robert Waller's book, *Slow Waltz in Cedar Bend.*

We hope those who purchase this cookbook enjoy it and share it with family and friends!

Sincerely,
The Cookbook Committee

Cover design, divider pages, and folk art graphics are by Teresa Hoffelmeyer of M.T. Woods, Winterset, Iowa. Additional designs are by Danielle Eivins.

Georgia Waller
"Artistry In Clay"

10/12/93

Dear Jana,

Enclosed find our favorite of favorite recipes for the Holidays. It comes from my father's mother. I grew up on it and so did our daughter Rachael. In our crazy lives, of late, it is sometimes all I make on a holiday!!!

I have been asked for recipes for several cookbooks of late and have turned them all down -- for once I begin -- where do I stop? However, for Madison County -- I cannot refuse! So here you are!

Sorry we missed the Covered Bridge Festival this year. We were on our way back from Europe. Today Robert leaves for his 2 week concert tour and next Tuesday I leave for Mexico to study Spanish. I won't be able to make this pie this year so I hope someone will get it from your book and make it (and enjoy it) for us!

Go well,

Georgia Waller

P.S. And --- it is so easy to make. Do be sure you use dark raisins and do send me a copy of this book. Thanks!

TABLE OF CONTENTS

M.T.

Standard Abbreviations

tsp. - teaspoon	qt. - quart
T. - tablespoon	oz. - ounce
C. - cup	lb. - pounds
f.g. - few grains	pk. - peck
pt. - pint	bu. - bushel

Guide to Weights and Measures

1 teaspoon - 60 drops	1 pound - 16 ounces
3 teaspoons - 1 tablespoon	1 cup - ½ pint
2 tablespoons - 1 fluid ounce	2 cups - 1 pint
4 tablespoons - ¼ cup	4 cups - 1 quart
5 ⅓ tablespoons - ⅓ cup	4 quarts - 1 gallon
8 tablespoons - ½ cup	8 quarts - 1 peck
16 tablespoons - 1 cup	4 pecks - 1 bushel

Substitutions and Equivalents

2 tablespoons of fat - 1 ounce
1 cup of fat - ½ pound
1 pound of butter - 2 cups
1 cup of hydrogenated fat plus ½ tsp. salt - 1 cup butter
2 cups sugar - 1 pound
2½ cups packed brown sugar - 1 pound
1⅓ cups packed brown sugar - 1 cup of granulated sugar
3½ cups of powdered sugar - 1 pound
4 cups sifted all-purpose flour - 1 pound
4½ cups sifted cake flour - 1 pound
1 ounce bitter chocolate - 1 square
4 tablespooons cocoa plus 2 teaspoon butter - 1 ounce of
  bitter chocolate
1 cup egg whites - 8 to 10 whites
1 cup egg yolks - 12 to 14 yolks
16 marshmallows - ¼ pound
1 tablespoon cornstarch - 2 tablespoons flour for thickening
1 tablespoon vinegar or lemon juice + 1 cup milk - 1 cup sour
  milk
10 graham crackers - 1 cup fine crumbs
1 cup whipping cream - 2 cups whipped
1 cup evaporated milk - 3 cups whipped
1 lemon - 3 to 4 tablespoons juice
1 orange - 6 to 8 tablespoons juice
1 cup uncooked rice - 3 to 4 cups cooked rice

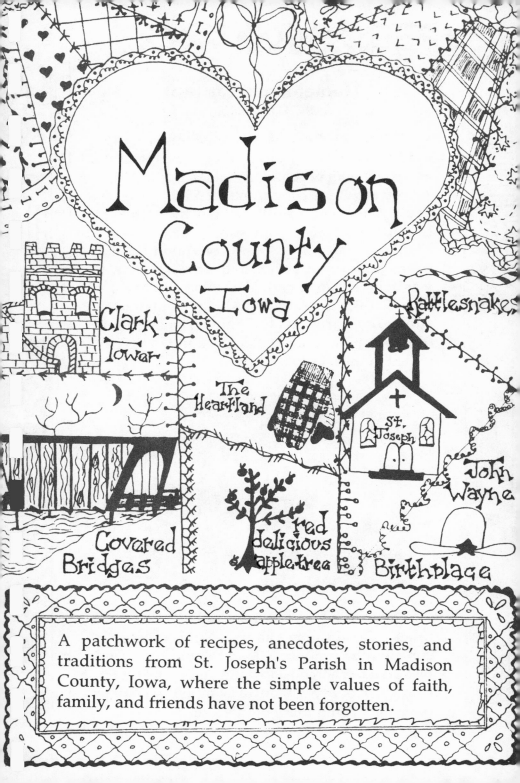

Madison County Iowa

Clark Tower

Rattlesnakes

The Heartland

St. Joseph

John Wayne

Covered Bridges

red delicious apple tree

Birthplace

A patchwork of recipes, anecdotes, stories, and traditions from St. Joseph's Parish in Madison County, Iowa, where the simple values of faith, family, and friends have not been forgotten.

Hometown Heartbeat

By: Mary Phillips

Winterset, Iowa, sits on the highest spot of Madison County and is bordered on the north and south with beautiful tree-laden, rolling hills. As you enter this community of 4,200 residents, you'll sense civic pride shown by well-kept lawns, homes, and businesses.

The focal point of the community is the courthouse in the center of the town square. It was built in 1876 of native limestone in the form of a Greek Cross, with its four wings facing streets of refurbished buildings. The interior is finished with native black walnut and oak milled in the county.

Descendants of early settlers, clubs, and other organizations have been generous in contributing money, land, buildings, and historical memorabilia to build and maintain the Madison County Historical Complex, second to none for a community of this size.

The complex has a furnished 1856 home complete with an outdoor stone privy and barn listed on the National Register, a museum filled with historical items, a country church, and several other buildings.

On the second weekend in October, Winterset is "bursting at the seams" as 50,000 people converge upon the area for the Covered Bridge Festival, held each year to honor the six covered bridges. A quilt show and the birthplace of John Wayne, Winterset's most famous personality, are additional "must sees" for festival visitors. There are many crafts, food stands, and continuous entertainment during these two days.

Winterset has 11 churches, 3 schools, an art center, library, hospital, swimming pool, six parks, and many friendly people.

Come visit us any time. You may even want to stay!

An Iowa Homecoming
(It was time my city-raised children recognized their roots.)
By: Debra Holliday

(This article appeared in both the "Denver Post" and the "Reader's Digest.")
(Reprinted with permission from Debra Holliday.)

Not long ago I went home for a few days -- home being Winterset, a very small town in the middle of Iowa. I haven't lived there for 20 years, yet whenever I go back, I'm home.

My Denver-born teenagers take great delight in the idiosyncrasies of small-town life, beginning with my phone call to reserve the motel room. The motel clerk asked for a local number in case there were problems with the reservation. I gave her my stepmother's number. "Oh," she said, "which one of the girls are you?"

Taken aback, I adjusted to the familiarity. "I'm Debbie, Dean Leslie's oldest daughter. I don't know if you knew him."

"My goodness, yes. All our kids had your dad as a music teacher in school. And they loved him."

"Well, thanks," I said. "And what is your name?"

"I'm Mrs. Matlage. My daughter-in-law is Sheri Blaschke, who lived next door to you."

"Oh, yes," I replied. "How is Sheri?"

By this time, my children were rolling their eyes and muttering, "I can't believe this. Is there anyone in that town she doesn't know?"

When we arrived, my kids stared in disbelief as we walked into a lobby filled with glass cases of antique plates and pitchers (unlocked, I might add). Not a soul was in sight. I rang the bell. We waited quite a while. My impatient city kids were accustomed to waiting in line, but waiting when no one else was around was something new. Eventually the proprietor came in from her house out back. "Had to get the cookies out of the oven," she said with a wink. The kids exchanged smirks.

We went to a local restaurant for a hamburger. The waitress set down our water glasses and stared for a few seconds. "Debbie," she asked cautiously, "is that you?"

"Yes and you're.....?" I knew she looked familiar.

"I'm Darcy's mother," she replied. And we were off. My kids scrunched down in their seats.

She took our order and soon another waitress and the cook came out to greet us. "Did you know," one asked the kids, "I used to babysit your mother when she was a little girl?" The kids may have been embarrassed, but they had to admit they had never received that kind of service in Denver.

Then came The Tour. My husband Randy and I drove past our childhood homes, our high school, the church, and where we were married. We pointed out my piano teacher's house, the woods where Randy had gone pheasant hunting, and Mayme's Hill, where every child in town had gone sledding.

On a walk around the town square, we ran into my third-grade teacher, my husband's second cousin, and one of my high school friends -- all of whom greeted us warmly and stopped to chat. It was as if our 20-year absence was only an intermission and now we were really home again.

My family and I were ready to return to Denver when I found myself low on cash and stopped at a local bank. There was only one teller in sight, a young woman I didn't recognize.

"We don't normally cash out-of-town checks," she said, "but I'll ask my supervisor."

She turned away and shouted toward an

office down the hall. "There's a woman here from Denver who wants to cash a check for $100."

"No out-of-town checks," came the reply.

"Too bad, Mom," my daughter said. "I guess even you can't bend these rules."

"Tell your supervisor I'm Dean Leslie's oldest daughter," I said. She relayed the message.

"Oh, then no problem," answered the voice. We were almost out the door when I heard the voice add, "And tell Debbie to say hello to Randy and have a safe trip home."

Now tell me, who couldn't love a town like that?

The John Wayne Birthplace
By: Jan Pergoli, Birthplace Director

(Reprinted with permission from the Madisonian.)

Even today, John Wayne is one of the most recognized people in American history. That recognition comes from the more than 200 motion pictures in which he appeared and his countless acts of charity. That's not surprising for someone born in the Midwest. And John Wayne was born in the heart of the Midwest . . . . Winterset, Iowa, to be exact.

Iowa's most famous native son, Marion Robert Morrison, arrived on the scene May 26, 1907, weighing in at a whopping 13 pounds. He was the son of the town pharmacist, Clyde and

Mary Brown Morrison, a telephone operator from Des Moines.

The modest four-room home where John Wayne was born is located downtown, two blocks south and one block east of the square, at 224 South 2nd Street, and it has been restored to its 1907 style with furnishings of the period.

In the kitchen you'll find a kerosene stove, ice box, ice tongs, and other items of the era along with a trundle bed where young Marion (John) likely slept while his mother worked nearby. The lace-curtained family parlor contains the original woodwork and stained glass; a potbellied stove, a fainting couch, and a rocking chair fill the room. The company parlor and the tiny bedroom now contain memorabilia from the Duke's long movie career. Included in the John Wayne Birthplace is the black eye patch he wore in the Academy Award winning movie "True Grit" and the suitcase he used in "Stagecoach." There also are special autographed

16

letters from John Wayne's friends: Jimmy Stewart, George Burns, Ronald Reagan, Maureen O'Hara, Lucille Ball, Gene Autry, Kirk Douglas, and Bob Hope. There also is an impressive photograph collection containing family photos and scenes from his movies.

C.H.I.R.C.H. - The Bridges of Scenic Madison County
By: Dave Braga, Madisonian Editor

(Reprinted with permission from the Madisonian.)

Madison County's six remaining covered bridges have a storied history with tales ranging from those of awe and horror to those of love and romance.

While Madison County's covered bridges carry with them a sense of local pride and treasure, most local folks would have a difficult time remembering the names of all the bridges. Here's a quick little trick which might help, however. It's "C.H.I.R.C.H." - each letter in the make-believe word can be used to quickly reference the names of all the remaining bridges: Cedar Covered Bridge; Hogback Covered Bridge; Imes Covered Bridge; Roseman Covered Bridge; Cutler-Donahue Covered Bridge, and Holliwell Covered Bridge.

Our most famous bridge is Roseman. It is the bridge that is mentioned in the book, The Bridges of Madison County by Robert Waller. Roseman Bridge is also known as the "haunted bridge."

Roseman Bridge

(Reprinted with permission from the Madisonian.)

One story has it that long ago a young man was falsely accused of theft by a father who resented his daughter's apparent interest in the boy. As was often the custom during pioneer days, "justice" was to be obtained quickly by means of a lynching. So, the father and two other men caught the stranger and strung him up from the center rafter of the Roseman bridge.

The men felt the nuisance to be rid of and forgotten about, when, to everyone's amazement, a hole appeared in the bridge's roof the next day and no trace of the hanged man was to be found.

Local legend also has it that there is a perpetual cold spot in the center of the bridge, even on the warmest days. And something happens to dogs that wander over the bridge which makes their hackles rise and often sets them to howling uncontrollably.

Perhaps the tale most often heard is that of one dark night in 1892. Two posses had formed to hunt an escapee of the Madison County Jail. The posses were approaching the bridge from each direction when they spotted the man entering the bridge. Both groups broke into a wild run so as to prevent the man from fleeing the bridge, and in all the excitement, their trapped victim is said to have uttered a wild cry in his panic and raised through the air, right on out through the roof of the bridge. In the stir that followed, one man was accidentally shot in the leg by another and the escapee was never found. It was decided that any man capable of such a feat must be innocent anyway.

Some men among the posse say the man climbed up the framework of the bridge and escaped through a hole already there. But no matter what the route of escape, the man's spirit is said to haunt the bridge on misty summer nights. Fishermen, among others, have vouched for the raucous laughter from atop the bridge, as

19

well as footsteps running across the roof. The escape hole has long since been mended, but signs of the repair job are still visible as the legends linger.

McBride - The Seventh Bridge
By: Teresa Hoffelmeyer

Until 1983, visitors to the Covered Bridge Festival were able to view not six, but seven covered bridges. Then, on the eve of the Covered Bridge Festival in 1983, the McBride bridge was burned to the ground.

Imagine the shock to our small community, awakening on the morning of the festival to learn that this historic landmark had been destroyed. The whole town was abuzz asking who and why.

We eventually learned that a young man, a resident of Madison County, had been the culprit. He had been jilted in a love affair and in an attempt to erase the painful memories had burned the bridge where the two sometimes met and where he had carved their initials into the worn wooden structure.

Interestingly, part of this man's restitution to the county was 150 hours of community service. These hours were spent at the Historical Complex restoring the Bevington House. After his hours were served, the Historical Society, pleased with his work, hired him for another year.

Clark Tower

By: Bill Sitton

(Reprinted with permission from the Madisonian.)

Driving into Winterset from the south on County Road P71, scan the wooded hillside above the Middle River, and you may catch a glimpse of what appears to be the turret of a castle.

Instead, you've just spotted one of Winterset's most fabled but least seen landmarks, Clark Tower.

The tower sits in the back of the Winterset City Park. It is accessible to cars or hikers by a winding, rocky road. Standing alone in the trees, Clark Tower provides a truly panoramic view of the Middle River Valley.

Clark Tower is a two-story, 25-foot tall structure dedicated to early Madison County pioneers Caleb and Ruth Clanton Clark. The tower, which is 12-foot in diameter, was built by descendants of the Clarks. It is constructed from native limestone excavated from within 200 feet of where the tower stands.

Clark Tower was dedicated in 1926-27. A narrow, hilly rock road is the only way to drive to the tower. This road is closed during the winter and during times of excessive rain. The tower is open year-round for people willing to hike the approximate two-mile round trip.

The Stone House
By: Teresa Hoffelmeyer

Long before Clark Tower was built, Caleb Clark built a stone house at the bottom of the hill below where Clark Tower is located. All that is now left of this house is the foundation, but a number of eerie legends are told about it. The site was originally the home of an Indian whose spirit is said to haunt the site. When Caleb Clark built this house, the head of the stone hammer he used in building kept flying off the handle. When the house was completed, he could get nothing to grow but weeds. Two other families lived in this house and had nothing but bad luck during their stay. It is now said that this is the late night meeting place of a group of Indian gentlemen-all long deceased.

Discoverer and Discovery of the Delicious Apple
By: Henry Miller

(Reprinted with permission from the Madison Co. Historical Society.)

Many Iowans probably have seen the original Delicious apple tree which grew on a farm two miles north of Peru, Iowa, 12 miles southeast of Winterset. However, few may know that we have those red Delicious apples only by the merest chance. The world is full of chances. Perhaps it was only one chance in a million that the Delicious tree sprouted and still less of a

23

chance that it fell into hands of a man who would know it and fight for it.

Jesse Hiatt was the youngest of twelve children and had ten of his own. He was born February 19, 1826, in Randolph County, Indiana, of Quaker parents. His father, William Hiatt, owned a farm and orchard and was known among his neighbors as an authority on fruit. He had developed some apple varieties of his own. So Jesse early on learned the art of planting and pruning and grafting and acquired an enduring life for it.

Hiatt was a slow-moving, slow-talking Quaker, known as a kindly man. All who knew him remember and were impressed by his kindness. He was a man "whose honesty could not be doubted." As was often true of Quakers, his religion molded his life in a vital way.

One day in the spring of 1872, Hiatt found that a Bellflower seedling in his orchard had died, but from the root had sprung a healthy shoot. He resolved to watch that apple sprout and see if it was worthwhile. He would give it a chance in the world. The sprout continued to grow, developing a round bushy top.

A few years later, the Bellflower reached the producing point. The first crop was meager. Upon tasting one of the apples, Hiatt decided then and there it was the best apple in the world. The flavor, like the aroma, was unlike any other apple. The shape was different. Each apple had a quintet of rounded knobs, well defined. This precluded it being a Bellflower apple, in the opinion of Jesse Hiatt -- a new apple altogether.

Thus, it came about that, in honor of his adopted state, Hiatt gave his new apple the name "Hawkeye", Iowa's nickname.

The tree produced every year afterward, until it was filling a barrel. But the top had blown over and the bark was sunburned, cracked, and peeling. He was taking no chances. He put a heavy cover about the trunk, tying it securely. When a freeze killed three-fourths of his orchard, it did not harm his Hawkeye.

It is one thing to be convinced you have the best apple in the world, but quite another to convince the world of it. Hiatt sent apples to the Iowa fairs. They got little notice. He tried to persuade his friends to promote the sale of his Hawkeye, but they could see no future in the apple.

Hiatt began carrying some of the prized apples with him and let people taste them. Nobody appeared to be interested, feeling that the apple was just ordinary. But Jesse Hiatt was stubborn. Nobody could convince him that he did not have the world's best apple.

At last, after 11 years of trying, in 1893, Hiatt sent four apples to a fruit show in Louisiana, Missouri. There they fell into the hands of a man who was looking for just such an apple. He was C.M. Stark, senior member of the Stark Brother's Nursery, who staged the annual show.

Stark always carried a little red book in his pocket. In it he was continually jotting down appropriate names for new fruit varieties as they occurred to him. So when he discovered a new variety, he usually had a name all ready in his little book.

For years, the book had retained the name Delicious. He was waiting for a fruit worthy of it. When he bit into the first apple in the lot from Madison County, Iowa, he had a sensation he never forgot. Here was the Delicious apple.

Stark would have written to Hiatt at once but in the confusion of the show, his name and address had been lost. Nobody knew where the apples had come from. He could do nothing but wait for another show on the bare chance that the unknown exhibitor would enter again.

There was one thing Jesse Hiatt had learned and that was patience. He forwarded apples to the Missouri show again in 1894. Stark went through the exhibits anxiously. He knew the apples with their streaked strawberry color the moment he unwrapped them. Now, he wrote to Hiatt and later made a trip to the orchard and secured permission to propagate the tree. Henceforth, the Hawkeye became the Delicious and eventually the nation's leading apple.

At the time of his death in 1898, the Delicious was still unrecognized and was not mentioned in his obituary. His death was not noticed by the state horticultural society.

In 1922, however, when the fiftieth anniversary of the Delicious was observed, Hiatt became very well known for his achievement.

The first Delicious tree lived and produced fruit until 1940 when it succumbed to the

Armistice Day storm as did many other apple trees in the state of Iowa. From its roots have sprung two sizable trees with the same luscious apples as the original. These trees along with the exact place of the old tree, are enclosed in a triangular fenced plot on what is now (1972) the Raymond Tracy farm.

Madison County, Iowa, is indeed proud to be the site of the origin of all Delicious apple trees in the world and is indebted to Jesse Hiatt for his alertness in discovering the fine qualities of this strange new apple, which became so valuable and useful to mankind.

Elma Tracy, her sister Irenee, and their brother Dick still own this farm. They have quite a collection of clippings from newspapers and magazines about the Delicious Apple Tree. Over the years, they and other family members have been visited by many a stranger wanting to see this historical site.

Elma writes that, "This past year, 1993, the last of the tree sprouts from the original tree only had 36 or 37 apples and they were of very poor quality. In 1992, however, we got nearly two bushels of pretty nice apples from the tree. Dick has farmed this place since the middle 1970's and last year he cut a 10' swath through the corn so the tree could be seen from the road."

NOTE: In our cookbook you will find an applesauce cake recipe submitted by Irenee. She and Elma make LOTS of applesauce, apple pies, and apple salad every year!!!

Rattlesnake Bites
Send Two Men To Hospital

By: Ted Gorman - July, 1986

(Reprinted with permission from the Madisonian.)

Does Madison County really have rattlesnakes?
Read the following accounts if you have doubts.

The severed head of a dead rattlesnake latched onto Ed Jensen's right thumb Saturday, injecting poisonous venom into his hand. Jensen was outside Winterset hunting rattlesnakes to use during the annual Covered Bridge Festival. This year's festival theme is "The Year of the Rattlesnake" and Jensen wanted to get some snakes to use for belts, hat bands, belt buckles, and other knick knacks.

"I'm hanging it up," Jensen said. Jensen said he's quitting rattlesnake hunting forever because he never realized the pain associated with a snake bite. "I didn't realize that much pain came from a rattlesnake bite," he said. "It went on for days."

Jensen was hunting with Brian Allen when the accident happened. They caught the snake and cut its head off before the accident.

When Jensen touched the back of the head, the snake opened its mouth and clamped onto his right hand with both fangs puncturing his hand.

"It's a natural reflex for snakes to do that," he said. After a while, the pain and burning

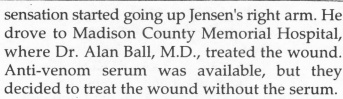

sensation started going up Jensen's right arm. He drove to Madison County Memorial Hospital, where Dr. Alan Ball, M.D., treated the wound. Anti-venom serum was available, but they decided to treat the wound without the serum.

"It was a foolish mistake," he said. "I've been hunting rattlesnakes for 39 years. It finally caught up with me."

"Don't worry, you snake haters," Jensen said, "there's at least a dozen other men around the county who like to look under rocks for ol' diamond back."

Another rattlesnake-biting accident took place last Friday when 18-year-old Brad McDonald was bitten. McDonald said the snake gave no warning before striking. "I was pulling fence wire north of town," McDonald said. "I was standing next to a corner fence post when I felt something sharp hit my left leg halfway up. I looked down and saw the snake and got out of there."

Both Jensen and McDonald are recovering this week and doing fine.

Madison County did away with its rattlesnake $1 bounty several years ago. Jensen said he doesn't think the bounty made any difference to hunters. "We like to hunt for the sport, not the money," Jensen said.

Recipes for Rattlesnake
From: Ed Jensen

CURING A RATTLESNAKE SKIN:
Cut the head off and hang by the tail. With a sharp knife cut center of belly from where the head was to the tail. Remove skin from snake body using hands and knife when necessary. Wash skin and remove all loose tissue. Lay the skin out flat on a board and tack the edges to keep it stretched out. Rub it well with salt a couple of times and let it cure.

COOKING RATTLESNAKE:
First skin and dress the rattlesnake, then cut the meat into 1 to 3 inch chunks and roll in flour or batter. Fry the meat in a deep-fat fryer just as you would chicken or fish.

Unrattled Mom
Shoots Rattlesnake
By: Tom Alex

(Reprinted with permission from the Des Moines Register, Copyright 1987, Des Moines Register & Tribune Co.)

Just call her Annie Oakley.

Though Marianne Fons knows more about quilting (she's written three books) than about guns, she saw her duty and she did it. When a 42-inch rattlesnake slithered into her rural

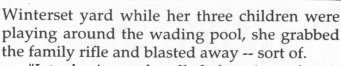

Winterset yard while her three children were playing around the wading pool, she grabbed the family rifle and blasted away -- sort of.

"I took aim and pulled the trigger but it didn't shoot," she said. "I cocked the gun again and a bullet fell out. Then I finally figured it out and fired from about six feet away."

Three Hits!

Bang! Bang! Bang! Three shots, three hits, one disabled rattler.

Marianne's husband John enjoyed the story so much he took out an advertisement in the Winterest Madisonian newspaper. It read: "To Marianne. Who called me and asked how to load the rifle over the phone. Who pulled 10 rounds from the cartridge belt, loaded six, dropped four, fired, and hit a 41-inch rattlesnake three times in our back yard under the oak tree. Nice shootin', honey. Next time try a little higher and to the right."

Marianne said she's, "just not the mountain woman type. I have no interest in guns or shooting. I don't like to kill anything, not even snakes. But when you have children I think you have to kill rattlesnakes when they're in your yard."

The snake met its fate a week ago Sunday. For her birthday last Saturday, John gave Marianne the gift that keeps on giving: a .410 shotgun. "My husband says they are much better for snake killing," said Marianne.

John and daughter Hannah, 11, skinned the rattler and ate part of it, but discovered it didn't taste as good as they thought it might.

Marianne killed a rattler in their yard with a shovel three years ago and her husband killed three rattlers last summer. Most of them have appeared under an oak tree about 25 feet from the house. The snakes are pretty common in Madison County.

"This time I wasn't even thinking about rattlesnakes," said Marianne, 38. "The children had been playing with the hose. When I heard this hissing sound I told them to turn off the hose."

"Hannah yelled to me that it was turned off and immediately, like a bolt out of the blue, I thought we must have another rattlesnake in the yard. I went outside and found our cat and the snake looking deeply into each other's eyes."

Marianne had one lesson with the family rifle last year, but couldn't remember the part about loading it. So she called her husband, who was visiting his great aunt at a local nursing home.

With the children -- Hannah, Mary (7), and Becky (4) -- watching safely behind her on the porch, Marianne marched up to the snake and let loose.

"The snake wasn't totally dead when my husband came home a few minutes later," said Marianne. "But it wasn't going anywhere, either."

John has made several targets for Marianne to use with her new shotgun. "They have pictures of little snakes on them," she said.

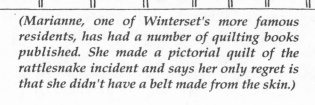

(Marianne, one of Winterset's more famous residents, has had a number of quilting books published. She made a pictorial quilt of the rattlesnake incident and says her only regret is that she didn't have a belt made from the skin.)

Macksburg, Home of the National Skillet Throwing Championship

By: Georgina Breakenridge

The National Skillet Throwing Championship has not brought any fortune to the small Madison County town of Macksburg, but it has brought a certain kind of fame. The first contest held some 15 years ago, although poorly organized, was the start of an annual media attraction which grew to national and then world-wide coverage.

The second year of the event was headlined by country music hall-of-famer Kitty Wells and attracted an estimated crowd of 5,000 plus. Considering Macksburg's total population of 130, this influx of humanity made for standing room only.

Perhaps the most noteworthy contest was what has been commonly referred to as, "The Year Japan Was Here." A film crew from Tokyo journeyed to Macksburg to tape the event for National Japanese television. On the way from the Des Moines airport, it was suggested that perhaps this film crew, actor, and directors, could get together as a team and compete. Instant approval was given by the Japanese and a team was formed. They won the World Championship that year and could boast that the World's Skillet Throwing Champs were from Japan!

Also there was the year the target dummy was kidnapped. Three fretful days passed before "Dumb-Dumb" was found, perched peacefully on the right-hand side of the two-holer in the city park.

Another year, much energy was expended as each team was required to throw a skillet by relays from Macksburg to Winterset. Teams left Macksburg at 8:00 in the morning throwing a skillet as they went. Some 6 hours later they were met at the Winterset city limits by County Sheriff Rex Rouse. The skillet thrown by the winning team now holds a place of honor in the Madison County Museum.

Since the first Skillet Throw in 1975, the championship has been reported on radio stations in 37 states and seen on television stations in 29 states, Japan, and the armed service network. Articles have appeared in scores of newspapers and letters have been received from all over the world.

The Annual Skillet Throw is held the third Saturday of June!

St. Joseph's Church: A Brief History Told with Humor and Love

L. MANTERNACH 90

Madison County and the ground upon which St. Joseph's Church, Rectory, and Parish Hall now stand was once native ground of the Fox and Sac Indians. Because of a treaty in 1842, these Indians agreed to move westward and the land was ceded to the U.S. government. Irish Catholic families were well represented among the first settlers eager to lay claim to this land. Their spiritual needs were periodically tended by circuit rider priests. Among these was Fr. John Brazill, famed pioneer, explorer, founder and builder, who built no less than ten churches outside of Des Moines. He and others came from the city at regular intervals and celebrated mass in the homes of parishioners.

In 1878 land was purchased for the building

of the first Catholic church in Winterset. The cost to build this wooden church was $1,500. Our present church was constructed in 1911 at a cost of $8,000. The beautiful stained glass windows depicting gospel stories were brought here from Munich, Germany. Our bell was a gift from Mary Monaghan and her brother, John. Sadly, the first funeral for whom this bell tolled was that of Mary Monaghan.

The priest at the time of the construction of the second church was Fr. James Troy. Mary McNamara wrote, "My father tried his best to have a spacious basement put under the church for future use on account of the heavy tile roof which he was not in favor of. My father knew what he was doing, for he was a heating and plumbing contractor for many years and had the contract for such large buildings as Fort Leavenworth Penitentiary and the buildings at Conception Abby. Anyhow, Fr. Troy wanted to build a church for show instead of for the future so there was just a hole instead of a basement."

Mary McNamara is no longer living, but we do have her written memories of St. Joseph's. She says, "My first memory of St. Joseph's was about 1902. My mother brought my brother and me out on the train from Des Moines, and we waited at the old St. Nicholas Hotel until my Uncle John picked us up and took us to the church. We were always thrilled to see Uncle John for he had five children several years older than we were. Some sort of a fund drive was going on at the church; it was new to me or I would not have remembered it. The priest asked Mr. Callahan what he could give. He replied, "I have debts of me own, Father, and me money won't reach."

"The church had an old pot bellied stove in the back on the west side and the choir loft was on the east side and raised several steps. They had an old pump organ and outside was a long hitch rack north of the rectory and church for those who drove a team of horses to Mass."

"A couple years later we moved from Des Moines to a farm my father owned 5 miles northeast of Winterset and we lived there two years before moving back to Des Moines. My mother was too lonesome and said no one passed by but the mailman."

It is also interesting to note that when the second church was built the first baby to be baptized in this church was Peter Cunningham. However, a little girl baby had been baptized several days previously in the rectory. They wanted a boy baby to be the first baby baptized in the new church.

Hutchings–Wintrode
503 East Jefferson

The historic Hutchings-Wintrode home was built in 1886. The original residents were J.J. Hutchings and his wife. J.J. Hutchings was a well respected business and civic leader who was president of one of two banks he established with C.D. Bevington. Sharing the home was their daughter Flora, her husband J.H. Wintrode, and their three children. J.H. Wintrode was a physician and banker.

In 1991, the home was purchased by Bill and Shirley Roach with the idea of starting a bed and breakfast. Using original photos, historic, and scientific techniques, the exterior is being restored. Bill has done extensive repair or replacement of overhangs and trim.

The interior of the home is also being lovingly restored. Decorated with Victorian charm and elegance and beautiful antiques, this bed and breakfast is a must for anyone with nostalgia for the Victorian era.

Appetizers, Dips & Beverages

Made with Love

Appetizers, Dips, Beverages

Apples with Caramel Dip

1 C. brown sugar
1 (8 oz.) pkg. Philadelphia
  cream cheese

1 tsp. vanilla
Apples

With an electric mixer, blend brown sugar, cream cheese, and vanilla. Wash, core, and slice apples. Dip apples into caramel sauce.

Karen Pommier
Pam Palmer

Buffalo Chips

1 lb. ground beef
1 lb. Jimmy Dean hot
  sausage
1 lb. Velveeta cheese

2½ loaves party rye bread
1 tsp. oregano
½ tsp. garlic salt
¼ tsp. red pepper

Fry meat and drain, then add cheese. Melt and add other ingredients. Spread on bread and bake at 400° for 5 minutes. Serve hot.

Frances Stevens

Appetizers & Dips

Cheerio Snack Mix

1 C. packed brown sugar
½ C. margarine
¼ C. light corn syrup
½ tsp. salt

½ tsp. baking soda
6 C. Cheerios
1 C. salted nuts
1 C. raisins

Grease 2 (13x9x2-inch) pans or 1 jelly roll pan (15x10x1-inch). Put brown sugar, margarine, corn syrup, and salt in 2-quart saucepan over medium heat, stirring constantly until bubbly around edges. Cook, uncovered for 2 minutes longer. Remove from heat and stir in baking soda until foamy and light colored. Pour over cereal, peanuts, and raisins in a greased 4-quart bowl. Stir until mixture is coated. Spread evenly in pan(s) and bake at 250⁰ for 15 minutes. Stir and let stand just until cool, about 10 minutes. Loosen with metal spatula. Let stand until firm, about 30 minutes. Break into bite-size pieces. Makes about 10 cups.

Kay Stoneking

Alpha Delta Epsilon Cheese Ball

1 large pkg. cream cheese
  (softened)
1 small pkg. cream cheese
  (softened)

1 small jar Roka cheese
2 small jars Old English
  cheddar cheese (sharp)
Chopped pecans

Mix in a bowl with electric mixer until blended well. Form into ball and roll in pecans and chill overnight.

Sue Stuchel

Spicy Cheesecake

2 (8 oz.) pkgs. cream cheese (softened)
2 C. shredded Monterey Jack cheese (8 ozs.)
1 (8 oz.) carton sour cream
3 eggs
1 C. salsa

1 (4 oz.) can diced green chili peppers
1 (8 oz.) carton sour cream
1 (6 oz.) can frozen avocado dip (thawed)
1 tomato (seeded & chopped)

Combine cream cheese and Monterey Jack cheese until light and fluffy. Beat in 1 carton sour cream. Add eggs all at once and beat at low speed just until combined. If you beat the mixture after adding eggs just until combined, the cheesecake is less likely to crack. Stir in salsa and chili peppers. Pour into 9-inch springform pan. Place on baking sheet and bake at 350° for 40 to 45 minutes or until center is almost set. Immediatly spread remaining sour cream over top of hot cheesecake. Cool on wire rack. Cover and refrigerate for 3 to 24 hours. Remove sides of pan and put dollops of avacado dip around edge. Sprinkle with chopped tomato and serve with tortilla or corn chips.

Ann Winjum

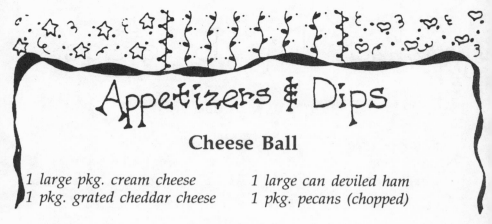

Appetizers & Dips

Cheese Ball

1 large pkg. cream cheese
1 pkg. grated cheddar cheese

1 large can deviled ham
1 pkg. pecans (chopped)

Let cream cheese set out until softened. Add cheddar cheese and deviled ham. Form into ball and roll in chopped pecans. Refrigerate for a few hours and serve with snack crackers.

Patricia Morris

Liver Cheese Ball

1 lb. liver cheese/
   Braunschweiger
¼ C. mayonnaise
2 tsp. dill pickle juice

1 tsp. Worcestershire sauce
¼ tsp. garlic salt
1 (8 oz.) pkg. cream cheese
¼ C. dried onion flakes

Cut liver cheese into pieces. Blend in mayonnaise, pickle juice, Worcestershire sauce, garlic salt, and cream cheese with a mixer. Add onion flakes. Pack into bowl lined with plastic wrap and let set overnight. Turn out on a plate and spread on your favorite crackers.

Debby Corkrean

Appetizers, Dips, Beverages

Pineapple Cheese Ball

16 ozs. cream cheese
1 (8½ oz.) can crushed
   pineapple
¼ C. minced green peppers

2 T. minced onion
1 T. seasoning salt
1 C. chopped pecans

Mash cream cheese with a fork and drain the crushed pineapple. Mix all ingredients together, except the pecans. Roll into a ball and chill for 1 hour, then roll ball in the pecans.

Joanne Nichols

Lo-Cal Chex Party Mix

3 C. Rice Chex
3 C. Wheat Chex
3 C. Corn Chex
3 C. Bran Chex
1 C. unsalted nuts

¼ C. margarine
1 T. Worcestershire sauce
1 T. water
¾ tsp. seasoned salt
½ tsp. garlic powder

Preheat oven to 250⁰. Mix cereals and nuts in a large bowl. Melt margarine. Add Worcestershire sauce, water, and seasonings to margarine. Pour margarine over cereals and nuts, mixing well. Bake on cookie sheets in oven for 1 hour, stirring every 15 minutes. Each ½ C. serving has 87 calories.

Sue Stuchel

Appetizers & Dips

Chicken Puffs

2 T. butter
1 egg
Dash of salt

¼ C. flour
¼ C. boiling water

CHICKEN FILLING:
2 C. finely chopped chicken
¼ C. finely chop celery
½ tsp. salt

2 T. chopped pimento
¼ C. mayonnaise
Dash of pepper

Melt butter in the boiling water. Add flour and a dash of salt, stirring vigorously. Cook and stir until mixture forms a ball that doesn't separate. Remove from heat and cool slightly. Add egg and beat vigorously until smooth. Drop dough onto greased baking sheet using 1 level teaspoon of dough for each puff. Bake at 400° for 20 minutes. Remove from pan, cool, and split. Makes 1 to 1½ dozen.

For Filling: Mix the ingredients and put in cooled puff shell. Can use other fillings such as tuna, ham, and beef.

Kathleen Kordick

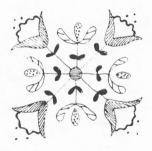

Appetizers, Dips, Beverages

Stuffed Croissant

18 croissants
2 (10 oz.) pkgs. chopped
  frozen spinach
2 C. mayonnaise
1 bunch chopped green onions

1 (2 oz.) pkg. Hidden Valley
  Ranch Dressing
1 (3 oz.) pkg. cream cheese
  (room temp.)

Steam spinach in steamer basket for 10 minutes. Drain and press all moisture out. Mix softened cream cheese with mayonnaise and blend well. Add spinach, dressing, and green onions. Let stand overnight. Split croissants and fill. Cut into 3 wedges.

Nancy M. Corkrean

Old English Dip

2 jars Kraft Old English
  cheese
2 C. mayonnaise
½ tsp. dry mustard

1 tsp. Worcestershire sauce
½ tsp. onion
Dash of garlic powder

Mash cheese with fork; add mayonnaise slowly and continue mashing. Add remaining ingredients and mix well. Chill overnight. Serve with crackers or veggies.

Val Herzog
(Algonquin, Illinois)

Appetizers & Dips

Pizza Pan Dip

1 (8 oz.) pkg. cream cheese
1 (8 oz.) carton sour cream
2 T. milk
2 tsp. lemon juice

½ head of lettuce
  (cut in small pieces)
1 C. grated cheddar cheese
1 tomato (sliced finely)
Taco sauce

Mix cream cheese, sour cream, milk, and lemon juice. Spread over pizza pan. Sprinkle lettuce, cheese, tomato slices, and taco sauce to taste over the cream cheese mixture. Serve with taco chips.

Marty Hester

7-Layer Dip

1 large can bean dip or
  2 small cans (refried beans
  can be substituted)
2 avocados (mashed)
1 pkg. taco mix

1½ C. sour cream
1 large onion (chopped)
2 tomatoes (chopped)
¾ lb. cheddar cheese (grated)

Spread bean dip in bottom of a 9x9-inch Pyrex dish or pan. Spread avocados over bean dip. Mix sour cream with taco mix and spread over avocados. Then layer onion, tomatoes, and grated cheese in the order listed above. Chill and serve with Tostada chips.

Wanda Martin

Egg Rolls

1 pkg. egg roll skins
1 beaten egg
4 C. cabbage (chopped fine)
1 bunch (5 or 6) green
   onions (chopped)
1 green pepper (chopped)
1 lb. ground pork

½ medium carrot
   (grated & chopped)
Soy sauce
¼ tsp. garlic salt
¼ tsp. pepper
Oil to fry finished egg rolls in

Brown pork with 2 tsp. soy sauce, garlic, salt, and pepper. In a large bowl combine ground pork and all ingredients, except skins, egg, and oil. Sprinkle generously with soy sauce and mix well. Spread out one skin and place 2 heaping soup spoons of mixture in center, fold as per instructions on egg roll skins package, and seal edge with beaten egg. Deep-fry in hot oil. (I use an electric skillet, turning once.) Fry until golden brown and crispy. Best when served immediately. Good served with rice.

Mary Ann Snyder

48

Appetizers & Dips
Shrimp Egg Rolls

14 to 20 frozen egg roll
  wrappers
Oil for frying in a Wok
½ lb. shrimp
1 tsp. sherry
1 tsp. salt
½ tsp. cornstarch
3 T. oil

2 C. finely diced celery
½ tsp. sugar
1 T. water
½ C. fresh bean sprouts
2 C. cut-up raw cabbage
1 C. finely chopped water
  chestnuts

Thaw egg rolls until pliable. Combine shrimp, sherry, salt, and cornstarch in small bowl. Let stand for 15 minutes. Heat 1 T. oil in Wok. Add shrimp mixture and stir-fry until shrimp are firm and pink. Spoon contents of Wok into large mixing bowl. Add remaining oil to Wok. Add celery and stir-fry for about 2 to 3 minutes. Add sugar and water. Cover and steam for 1 minute. Uncover and stir-fry until liquid evaporates. Add to shrimp mixture. Add remaining ingredients and blend. Cool. Use about ¼ C. filling for each egg roll. Place filling diagonally across the center of egg roll wrapper. Lift the lower triangle of wrapper over the filling and tuck the point under it, leaving the upper point of wrapper flat. Bring the two end flaps up and over the enclosed filling. Press flaps down firmly. Dip your fingers in cold water and brush them over the upper exposed triangle of dough. Then roll the filled portion over it until you have a neat package. Cold water seals the edges and keeps the package intact. Fill Wok with oil to 3-inch depth. Heat to 375⁰ (191⁰). With tongs lower 4 egg rolls into the hot fat. Fry for 3 to 4 minutes or until golden brown and crisp. Drain on paper towels. Dip in mustard or sweet and sour sauce.

Bill Camp

"Bill loves to cook, when he isn't driving a bus. He likes to cook Chinese. When he deicdes to do this he has us all help cut the vegetables and makes it a family cooking experience, but he does most of it. Everytime he cooks Chinese - he gets us all in the act, but the "wife" gets to clean up."

Spring Rolls/Egg Rolls

1 lb. (450 g) uncooked
   medium shrimp
1 lb. uncooked boneless
   lean pork
4 ozs. (115 g) fresh
   mushrooms (cleaned)
8 green onions
1 red pepper (seeded)
8 ozs. (225 g) Chinese
   cabbage (about ½ head)

1 can (8 ozs. or 225 g) water
   chestnuts (drained)
3 T. soy sauce
2 tsp. grated ginger root
1 tsp. sugar
½ tsp. salt
¼ C. water
1½ T. cornstarch
24 spring rolls or egg roll
   wrappers
3 C. vegetable oil

Remove shells and back veins from shrimp. Remove and discard
fat from pork. Finely chop shrimp, pork, mushrooms, onions, pepper, cabbage, and water chestnuts using cleaver, sharp knife, or food
processor. Transfer all chopped ingredients to large mixing bowl.
Add soy sauce, ginger, sugar, and salt; mix well. Mix water and
cornstarch in small bowl until blended. Place ¼ C. of the pork mixture evenly across a corner of each wrapper. Brush cornstarch mixture evenly over all edges of wrappers. Carefully roll wrappers
around filling, folding in the corners. Heat oil in Wok over high heat
until it reaches 375°. Fry 3 or 4 rolls at a time in the hot oil until
golden, 3 to 5 minutes. Drain on absorbent paper. Makes 2 dozen.

Marvin & Mira Imes

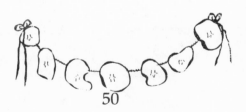

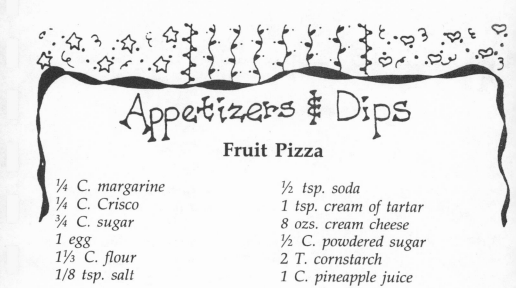

Appetizers & Dips

Fruit Pizza

¼ C. margarine
¼ C. Crisco
¾ C. sugar
1 egg
1⅓ C. flour
1/8 tsp. salt

½ tsp. soda
1 tsp. cream of tartar
8 ozs. cream cheese
½ C. powdered sugar
2 T. cornstarch
1 C. pineapple juice

Cream oleo, Crisco, and sugar. Add egg, then add salt, soda, cream of tartar, and flour. Pat into an ungreased pizza pan and bake at 400° for 10 minutes. Let cool. Blend cream cheese and powdered sugar; spread over cooled crust. You can use a variety of fresh or canned fruit. Pineapple, kiwi, strawberries, apples, bananas, blueberries, or whatever fruit happens to be in season. Fresh fruit is best. Thicken pineapple juice with cornstarch. Pour over fruit and crust making sure all the fruit is covered. Chill.

Cheryl Emanuel

Ham Cubes

2 T. mayonnaise
2 T. horseradish
1 tsp. Worcestershire sauce
½ tsp. seasoned salt

8 ozs. cold cream cheese
(cubed)
2 pkgs. sliced ham
(luncheon meat)

In blender combine mayonnaise, horseradish, Worcestershire, salt, and cream cheese. Spread between 6 slices of ham. Wrap in foil and freeze for 2 hours. Remove and cut into cubes 1 hour before serving with toothpicks.

Maureen Roach

Hot Mexican Dip

1 lb. ground beef
1 diced onion
1 diced green pepper

⅓ bottle mild taco sauce
1 lb. Velveeta cheese
1 T. chili powder

In a skillet brown ground beef, drain. Add the onion and green pepper. Remove from heat and stir in the cheese. Add the taco sauce and chili powder. Stir well and pour into a crock pot to keep warm. Serve with chips or party rye bread.

Pam Palmer

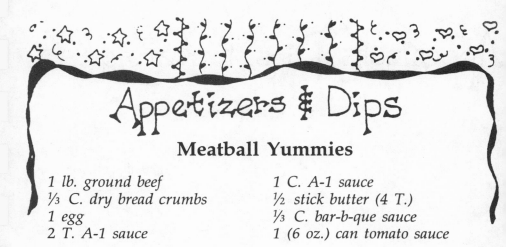

Appetizers & Dips

Meatball Yummies

1 lb. ground beef
⅓ C. dry bread crumbs
1 egg
2 T. A-1 sauce

1 C. A-1 sauce
½ stick butter (4 T.)
⅓ C. bar-b-que sauce
1 (6 oz.) can tomato sauce

Combine beef, bread crumbs, egg, and 2 T. A-1. Mix and shape into 1-inch meatballs. Place into microwave-safe dish and microwave on High setting until pink color changes to brown (about 5 minutes). Transfer to saucepan (discard drippings). Combine remainder of ingredients over meatballs. Simmer, covered at least 15 minutes.

"This meatball recipe is one of my husband's favorites. Served with buttered noodles, it makes a quick delicious dinner."

Joy Drury

Lime Pickles

7 lbs. sliced cucumbers
  (sliced round)
2 C. lime, well dissolved
  in 2 gallon of cold water
2 qts. vinegar

10 C. sugar
2 T. salt (not iodized)
1 T. mixed pickling spices
  (tie in a bag)
1 tsp. celery seed

Put sliced cucumbers in lime water and let stand for 24 hours. Rinse very well (2 or 3 times). Put in clear water and let stand overnight. Handle very carefully as they should be real crisp. For the syrup, mix the last 5 ingredients and bring to a boil and pour over pickles. Let stand for 24 hours, then boil syrup and pickles hard for 35 to 40 minutes. Seal. Makes 10 to 11 pints.

Veronica Klug

Pickle Sticks

1 head of dill
1 garlic bud

2 tsp. salt
1 whole red pepper (uncut)

SYRUP:
3 C. water
1 C. vinegar

3 C. sugar

Use medium or oversize cucumbers. (The bigger the better.) Peel, quarter, and remove seeds. Loosely pack in jars. To each jar add the first 4 ingredients. Mix together the water, sugar, and vinegar for syrup. Bring to boil and pour over pickles and seal. Put jars in canner and bring to boil (no longer). Remove canner from heat and let stand to cool.

Shirley Bush

Just Good Pickles

1 qt. jar sliced dill pickles
2 C. sugar

¼ C. water

Drain the pickles. Empty pickle slices in a mixing bowl. Add the sugar and water, stirring with a rubber spatula. When sugar is dissolved put the pickles back in the jar.

Mildred Waltz

Appetizers & Dips

Very Easy Refrigerator Pickles

4 C. sugar
4 C. dark cider vinegar
½ C. pickling salt
1⅓ tsp. tumeric

1⅓ tsp. mustard seed
1⅓ tsp. celery salt
4 onions (sliced thin)
Cucumbers (sliced thin)

Mix sugar, vinegar, and water together. DO NOT HEAT! This syrup is used cold. Wash and sterilize 4 quart jars. Slice 1 onion in each jar first. Slice thin enough cucumbers to fill jars. Stir syrup well and pour over cucumbers. Screw lids on tightly. Place in refrigerator a week before using. Keep cucumbers in refrigerator. Will keep refrigerated for 1 year if you can keep them around that long before they're eaten.

Veronica Klug

Baked Praline Popcorn Crunch

1 C. butter
2 C. brown sugar
½ C. light corn syrup
1 tsp. salt
½ tsp. baking soda

1 tsp. vanilla
6 qt. popped popcorn
1½ C. pecan halves
1 C. sunflower nuts

Bring butter, sugar, syrup, and salt to a boil, stirring constantly. Boil, without stirring for 5 minutes. Remove from heat and stir in soda and vanilla. Pour syrup over mixture of corn, nuts, and pecans. Mix well. Bake in 2 large shallow pans at 250⁰ for 1 hour, stirring every 15 minutes.

Mary Brayton

Appetizers, Dips, Beverages

Caramel Corn

2 C. brown sugar
2 sticks margarine
½ C. corn syrup
1 tsp. salt

1 tsp. baking soda
15 C. popped corn
   (1½ C. unpopped)

Boil the first 4 ingredients together for 5 minutes. Remove from heat and add 1 tsp. baking soda. Mix quickly. Pour hot mixture over popped corn in large stainless steel mixing bowl. Mix well and bake at 200° for 1 hour, stirring every 15 minutes. When cool, store in airtight container.

"Once you get started eating this it is almost impossible to put down!!!"

Teresa Pearson

Margaret's Parmesan Pepper Popcorn

2 qts. popped corn
¼ C. grated Parmesan cheese

1 tsp. lemon pepper
Melted butter

Sprinkle cheese and lemon pepper over popped, buttered corn. Enjoy!

Jeanette Neel

Appetizers & Dips

Potato Skins

6 medium potatoes
1 lb. hamburger
½ C. onions (chopped)
1 tsp. pepper
1 tsp. salt
1 pkg. taco seasoning

1 (12 oz.) pkg. mozzarella
  cheese
2 (12 oz.) pkgs. cheddar cheese
Onion chives
Bacon bits
Sour cream

Brown hamburger with onions. Add salt and pepper. Drain grease. Add taco seasoning and simmer. Bake potatoes and cut in half lengthwise. Scoop out center of potato, leaving ¼-inch around edges. Place potatoes in baking dish and sprinkle with cheddar cheese. Add about 2 T. seasoned hamburger and top with mozzarella and cheddar cheese. Sprinkle on onion, chives, and bacon bits. Heat until cheese is melted and serve with sour cream.

Teresa Hoffelmeyer

Salmon Appetizers

1 (15 oz.) can salmon or
  2 C. cooked salmon
1 (8 oz.) pkg. cream cheese
4 T. mild or medium salsa

2 T. fresh parsley
1 tsp. dried cilantro
¼ tsp. ground cumin (opt.)
8 flour tortillas (8 inches)

Drain salmon and remove bones. In a small bowl combine salmon, cream cheese, salsa, parsley, cilantro, and cumin. Spread 2 T. salmon mixture over each tortilla. Roll each tortilla up tightly and wrap each with plastic wrap. Refrigerate for 2 to 3 hours. Slice each tortilla into bite-size pieces. Makes 48 appetizers.

Fonda Bass

Sesame Chicken Wings

2½ lbs. chicken wings
½ C. soy sauce
⅓ C. water
¼ C. sugar
2 T. sesame or olive oil

4 green onions with tops
   only (sliced)
½ medium onion (sliced)
2 cloves of garlic (minced)
1 to 2 T. sesame seeds &
   pepper, to taste

In a large plastic bag or glass dish combine all ingredients, but chicken wings, to make a marinade. Add chicken to marinade. Coat well, cover, and refrigerate for 2 to 3 hours or overnight, turning occasionally. Remove chicken to a shallow rack in a baking pan. Discard marinade. Bake, uncovered at 350⁰ for 30 minutes. Turn and bake for 20 minutes longer or until tender. Makes 6 to 8 appetizer servings.

Fonda Bass

Shrimp Dip

1 (8 oz.) pkg. cream cheese
3 T. chili sauce
½ tsp. onion juice
2 cans shrimp

½ C. Miracle Whip
2 tsp. lemon juice
¼ tsp. Worcestershire sauce

Drain and rinse shrimp. Mix all ingredients and fold in shrimp.

Carita Kelleher

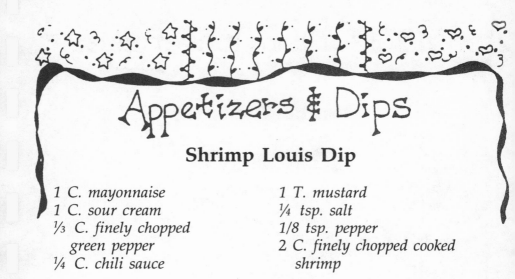

Appetizers & Dips

Shrimp Louis Dip

1 C. mayonnaise
1 C. sour cream
⅓ C. finely chopped
 green pepper
¼ C. chili sauce

1 T. mustard
¼ tsp. salt
1/8 tsp. pepper
2 C. finely chopped cooked
 shrimp

Mix all together, cover, and chill. Makes 3 cups.

Joanne Nichols

Tortilla Roll-Ups

1 (8 oz.) pkg. cream cheese
 (softened)
1 C. sour cream
1 C. grated cheddar cheese
2 T. chopped black olives

Chopped green onion
 (about 3)
¼ tsp. garlic powder
4 large flour tortillas

Mix together cream cheese, sour cream, grated cheese, olives, onions, and garlic powder. Spread on tortillas. Roll them up and store them overnight in the refrigerator. The next day slice and serve with salsa, if desired.

Berta says: "This is always requested when we have "food day" at work."

Berta Kordick
Bev Maxwell
Pam Palmer

Appetizers, Dips, Beverages

Witches Brew

1 C. blood drops (1 pkg. red hots)
1 C. owl eyes (1 pkg. peanuts)
1 C. chicken toenails (1 pkg. corn candy)
1 C. colored flies (1 pkg. M & M's)
1 C. cat's claws (1 jar sunflower seeds)
1 C. dead ants (½ lb. raisins)
1 C. chicken gizzards (1 can shoestring potatoes)
1 C. bat bones (1 bag straight pretzels)
1 C. ghost noses (1 bag miniature marshmallows)

Mix ingredients and serve in a Halloween pumpkin.

Jeanette Neel

Won Tons

2 lbs. browned ground beef
½ C. soy sauce
2 T. chopped green onion
1 T. sesame oil
1 T. sugar
¼ C. water

1/8 tsp. pepper
1/8 tsp. garlic salt
1 egg
1 lb. pkg. Won Ton skins
3 C. oil

Mix together the first nine ingredients. Fill the Won Ton skins and cook in oil until a golden brown.

Joan Hilton

Beverages

Instant Cappuccino

1 C. instant coffee creamer
1 C. instant chocolate
   drink mix
⅔ C. instant coffee

½ C. sugar
½ tsp. ground cinnamon
¼ tsp. ground nutmeg

Combine all ingredients and mix well. Store in airtight container. When ready to use mix 2 T. per coffee cup of hot water. Top with whipped cream sprinkled with nutmeg or chocolate shavings.

Teresa Hoffelmeyer

Hot Apple Cider

3 (3-inch) sticks cinnamon
2 tsp. whole cloves
1 whole nutmeg or
   ½ tsp. ground

½ gallon apple cider
1 C. sugar
2 C. orange juice
½ C. lemon juice

Tie spices in cheese cloth. Stir sugar into cider in large saucepan. Add spices and simmer for 15 minutes. Remove spices and stir in orange and lemon juice, continuing to heat until served. (Can use crock pot.)

Bev Maxwell

61

Appetizers, Dips, Beverages

Mulled Cider

1 gallon apple cider
1 qt. pineapple juice
1 (6 oz.) can concentrated
   orange juice

2 or 3 cinnamon sticks
Whole cloves in whole orange

Heat all ingredients together and serve from crock pot.

Shirley Bittinger

Frozen Cooler

1 (12 oz.) can orange juice
   (thawed)
1 (12 oz.) can lemonade

3 tea bags
2 C. brandy or vodka
2 C. sugar

Heat 7 C. of water and add sugar and dissolve. Heat 1 C. water, and add tea bags and let set for 10 minutes. Mix with sugar-water. Add juices and brandy. Mix and freeze. Serve with sour mix.

Sheila Algreen

Beverages

Hot Chocolate Mix

1 (8-quart) box powdered milk
(Carnation)
1 (1 lb.) box (Nestle's)
chocolate milk drink

1 (6 oz.) jar cream substitute
powder (Pream)
1¼ C. sugar

Mix all ingredients together well. Use 3 T. mix for 1 C. hot chocolate.
Use hot water for liquid. Good and goes a long way.

Ruth Cunningham

Lambs Wool
(The traditional Old English Wassail Drink)

6 apples (cored)
2 pts. ale (4 C.)
1 pt. sweet wine (2 C.)

1 tsp. allspice
1 stick cinnamon
½ C. brown sugar

Bake apples in baking pan at 450⁰ for 1 hour or until very soft.
Remove skins and mash the pulp in a large bowl. Heat slowly the
ale and wine with the sugar and spices. When heated pour over apples in large punch bowl and serve. (For a non-alcoholic drink, you
may use 2 quarts of apple cider in place of ale and wine.)

*"The name sounds strange, but refers to the whiteness of the flesh of the apples
as they float in the ale or cider. Traditionally served on the Twelfth-Eve, January
5th."*

Phyllis Patrick

Appetizers, Dips, Beverages

Orange Julius

1 (6 oz.) can frozen orange
    juice (slightly thawed)
½ C. sugar
1 C. milk

1 C. water
1 tsp. vanilla
2 trays ice cubes

In an electric blender put juice, sugar, milk, water, and vanilla. Add approximately 8 ice cubes at a time. Continue blending and adding ice cubes until desired consistency.

Karen Pommier
Cindy Pottebaum

"Redeye"

A must for all of our weddings was a drink called "REDEYE." It was made with burnt sugar, water, and 190 proof alcohol.

A very small amount in small cups or glasses was given to each guest as he or she entered the wedding reception.

This drink was very potent and a small shot was all you wanted if you were to enjoy the remainder of the wedding festivities. The drink was well named.

My Dad made "Redeye" when each of our four children were married.

Shirley Privratsky

Beverages

Russian Tea or Spiced Tea

1¼ C. Tang
⅓ C. instant tea

½ C. sugar
1 tsp. cinnamon

This tea was a real favorite served to the children who attended the Herb Shop during Vacation Bible School. It is delicious served hot or cold. Combine all ingredients. To make 1 C. of tea put 2 to 3 tsp. in mug with boiling water. Store mix in airtight container.

Teresa Pearson

St. John's Wine

(Serve December 27th the Feast Day of St. John the Evangelist.)

1 qt. cranberry juice
1 qt. apple juice
½ gallon red wine
15 whole cloves

3 sticks cinnamon
1 tsp. ground cinnamon
½ C. sugar

Decorate with orange slices and simmer for 30 minutes.

"Legend has it that the Emperor Domitian tried to kill St. John by ordering him to drink a cup of poisoned wine. St. John took the cup, blessed it and the poison slithered away in the form of a snake. In some countries it has become a tradition that on this feast day the father of the family blesses a cup of wine and everyone says, "I drink to you in the love of St. John."

Teresa Hoffelmeyer

Appetizers, Dips, Beverages

Father & Son
By: Fr. Frank Palmer

When I was first ordained, I was assigned as an associate pastor to a pastor who was a Monsignor in Council Bluffs, Msgr. Moriarty. Msgr. was much older, had graying hair, and was a bit portly. I, like most newly ordained priests, appeared somewhat boyish. The fact that I was not very tall (5'3"), I am sure, contributed to this boyishness.

We would be seen together, Msgr. and I, by parishioners in various aspects of our ministry. We would also be seen by neighbors on the street. We would often walk together after Mass to the nearby hospital for breakfast and visit patients afterwards. However, when walking, Msgr. had a habit of walking fast; I often would trail him by a few steps.

We had some non-Catholic neighbors, one of whom had two children around the ages of 7 and 8. They would often see Msgr. and me walking to the hospital. They frequently waved and seemed quite friendly.

One Saturday morning they were out selling Girl Scout cookies (the older apparently was in the Scouts). They had decided to call on the rectory to make a possible sale. They rang the rectory door bell, and since it was usually my duty to answer the door when I was in, I came bouncing down the steps from my room. When I opened the door, the older girl said, "Is your daddy in? Would he like to buy some cookies?"

Breads

Breads

St. Joseph's Day
By: Fr. Palmer

The feast day of St. Joseph was a significant day in our parish. What made it significant was bread . . . loaves of bread.

There was this Italian woman in the parish, quite robust, and always wearing black who on this feast day would hand out little loaves of freshly baked bread to all who were in church that morning. That included all of the grade school, for we began our school day by attending Mass . . . some 230 children.

After the end of Mass, "Bambino", as we called her, would come to the center of the sanctuary. At each side of her would be baskets of freshly baked bread. We would come up by class, one by one and she would hand each of us a loaf. It smelled so fresh and was quite tasty. How delighted we were! It was really good. Many of us would come around for seconds once everyone had gone through the line.

How did Bambino come to hand out the bread? The story was that she had a great devotion to St. Joseph and that was her way of honoring him. Whatever the reason, it did not matter to us kids. What I remember was her tasty bread and her generosity!

Apple Bread

2 C. sugar
1 C. oil
3 eggs (beaten)
3 C. flour
1 tsp. salt

1 tsp. cinnamon
1 tsp. soda
2 tsp. vanilla
3 C. peeled & chopped apples
1 C. nuts

Beat together sugar, oil, and eggs. Sift together flour, salt, cinnamon, and soda. Add to liquid mixture. Add vanilla, apples, and nuts to mixture. Put into two loaf pans sprayed with Pam. Sprinkle tops with sugar. Bake at 325° for 1 hour or until done.

Rosemary Stuchel

Banana-Blueberry Bread

2 C. Bisquick baking mix
¾ C. quick-cooking oats
⅔ C. sugar
¼ C. milk
2 eggs (beaten)
1 C. mashed ripe bananas
1 C. fresh or frozen blueberries

Mix all ingredients, except blueberries, until moistened. Beat vigorously for 30 seconds. Fold in blueberries and pour in a greased and floured 9x5x3-inch loaf pan. Bake at 350⁰ for 50 to 60 minutes or until wooden pick inserted in center comes out clean. Cool for 10 minutes. Remove from pan.

Marianne Eivins

Banana Nut Bread

½ C. margarine
½ C. sugar
3 eggs
2¾ C. flour (sifted)
1½ tsp. baking powder
½ tsp. soda
1 tsp. salt
1½ C. ripe bananas (mashed) (about 3 medium)
⅓ C. chopped walnuts

Preheat oven to 350⁰. Cream together margarine and sugar. Add eggs and beat well. Sift together dry ingredients. Add to eggs alternately with banana, mixing well after each addition. Stir in nuts. Turn into 9x5-inch loaf pan coated with vegetable pan spray. Bake for 50 to 60 minutes or until done. Remove from pan and cool on rack.

Shirley Bush
Rosemary Stuchel

Breads

Beer Bread

1 can beer
3 C. self-rising flour

⅓ C. sugar

Mix all ingredients together. Batter will be lumpy. Place in greased bread pan and bake at 350⁰ to 375⁰ for 1 hour. This goes great with soups and salads.

Nancy M. Corkrean

Biscuit Mix

8 C. flour
¼ C. baking powder

2 tsp. salt
1 C. shortening

Sift together first 3 ingredients. Cut in shortening with fork or pastry blender until mix resembles coarse crumbs. Cover and store in refrigerator for up to one month.

To Use: Add ½ C. milk to 2 C. of biscuit mix. Turn onto floured surface and knead lightly. Pat or roll to ½-inch thick, cut with cutter, and bake in hot 450⁰ oven for 12 to 15 minutes. Yield: 10 to 12 biscuits.

Margaret Tiernan

Buttermilk Biscuits

1 pkg. dry yeast
¼ C. warm water (115°)
2½ C. flour
½ tsp. baking soda
1 tsp. baking powder

1 tsp. salt
2 T. sugar
½ C. shortening
1 C. buttermilk

Dissolve yeast in warm water and set aside. Mix dry ingredients in order given. Cut in shortening. Stir in buttermilk and yeast mixture. Blend well. Knead lightly on floured board, roll out ½-inch thick, and cut with biscuit cutter. Place on greased cookie sheet. (I usually place 2 biscuits together, one on top of the other.) Let dough rise in warm place, about ½ hour before baking. Bake at 400° for 12 to 15 minutes.

Teresa Hoffelmeyer

Cranberry Nut Bread

3 C. sifted all-purpose
  flour
1 C. sugar
4 tsp. baking powder
1 tsp. salt
1 beaten egg

1½ C. milk
2 T. salad oil
1 C. coarsely chopped
  cranberries
½ C. chopped nuts

Sift together dry ingredients. Combine egg, milk, and salad oil. Add to dry ingredients, stirring just until moistened. Stir in cranberries and nuts. Turn into greased 9x5x3-inch loaf pan. Bake at 350° for about 1¼ hours or until done. Remove from pan and cool on rack.

Larry Lantz

Breads

Butterhorns

1 pkg. dry yeast
¼ C. water
¾ C. milk (scalded)
½ C. oleo

½ C. sugar
1 tsp. salt
3 beaten eggs
4½ C. flour

Soften yeast in warm water. Combine milk, oleo, sugar, and salt. Add eggs, then flour. Mix until smooth. Cover and let rise until double in size. Divide dough and roll out on floured surface. Brush with melted oleo. Cut into wedge shapes and roll-up. Brush top of each roll with oleo and let rise, then bake at 350⁰ until done. Brush again after baked.

"I triple this recipe for my family every holiday. I even have to hide these in order to have them for dinner!"

Luella Fairholm

English Muffin Bread

2 pkgs. dry yeast
6 C. unsifted flour
1 T. sugar
¼ tsp. baking soda

½ C. water
2 tsp. salt
2 C. milk

Combine 3 C. of flour and dry ingredients. Heat liquids until very warm (120⁰ to 130⁰). Add to dry ingredients and beat well. Stir in remaining flour. Bake in two greased and sprinkled with cornmeal loaf pans. Sprinkle cornmeal on top, cover, and let rise for 45 minutes in a warm place. Bake at 400⁰ for 25 minutes.

Joann Ritter

Cheese Casserole Bread

2¼ C. all-purpose flour
¼ C. grated Parmesan
   cheese
2 T. snipped parsley
1 pkg. active dry yeast
¼ tsp. baking soda

1 C. cream-style
   cottage cheese
⅓ C. water
2 T. butter or
   margarine
1 egg

In a large mixer bowl combine 1 C. of the flour, Parmesan, parsley, yeast, and soda. Heat together the cottage cheese, water, and butter just until warm (115 to 120 degrees), stirring constantly to melt butter. Add to dry mixture, then add egg. Beat at low speed with electric mixer for ½ minute, scraping sides of bowl constantly. Beat for 3 minutes at high speed. By hand, stir in remaining flour and turn into greased bowl. Cover and let rise until double (about 1½ hours). Stir down and spread evenly in a greased 1½-quart casserole. Let rise until nearly double (about 40 minutes). Bake at 350⁰ for 50 to 55 minutes. Cover top with foil if bread browns too quickly. Remove from casserole and let cool. Makes 1 loaf.

Jill Kordick

73

Garlic Bubble Bread

Frozen white bread loaf
¼ C. oleo (melted)
1 beaten egg

1 T. dried parsley flakes
1 tsp. garlic powder
¼ tsp. salt

Thaw frozen bread loaf according to package. Cut bread into walnut-sized shapes and dip into the mixture of oleo, egg, parsley flakes, garlic powder, and salt. Place into greased loaf pan, cover, and let rise. Bake at 350° until brown.

Kelly Stevens

Easy Dill-Onion Bread

3 C. all-purpose flour
1 pkg. active dry yeast
1¼ C. milk
2 T. sugar

2 T. butter or margarine
2 tsp. dried dill seed
2 tsp. instant minced onion
1 egg

In a small mixer combine 1½ C. of the flour and the yeast. In saucepan heat milk, sugar, butter, dill seed, onion, and 1 tsp. salt just until warm (115°-120°), stirring constantly to melt butter. Add to dry mixture and add egg. Beat at low speed with electric mixer for ½ minute, scraping bowl. Beat for 3 minutes at high speed. By hand, stir in remaining flour. Cover and let rise until double (30 to 45 minutes). Stir down. Spread evenly in a greased 9x5x3-inch loaf pan. Let rise until nearly double (about 30 minutes). Bake at 350° for 25 to 30 minutes. Cover loosely with foil if bread browns too quickly. Remove from pan and let cool. Makes 1 loaf.

Jill Kordick

Homemade Bread

"This recipe is from my Aunt Helen King of St. Patrick's."

2 pkgs. yeast
4½ C. lukewarm water
½ C. sugar
2 T. salt

½ C. melted shortening
2 T. vinegar
12 C. flour

In a large mixing bowl dissolve yeast in warm water. Stir in sugar, salt, shortening, and vinegar. Add 6 C. of flour and beat well. Stir in remaining flour and let rest for 10 minutes. Turn on a lightly floured board and knead until smooth and satiny. Return to oiled bowl, cover, and let rise in warm place until double in bulk. Turn onto a floured board and cut into 4 or 5 parts with a knife. Run a rolling pin over dough to remove air pockets. Shape into loaves. Place in oiled loaf pans. Cover and let rise until doubled in bulk. Bake at 350⁰ for 45 to 50 minutes.

Variations: Eggs may be added to make richer and 6 C. of whole-wheat flour may be substituted for 6 C. of white flour.

"I make this for Thanksgiving dinner and my big boys can't get enough."

Peggy Barker

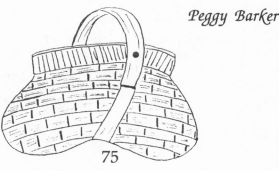

Hot Cross Buns

4¾ to 5½ C. flour
⅓ C. sugar
1½ tsp. cinnamon
¼ tsp. ground nutmeg
2 pkgs. active dry yeast
¾ C. milk

½ C. water
¼ C. butter
3 eggs (room temp.)
8 ozs. pitted dates (chopped)
1 egg white, lightly beaten
   with 1 T. water

In a large bowl, combine 1½ C. flour, sugar, cinnamon, salt, nutmeg, and undissolved yeast. Heat milk, water, and butter until hot (125° to 130°). Gradually add to dry ingredients and beat for 2 minutes at medium speed of mixer. Add eggs and ½ C. flour; beat for 2 minutes at high speed, scraping bowl occasionally. With spoon, stir in enough additional flour to make soft dough. Knead on lightly floured surface until smooth and elastic, about 8 minutes. Cover and let rest on board for 20 minutes. Punch dough down and turn out onto lightly floured surface. Knead in dates. Divide dough into 18 equal pieces and form into smooth balls. Place balls on greased baking sheets, 2-inches apart, or in two greased 8-inch square baking pans. Cover and let rise in warm place until doubled in size, about 30 minutes. Brush with egg white mixture. Bake at 375° for 20 minutes or until done. Remove from pans and cool on wire racks. Drizzle with vanilla frosting: 1½ C. sifted confectioner's sugar, 1 to 2 T. milk, and ½ tsp. vanilla.

"Our family traditionally eats these buns on Good Friday. The custom of serving hot cross buns on Good Friday is said to have originated at St. Alban's Abbey in England where a monk there served these special buns, marked with a cross, to the poor on Good Friday in 1361."

Teresa Hoffelmeyer

Aunt Lizzie's Irish Soda Bread

4 C. flour
2 tsp. soda
1 tsp. salt
½ C. sugar

1½ C. raisins
2 C. buttermilk
1 egg

Mix all the dry ingredients together. Stir in buttermilk, 1 beaten egg, and raisins. Mix to a smooth consistency and place in a greased and floured pan. Sprinkle top with flour. Poke 4 to 5 holes in the top and bake at 350° for 1 hour.

Karen Gronemeyer

Church Picnics
By: Karen Gronemeyer

My father tells us of the church picnics that were weekly social gatherings during the summer months in rural Iowa. He was a young bachelor, living with Grandpa on the home farm after serving in WWII and on Sunday they would attend one of the church picnics in the area.

The women would cook for several days before the event and the menu usually included fried chicken, potatoes and gravy, fresh peas and beans, bread, pies, and cakes.

The men would be in charge of the beer that was usually placed in a horse trough with ice. They were also in charge of the games which included paddle wheel, chuck-o-luck, and bingo.

Children would play and then nap on blankets or coats on the lawn. At night there was usually a dance.

These events were important fundraisers and could raise as much as $1,000 or $1,500 for the local parish.

77

Breads

Irish Yeast Bread

5 to 6 C. flour
½ C. sugar
2 T. yeast
¾ tsp. salt
1 C. chopped dates

1 C. hot water
½ C. melted butter
2 eggs (stirred)
⅓ C. mashed potatoes
2 (9x5-inch) baking pans

Dissolve yeast in water with 1 tsp. of the sugar. Let sit for 10 minutes to proof yeast (should be bubbly). Add remaining ingredients, except flour, and stir to blend. Gradually add enough flour to make a batter consistency, then stir 200 strokes. Add enough flour to make a soft dough. Turn out onto floured surface and knead for 5 to 10 minutes, adding remaining flour as needed. There may be flour leftover. Let rise for 1 hour or until double. Punch down and let rest for 15 minutes. Shape into 2 loafs and place in oiled bread pans. Let rise until double, about 25 to 40 minutes. Bake at 350° for 30 to 40 minutes (until loaves are brown and sound hollow when tapped).

"This is a must for St. Patrick's Day or any holiday. Especially delicious warmed for breakfast."

Georgia Ryan

Kolaches

2 pkgs. yeast (I use
   quick rise), dissolved
   in ¼ C. water &
   1 tsp. sugar
1 tsp. salt
1 C. potato water

½ C. milk
⅓ C. sugar
¼ C. margarine
1 egg
4½ to 5 C. flour

FILLING:

1 pkg. seedless prunes
   (cooked)
1½ tsp. cinnamon

Add ½ C. sugar to
   12 ozs. of prunes

Melt margarine. Scald milk and potato water. Add salt and sugar. Cool. Pour dissolved yeast and beaten egg into mixture. Add flour and knead dough in the bowl as the dough will be sticky. Grease top of dough, cover, and let rise. (Quick rise yeast for 30 minutes, other yeast for 1 hour.) Remove from bowl and place on floured board and form into 2-inch balls. Place balls in a greased pan and grease tops. When balls are about half risen add filling by making a hole in center of ball, deep as possible, so filling will not come out when dough is done raising. Bake at 350° until golden brown. Remove from oven and lightly grease the edges of the kolaches.

"This was a tradition in our house, every weekend these were made for our Sunday dinner."

Martha Street

Breads

Help In Stormy Weather

By: Martha Street

"When a storm is brewing and the wind is blowing, we light a portion of a palm and say the 10 Commandments. I always repeat it another time, praying and lighting the palm twice. We have done this ever since I can remember. My mother handed down this tradition. It seems to work as the storm passes quickly."

Plum Bread

1 C. Wesson Oil
2 C. sugar
3 eggs
3 small (4 oz.) jars baby food
  (plums with tapioca)
2½ C. flour

½ tsp. salt
1 tsp. cinnamon
1 C. buttermilk (or 1 C. milk
  with 1 tsp. vinegar)
2 tsp. baking soda

Add ingredients in order given using a electric mixer. Grease two loaf pans and divide mixture into them. Bake at 350⁰ for 30 minutes, then lower heat to 325⁰ and continue baking for an additional 30 minutes. Take out of pans quickly and let cool on rack.

Karen Pommier

Kringle Bread

1 C. milk (warm)
½ C. warm water
1 pkg. dry yeast
2 eggs (beaten)
2 tsp. vanilla

4 C. flour
1 tsp. salt
¼ C. sugar
1 C. oleo

FRUIT FILLING:
2 C. dried apricots
  (chopped)
1 C. raisins
1 C. prunes

½ C. dates
1 C. sugar
2 C. water
3 T. lemon juice

For Bread: Mix all liquid ingredients together. Stir in flour, salt, and sugar together with a fork. Cut oleo into flour mixture like pie crust, then stir liquid ingredients into oleo and flour mixture. Mix well - will be moist batter. Cover and chill at least 2 hours or overnight. Grease hands well. Take ⅓ of dough and pat out on well floured board to about 8x12-inch size. Spread with soft oleo and sprinkle well with cinnamon and brown sugar. Fold edge near you just past center, then bring far edge to barely overlap center. Spread ¼ C. fruit filling, then fold far edge clear over to edge close to you. Pinch edges together, also ends, and place on well-greased pan or cookie sheet. Let rise for 1 to 1½ hours. Repeat above procedure to the other two balls of dough. Bake for 30 minutes until light brown in 350⁰ oven. Ice with 1½ C. powdered sugar, 2 T. milk, and ½ tsp. almond extract. Decorate with candied cherries.

For Filling: Mix all ingredients together and cook for 5 minutes until slightly thickened.

Shirley Bittinger

Breads

Pretzels for Lent

1½ C. warm water
1 pkg. active dry yeast
½ tsp. sugar
½ tsp. salt

4½ to 5 C. flour
1 beaten egg (for glaze)
Coarse salt

Add dry yeast, sugar, and salt to warm water in bowl, stirring to dissolve. Mix in flour, forming a ball. Knead on lightly floured board and let rest for 1 hour or more. Roll pieces of dough 6-inches long and ½-inch thick. Form pretzel shape and place on cookie sheet. Brush with beaten egg and sprinkle with coarse salt. Bake at 425° for 12 to 15 minutes. Makes 30 pretzels.

The pretzel is shaped in the form of arms crossed in prayer. (At one time the custom was to fold your arms over your chest to pray.) Monks would make these breads and give them away to remind people to pray more during Lent and to reward children for learning their prayers.

Teresa Hoffelmeyer

No-Knead Raisin Loaf

5 C. flour
1 C. uncooked quick-
   cooking oats
2 pkgs. active dry yeast

½ C. light molasses
⅓ C. shortening
2 eggs
2 C. dark seedless
   raisins

In a large bowl add 3 C. flour, oats, yeast, and salt. In a medium saucepan over low heat, heat 2 C. of water, molasses, and shortening until very warm (120^0-130^0). (Shortening does not need to melt.) With mixer at medium speed add liquid to dry ingredients and beat for 2 minutes with spoon. Stir in eggs, raisins, and 2 C. flour. Cover with waxed paper and refrigerate for 3 hours. Grease a 3-quart round casserole dish. With well greased hands, shape dough (do not knead) into a large ball and place in casserole. Cover with towel and let rise in warm place (80^0-85^0) until doubled, about 1 hour. Bake at 350^0 for 1 hour and 10 minutes or until golden brown. Cool in casserole for 10 minutes, then remove to rack to cool completely.

"My mother-in-law, Frances Corkrean always made raisin bread on Christmas Eve. It was served to her family after Midnight Mass on Christmas Eve.

To carry on this tradition, I still make it for our family to be served after Midnight Mass."

Nancy M. Corkrean

Breads

Poppy Seed Bread

4 eggs
3¼ C. sugar
2¼ C. milk
¾ tsp. vanilla
4½ C. flour

1½ C. oil
¾ tsp. butter flavoring
2¼ tsp. baking powder
1 tsp. salt
2¼ tsp. poppy seed

GLAZE:
¾ tsp. almond flavoring
¾ tsp. butter flavoring
¾ tsp. vanilla

1 C. sugar
⅓ C. orange juice

Grease and flour three large loaf pans. Mix ingredients together and put in pans. Bake at 325⁰ for 1 hour. Let cool for 3 to 4 minutes. Remove from pans and glaze immediately.

Frances Stevens

Strawberry Bread

4 eggs
1¼ C. salad oil
2 (10 oz.) pkgs. strawberries
   (blended)

3 C. flour
1 tsp. soda
1 tsp. salt
1 C. nuts

Mix in order given and pour into two greased and floured loaf pans. (Joan puts waxed paper on bottom first.) Bake at 350⁰ for 45 to 60 minutes.

Joan Hilton
Frances Radke

Oatmeal Raisin Bread

2 pkgs. dry yeast	2½ tsp. salt
½ C. warm water	2 eggs
1½ C. boiling water	5½ to 6 C. flour
1 C. oatmeal	1 C. raisins
½ C. brown sugar	⅓ C. sugar
7 T. soft butter	3 tsp. cinnamon

In a cup, dissolve yeast in warm water and let stand for 5 minutes or until foamy. In a large bowl, stir boiling water, oats, brown sugar, 3 T. butter, and salt until lukewarm. Beat in eggs, 2 C. flour, raisins, and yeast mix. Stir in remaining flour gradually until a stiff dough is formed. On a floured surface knead dough until smooth and elastic. Place in greased bowl and turn to coat surface. Cover and let rise in a warm place, until doubled, about 1½ hours. Mix sugar and cinnamon. On a floured surface, roll half of dough into a 15x9-inch rectangle. Spread with 2 T. butter and sprinkle with ½ of sugar mixture. Roll from short side and place in greased 8½ x4½ -inch loaf pan. Repeat with second half. Cover and let rise until almost double, about 45 minutes. Bake in preheated 350⁰ oven for 45 to 55 minutes or until well browned. Cool. Makes two loaves.

Jana Corkrean

85

Breads

Rich Egg Batter Bread

2 T. softened butter
6½ C. sifted flour
2 C. very warm water
   (120° to 130°)

3 eggs
2 T. sugar
2 pkgs. active dry yeast
2 tsp. salt

Mix together 1½ C. flour, sugar, salt, and yeast in a large bowl. Add butter. Gradually add water to dry ingredients and beat for 2 minutes at medium speed of electric mixer. Add eggs and ½ C. flour; beat for 2 minutes at high speed. Stir in enough remaining flour to make a soft dough. Cover and let rise until doubled, about 35 minutes. Stir down and turn into two well-greased 1½-quart casseroles. Cover and let rise until doubled, about 40 minutes. Bake at 375° for 35 minutes or until done. Makes 2 loaves.

Jill Kordick

Unleavend Communion Bread

1 C. white flour
3 C. whole-wheat flour
1½ tsp. soda
1½ tsp. salt

1½ C. water
4 T. oil
6 T. honey

Knead and roll dough ¼-inch thick. Cut with 2 lb. coffee can. Dent with two smaller circles and then cut an X on top. Bake at 350°.

Jo Agan

St. Lucia's Wreath

6½ to 7 C. flour
½ C. sugar
2 tsp. salt
¾ tsp. cardamon
2 pkgs. active dry yeast
¾ C. milk

½ C. water
½ C. butter
3 eggs
1 T. milk
1 egg

GLAZE:
¾ C. powdered sugar   1½ to 2½ tsp. milk
¼ tsp. vanilla

Grease a large cookie sheet. Spoon flour into measuring cup and level off. In a large bowl, combine 2 C. flour, sugar, salt, cardamon, and yeast. In saucepan heat ¾ C. milk, water, and butter to 120°. Add warm liquid and 3 eggs to flour mixture. Blend at low speed until moist, then beat for 3 minutes at medium speed. Stir in an additional 4½ to 5 C. of flour until dough pulls away from sides of bowl. On floured surface, knead ¼ to ½ C. flour until dough is smooth (10 minutes). Place dough in greased bowl and cover. Let rise until doubled, about 1½ hour. Punch down and divide dough in half. Let rest for 15 minutes on counter, covered with a bowl. Shape each half into 45-inch rope. Twist ropes together and place in ring on cookie sheet. Pinch ends to seal. Cover and let rise until doubled in a warm place, about 1 hour. Heat oven to 350°. Combine 1 T. milk and 1 egg. Brush over wreath and bake at 350° for 25 to 35 minutes. Remove wreath from cookie sheet immediately. Cool on wire rack. Drizzle with glaze. To decorate add 3 or 4 candles and ribbon or greenery.

Teresa Hoffelmeyer

Breads

St. Lucia

St. Lucia's feast day is December 13th. On the Sunday nearest her feast day, our parish remembers this young saint in a special way:

When the children come forward to receive their blessing at the end of Mass, Father tells them the story of St. Lucia:

St. Lucia was a Christian martyr, killed around 304 A.D. It is said that a rejected suitor denounced her as a Christian. According to legend, her eyes were plucked out during her torture and then miraculously restored. In the end, she was killed by a sword.

In Swedish homes, the oldest daughter serves special breads, like "St. Lucia's Wreath," to her family for breakfast on this feast day. She may wear a wreath with several candles upon her own head while serving the bread. This symbolizes St. Lucia's martrydom, as martyrs are said to wear crowns in heaven.

In our parish, each child receives a construction paper wreath "crown" upon his or her head. Then, after Mass, at the Parish Hall, the Junior High girls wear candle wreaths upon their heads, LEAVING THE CANDLES UNLIT, and serve braided bread to parishioners.

Zucchini Bread

2 C. sugar	1 tsp. baking soda
3 eggs	1 tsp. baking powder
1 C. oil	1 tsp. salt
2 C. zucchini	½ C. milk
(peeled & grated)	1 tsp. vanilla
3 C. flour	⅔ C. chopped nuts
1 tsp. cinnamon	Raisins (optional)

Blend by hand the sugar, eggs, and oil. Stir in zucchini. Add the remaining ingredients, except the nuts. Blend thoroughly, then add nuts or raisins, if desired. Pour into greased and floured loaf pans, filling them half full. (I use 3 fruit cans for nice round loaves.) Bake at 325° for 60 to 65 minutes. Test with a toothpick. Makes 2 regular loaves or 4 little ones. Freezes nicely.

Pam Palmer

89

Breads

Zucchini Bread

2 C. sugar
3 eggs
1 C. oil
2 tsp. vanilla
2 C. shredded unpeeled
   zucchini
1 (15¼ oz.) can crushed
   pineapple (drained)

3 C. flour
2 tsp. baking soda
1½ tsp. cinnamon
1 tsp. salt
¾ tsp. nutmeg
¼ tsp. baking powder
1 C. chopped dates
½ C. chopped pecans (optional)

Beat eggs, oil, sugar, and vanilla until thick. Stir in remaining ingredients and mix well. Pour into two greased 9x5-inch loaf pans. Bake at 350° for about 1 hour or until wooden pick comes out clean. Cool on rack and serve. Keeps well wrapped in freezer.

Josephine Sitkiewicz
Barb Schmitz

Banana-Oatmeal Muffins

1 C. flour
½ C. sugar
2½ tsp. baking powder
¾ C. oats
¼ tsp. baking soda

1 egg
3 T. oil
½ C. mashed banana
½ C. milk

Sift dry ingredients and set aside. Mix other ingredients together and add to dry. Stir until moistened. Batter will be slightly lumpy. Bake at 400° for 15 to 20 minutes.

Cindy Watson Pottebaum

Applesauce Bran Muffins

3 C. All-Bran cereal
2 C. milk
1 C. unsweetened
  applesauce
2 eggs
⅓ C. vegetable oil

4 tsp. baking powder
½ tsp. salt
¾ C. brown sugar
  (packed)
1 T. cinnamon
2½ C. flour

Preheat oven to 375⁰. In a large bowl combine cereal, milk, and applesauce; allow to sit for 10 minutes. Beat in eggs and oil. In a separate bowl, stir together all remaining dry ingredients. Fold dry ingredients into cereal mixture, just until moistened. Spoon into 24 muffin tins, sprayed with non-stick cooking spray. Bake at 375⁰ for 15 to 18 minutes. Yield: 24 muffins.

Rosemary Stuchel

Orange-Oatmeal Muffins

½ C. oats
1½ C. flour
1¼ tsp. baking powder
¼ tsp. baking soda
½ C. sugar

½ C. oil
¼ C. frozen orange
  juice
¼ C. water
1 egg

Sift dry ingredients together in a bowl. Mix all other ingredients together and add to dry ingredients. Stir only until moistened - the batter will be slightly lumpy. Sprinkle with sugar and cinnamon before baking. Bake at 400⁰ for approximately 15 minutes.

Cindy Watson Pottebaum

91

Breads

Whole-Wheat Muffins

2 eggs (well-beaten)
¾ C. melted shortening
¾ C. brown sugar
2 C. buttermilk

4 C. whole-wheat flour
2 tsp. soda
½ C. wheat germ

Mix well and bake at 350⁰ for 15 to 20 minutes. Makes 2 dozen muffins. I freeze them and reheat in microwave for breakfast or a healthy snack.

Jean Pletchette

Best Cinnamon Rolls

2½ C. lukewarm water
2 pkgs. yeast
1 box yellow cake mix
1 C. all-purpose flour
3 eggs
⅓ C. oil

1 tsp. salt
5¼ C. flour
Soft margarine
Sugar
Cinnamon

Dissolve yeast in water for about 3 minutes. Add cake mix, 1 C. flour, eggs, oil, and salt. Beat with beater until bubbles appear. Slowly add 5¼ C. flour and stir until you have made a soft dough. Knead for about 8 to 10 minutes. Let rise until double. Roll out to about ¼-inch thick. Spread with margarine and sprinkle with sugar and cinnamon. Roll up jelly roll style and stretch. Cut and place each roll cut side up on a greased pan. Allow to rise until double and bake at 350⁰ for 20 to 30 minutes. Ice with powdered sugar frosting.

Marvin & Mira Imes

Custard Sweet Rolls

2 pkgs. yeast, dissolved in 1 C. warm water
½ C. melted oleo
2 tsp. salt
1 egg
1 box vanilla instant pudding mix
1 C. warm water in addition to the 1 C. added to the yeast
1 C. warm milk
7 or 8 C. flour

Dissolve yeast in 1 C. warm water. Mix the next 6 ingredients and add the yeast. Stir in flour. Knead until smooth. Let rise, roll out ½ of dough at a time. Spread with butter, brown sugar (I use ½ white sugar), and cinnamon. Roll-up and slice. Place in greased baking dish and let rise again. Bake at 350⁰ for 20 to 25 minutes.

For Glaze: Mix 1 C. brown sugar, 1 C. powdered sugar, and enough milk to make a thin paste. Ice while rolls are still hot.

Maxine Brunsmann

93

Breads

Feather Rolls
"Family favorite as Cinnamon Twist"

1 C. mashed potatoes (hot)	½ C. sugar
½ C. butter	1½ tsp. salt
2 pkgs. yeast	1½ C. potato water
1 egg + 1 egg yolk (beaten)	6 C. flour (sifted) (approx.)

Beat hot mashed potatoes, sugar, butter, and salt together until blended. Beat egg and egg yolk until light. Dissolve yeast in 4 T. warm potato water. Combine potato mixture with egg mixture and the rest of potato water. Stir in yeast and half of flour, beating until smooth, then add more flour to make soft dough. Knead on a lightly floured board until smooth and satiny. Put dough in greased bowl, cover, and let rise to double in bulk. If you have time, punch down and let rise again. At this time you can shape them and put them on greased baking sheet or punch down and store in refrigerator for later.

For Cinnamon Twist: Take enough dough that you think will make a nice size roll. Pull long, dip in butter, then in cinnamon-sugar mixture and twist. Let rise until doubled or light. Bake at 325⁰ for 30 minutes (approximately) or if freezing, 400⁰ for 15 minutes. Cool and wrap.

Delores Nicholson

Overnight Sweet Rolls

3 C. warm water
1 tsp. yeast
1 C. sugar
1 T. salt

2 eggs
½ C. shortening
10 or more C. of flour

SYRUP:
¾ C. brown sugar
¾ C. oleo

1 tsp. white Karo syrup

Starting at 5:00 p.m. mix the ingredients with enough flour, so that it is just past the sticky stage. Put into a greased pan, cover, and push down every hour. At 10:00 p.m. place equal amounts of brown sugar and oleo into 9x13-inch pan and melt slowly on stove. (Optional: Add 4 ozs. pecans.) Recipe will make 50 to 60 medium rolls, so you will need to prepare three 9x13-inch pans. Roll the dough out after dividing it in half, then spread with oleo and sprinkle with brown sugar. Form into a long roll, about 2-inches in diameter, cutting not more than 1-inch thick and place into pans, about 20 to a pan. Place on table and cover with towel and let raise overnight. Bake at 400° for 20 minutes. Take from oven and immediately turn pan over on foil and let stand for a minute to let drip.

Jo Agan

Orange Rolls

1 C. milk
½ C. shortening
⅓ C. sugar
1 tsp. salt
1 pkg. yeast

¼ C. warm water
2 eggs (beaten)
¼ C. orange juice
Grated peel of 2 oranges
5 to 6 C. flour (divided)

Heat milk, shortening, sugar, and salt. Cool to lukewarm. Dissolve yeast in warm water. In a large bowl combine yeast with milk mixture, eggs, juice, peel, and 3 C. flour. Mix well, then add remaining flour to form a soft dough. Knead and place in a greased bowl. Cover and let rise for 1½ hours or until doubled in size. Punch down and let rest for 15 minutes. Roll dough into a rectangle. Cut into 16x1-inch strips, tie in knots, and place on a greased cookie sheets. Cover and let rise until double, about 1 hour. Bake at 400° until golden brown. Cool and spread with following glaze.

GLAZE:
2 T. orange juice
2 tsp. grated orange peel

1 C. powdered sugar

Spread glaze over rolls.

Shirley Privratsky

96

Sticky Buns

1 C. milk	1 egg
½ C. sugar	⅔ C. light brown sugar
1 tsp. salt	1½ tsp. cinnamon
1 env. dry yeast	½ C. light corn syrup
½ C. butter	½ C. pecans (optional)
(¼ C. for dough &	¾ C. raisins (optional)
¼ C. for sticky)	

Heat milk. Dissolve yeast in ½ C. warm water. Mix sugar, salt, yeast, ¼ C. butter, egg, and 3 C. flour. Add milk and stir in rest of flour and knead. Let rise until double. Punch down and prepare the topping for rolls. Mix ¼ C. butter, corn syrup, and brown sugar. Put in the bottom of a 9x13-inch pan. Roll dough out and spread with butter, 2 T. sugar, 1 tsp. cinnamon, nuts, and raisins. Roll up as for jelly roll. Cut into rolls and put on top the sticky mixture in pan. Let rise again. Bake at 350⁰ for about 25 minutes or until lightly brown. Immediately invert onto waxed paper. Makes 12 very large rolls.

Linda Hermanstorfer

TIP: If you dissolve yeast in liquid, the liquid temperature should be 110°-115°. If you use the mixer method and yeast is blended with dry ingredients before adding liquid, the liquid should be 120°-130°.

Breads

'Kids in Church'
By: Cindy Watson Pottebaum

My husband Jim and I like to sing at church services and we have encouraged our children to sing starting at an early age.

Our daughter Kate was about three years old when she started holding the hymnal and flipping through the pages. One Sunday morning during the celebration of the Eucharist, while the congregation was singing the "Holy, Holy," she started singing the ABC song at the top of her lungs. She got some strange looks and smiles from those nearby but she didn't pay any attention. Then as the congregation sang the "Great Amen," she started in again with the ABC song at the top of her lungs. When she finished I leaned over and whispered that she should sing the same songs as us. Kate said, "But Mommy, I don't know any of those 'God songs'."

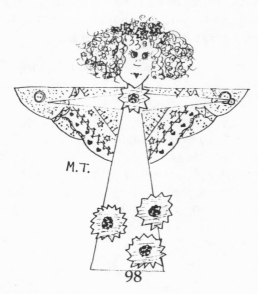

M.T.

Brunch

Brunch

Our parish has a number of brunches throughout the year to celebrate various events. We have a St. Nicholas Brunch and a Palm Sunday Brunch for everyone in the parish. We also have a First Communion, Confirmation, and Graduation brunch for the students involved and their families. In this section of our cookbook, you will find some of our favorite brunch recipes.

Fruit Slush

1 (6 oz.) can frozen lemonade
1 (6 oz.) can frozen
   orange juice
2 C. sugar
4 C. water
1 (11 oz.) can mandarin oranges
   (drained)

1 can pineapple tidbits or
   chunks (15 oz., drained)
1 (10 oz.) frozen small carton
   strawberries
3 bananas (sliced)

Mix sugar and water in pan and warm to dissolve sugar completely. Add lemonade and orange juice; stir. Add fruit and pour into 9x13-inch Tupperware container or glass baking dish. Freeze. Remove from freezer for 20 to 30 minutes before serving. (Juices from oranges and pineapple may be used instead of water to complete the 4 C. of water.) (Can be frozen in individual plastic cups.)

Marilyn Mc Namara

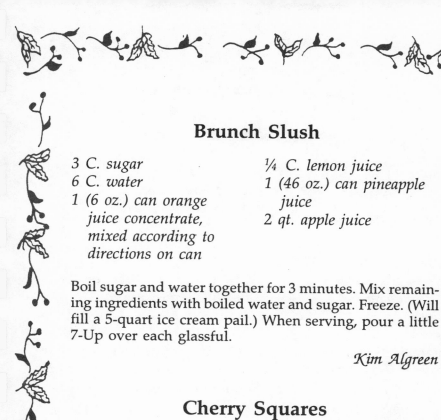

Brunch Slush

3 C. sugar
6 C. water
1 (6 oz.) can orange
   juice concentrate,
   mixed according to
   directions on can

¼ C. lemon juice
1 (46 oz.) can pineapple
   juice
2 qt. apple juice

Boil sugar and water together for 3 minutes. Mix remaining ingredients with boiled water and sugar. Freeze. (Will fill a 5-quart ice cream pail.) When serving, pour a little 7-Up over each glassful.

Kim Algreen

Cherry Squares

½ C. Crisco
½ C. margarine
1¾ C. sugar
4 eggs
1 tsp. vanilla
½ tsp. almond extract

3 C. sifted flour
1½ tsp. baking powder
½ tsp. salt
1 can Wilderness cherry
   pie filling

Beat together Crisco and margarine; add the sugar, eggs, vanilla, and almond flavoring. Alternately add and beat in the flour, baking powder, and salt which have been sifted together. Pour ⅔ on a greased 10x15-inch cookie sheet (jelly roll pan with sides). Spread out evenly. Drop cherry pie filling by teaspoon over the batter. Top by adding by teaspoon the remaining ⅓ of the batter. Bake at 350° until light brown, about 25 minutes. Cut in squares.

Anna King
Ruth Eivins

Brunch

Coffee Cake

2 C. flour
2 eggs
1 C. sugar
1 C. milk

4 T. shortening
1 tsp. salt
4 tsp. baking powder

TOPPING:
½ C. brown sugar
2 tsp. cinnamon
2 T. flour

2 T. butter or margarine
Finely chopped nuts

Mix ingredients together and beat for 3 minutes on high speed. Pour in a greased 9x13-inch and sprinkle with the brown sugar mixture. Bake at 350⁰ for approximately 40 minutes or until it tests done.

"This was a recipe of Marguerite Gallery's. Now and then after 8:00 mass she would have us stop by and she would put it in the oven. We would savor the aroma while baking and later enjoy the cake and coffee. Fond memories and good times."

Mildred Waltz

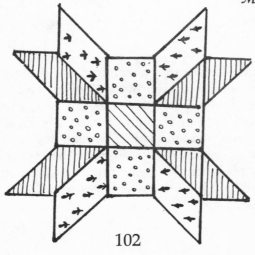

102

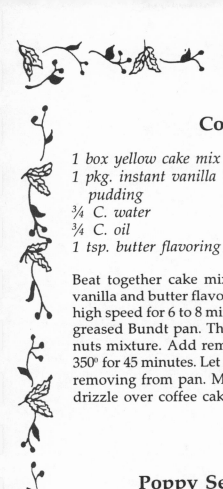

Coffee Cake

1 box yellow cake mix
1 pkg. instant vanilla
   pudding
¾ C. water
¾ C. oil
1 tsp. butter flavoring

1 tsp. vanilla
4 eggs
1 tsp. cinnamon
¼ C. white sugar
¼ C. nuts

Beat together cake mix, pudding, water, and oil. Add vanilla and butter flavoring. Add eggs, 1 at a time. Beat at high speed for 6 to 8 minutes. Pour half of mixture in well greased Bundt pan. Then add the cinnamon, sugar, and nuts mixture. Add remaining cake mixture and bake at 350⁰ for 45 minutes. Let stand for at least 10 minutes before removing from pan. Make a powdered sugar glaze and drizzle over coffee cake while still warm.

Barbara Corkrean
Bev Maxwell

Poppy Seed Brunch Cake

3 eggs
2 C. sugar
1 C. vegetable oil
3 C. flour

1½ tsp. soda
1 tsp. salt
1 can evaporated milk
¼ C. poppy seeds

Mix the eggs, sugar, and oil very well for 3 minutes. Sift flour, soda, and salt. Add flour mixture alternately with evaporated milk. Stir in poppy seeds. Bake in a greased Bundt pan at 350⁰ for 45 to 50 minutes.

"I have made this without the poppy seeds and it makes a delightful pound "type" cake to serve with fresh strawberries or fudge sauce."

Linda Hermanstorfer

Brunch

Sour Cream Coffee Cake

½ C. margarine
1 C. sugar
1 egg
1 C. sour cream

2 C. sifted flour
1 tsp. baking soda
1 tsp. vanilla

TOPPING:
1 C. flour
½ C. sugar

½ C. margarine

Cream margarine, sugar, and egg together. Add dry ingredients to creamed mixture. Alternate with sour cream and vanilla. Use a fork or pastry blender to combine topping. Add topping and bake in a greased and floured 15½ x10½ x1-inch pan at 350⁰ for 20 minutes. Remove from oven and let cool a few minutes. Drizzle powdered sugar frosting over top.

Val Herzog

Springtime Coffee Cake

1 pkg. lemon cake mix
1 can peach pie filling
3 eggs

½ tsp. lemon juice
½ C. nuts

TOPPING:
½ C. sugar
½ C. flour

¼ C. butter
½ tsp. lemon juice

Combine dry cake mix, eggs, pie filling, lemon juice, and nuts. Blend at low speed of mixer. Spread batter in greased 13x9x2-inch pan. Combine topping and sprinkle over cake mixture. Bake at 350⁰ for 40 to 50 minutes. (If desired mix some powdered sugar and water together. Drizzle over top when cooled.) Other pie fillings may be used - apricot, raisin, cherry, etc.

Ginny Hoffelmeyer

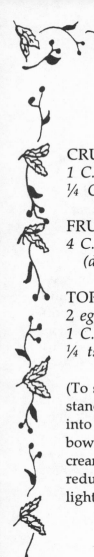

Kuchen

CRUST:
1 C. flour ¼ tsp. salt
¼ C. confectioner's sugar ½ C. butter

FRUIT FILLING:
4 C. fruit (peaches, cherries, etc.)
  (drained)

TOPPING:
2 eggs 3 T. flour
1 C. sugar 1 C. sour cream
¼ tsp. salt

(To sour cream, add 1 T. lemon juice or vinegar and let stand for 5 minutes.) Combine crust ingredients and pat into 13x9-inch pan. Arrange fruit over crust. In another bowl beat eggs well, then add sugar, salt, flour, and sour cream. Pour over fruit and bake at 450° for 10 minutes then reduce heat to 325° for remaining 35 minutes. Should be lightly browned on top when done.

Phyllis Patrick

Brunch

Marge's Christmas Coffee Cake

1 C. scalded milk
¼ C. butter
½ C. sugar
1 tsp. salt
2 cakes yeast
¼ C. lukewarm water

2 eggs
4¾ C. flour
2 (8 oz.) can Solo brand
   fillings: apricot, almond
   paste, poppy seed or
   prune

Pour scalded milk over butter, sugar, and salt, stirring well. Dissolve yeast into lukewarm water with a pinch (¼ tsp.) of sugar. Cool milk mixture to lukewarm and add yeast. Let set for a few minutes until yeast begins to work. Add well beaten eggs, then gradually add flour and stir well after each addition of flour to form a soft dough. Turn out onto floured surface and knead until smooth and elastic. Form into ball and place in greased bowl. Let rise until double. Cut into 4 parts and roll each into rectangle approximately 10x12-inches and brush with warm melted butter. Spread with ½ can filling. Roll up and pinch seam shut and place seam side down on greased cookie sheet. Cut slits in top of roll, cover, and let raise until double. Bake at 350⁰ for 25 minutes. Frost with the following while still warm:

1 C. powdered sugar
½ tsp. vanilla or almond
   extract

2-3 T. milk, enough to
   make frosting fairly thin

Frost coffee cakes and decorate with red and green cherries (cut in half and drained). Sprinkle with nuts. Can place on cardboard cut to size, covered with foil and wrapped with Saran wrap. Trim with a Christmas ribbon for gift giving.

"Grandma Marge (Dick's Mother) delivered these Christmas Eve Day to each of her 10 children and their families so we could enjoy Christmas morning. We all looked forward to this delicious family tradition."

Fonda Bass

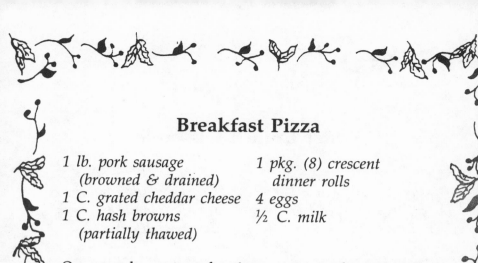

Breakfast Pizza

1 lb. pork sausage
  (browned & drained)
1 C. grated cheddar cheese
1 C. hash browns
  (partially thawed)

1 pkg. (8) crescent
  dinner rolls
4 eggs
½ C. milk

On a round or rectangular pizza pan, greased, pat out rolls, sides touching, and flute edges. Layer in order: sausage, cheese, and hash browns. Beat eggs and milk together. Drizzle on top and bake at 325° for 20 to 25 minutes.

Debby Corkrean

"Roger's Breakfast Pizza"

1 can refrigerator biscuits
4 eggs
½ C. milk
Ham or cooked bacon
  (chopped)

American cheese slices
1 green onion (chopped)
  (optional)
Mushroom pieces
  (optional)

Grease the bottom of a 13x9x2-inch cake pan (or smaller). With rolling pin, roll out the refrigerator biscuits to about ¼-inch thick, then set in bottom of pan. Beat eggs with a whisk, then stir in milk. Place the ham or bacon on top of the biscuits, then the onions and mushrooms. Over this, place the cheese slices. Pour the egg and milk mixture over everything and bake, uncovered for 15 minutes.

"This easy casserole is an original recipe and a real favorite of our kids."

Cheryl Weltha

Brunch

Easter Brunch Casserole

SAUCE:

8-10 slices diced bacon

1 (4 oz.) pkg. chipped beef

¼ C. butter

1 (2 oz.) can sliced mushrooms

1 qt. milk (may use
Half & Half)

SCRAMBLED EGGS:

16 eggs

¼ C. melted butter

1 C. milk

¾ tsp. salt

Make sauce by frying bacon, then remove from heat. Add chipped beef, butter, mushrooms and mix well. Sprinkle ½ C. flour and pepper, to taste over bacon, beef, and mushrooms. Add 1 quart of milk. Cook on medium-high heat, stirring constantly until thickened; set aside. Combine eggs, milk, and salt. Melt butter in a large skillet and scramble until cooked through. Use shallow 9x13-inch baking dish and alternate layers of eggs and sauce. (Be sure to keep eggs moist to prevent darkening.) You may cover and refrigerate at this point. To serve, heat covered at 275⁰ for 40 minutes until heated through and bubbly. Do not overbake as eggs will discolor.

"This recipe was prepared by my mother-in-law every Easter and Christmas morning. She was the best mother-in-law anyone could ever have. Now, I never miss preparing this dish on Easter and Christmas mornings. These holidays aren't the same without it. My family always looks forward to our holiday breakfasts. I prepare the casserole the night before. I hope someone else can enjoy it as much as we have."

Joy Drury

108

Brunch Casserole

1 (10 oz.) pkg. hash
   browns
¼ C. onion
2 T. parsley
¼ C. butter
½ C. flour
1½ C. milk

1 tsp. salt
¼ tsp. pepper
1 C. commercial sour
   cream
1 lb. sausage
8 cooked scrambled eggs

Cook hash browns according to package directions and drain grease. Stir in onion and parsley. Place in greased 9x13-inch pan. Melt butter. Add flour, salt, and pepper. Add milk and cook until it thickens. Stir in sour cream and remove from heat. Cover the potatoes with sausage. Pour half the sauce over the sausage. Cover with scrambled eggs and then pour remaining sauce on top. Bake at 350⁰ for 30 minutes.

P.J. Hoffelmeyer

Potato & Sausage Casserole

1 lb. pork sausage
1 can cream of chicken
   soup
¾ C. milk

¼ C. chopped onion
4 C. sliced raw potatoes
Grated cheese

Brown sausage and drain well. Put potatoes in bottom of pan. Add sausage and cover with soup mixture. Bake at 350⁰ for 1¼ to 1½ hours. Add cheese when almost done.

Jana Corkrean

Egg Casserole

1 box seasoned croutons
Cubed ham or bacon
6 beaten eggs (I use a
   couple more)
½ tsp. dry mustard

¼ lb. butter
½ lb. Velveeta cheese
   (cubed)
2 C. milk
½ tsp. salt

Cover bottom of greased 9x13-inch pan with croutons. Sprinkle bacon or ham over croutons. Add cheese. Mix together eggs, milk, dry mustard, and salt. Pour over croutons, meat, and cheese. Melt butter and pour over top. Cover and refrigerate overnight. Bake at 350° for 1 hour, uncovering for the last 10 minutes.

Sue Stuchel
Joanne Nichols

24 Hour Breakfast

12 slices bread (cubed)
½ lb. American cheese
   (2 C. grated)
2 to 3 C. cubed ham or
   1 lb. cooked sausage

6 to 8 eggs
2 C. milk
1 tsp. salt
½ C. melted oleo

Grease an 8x12-inch baking dish. Put half of bread cubes on bottom. Cover with half of cheese and ham. Repeat with remaining bread, ham, and cheese. Combine eggs, milk, and salt. Pour over bread and other ingredients. Drizzle melted oleo over top. Cover casserole and refrigerate overnight. Bake at 325°-350° for 1¼ hours, uncovering for the last 15 minutes of baking.

"This casserole is great to fix for large family gatherings. Can be baking while you get dressed in A.M. Good with fresh fruit and rolls."

Shirley A. Bittinger

110

Microwave Omelet Surprise

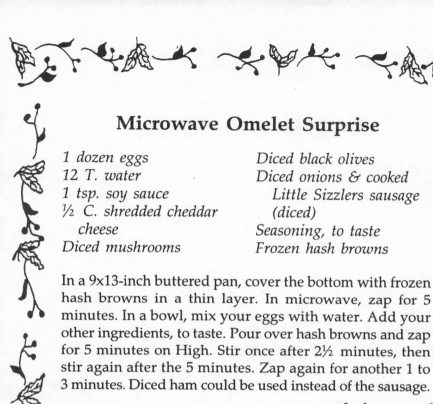

1 dozen eggs
12 T. water
1 tsp. soy sauce
½ C. shredded cheddar
   cheese
Diced mushrooms

Diced black olives
Diced onions & cooked
   Little Sizzlers sausage
   (diced)
Seasoning, to taste
Frozen hash browns

In a 9x13-inch buttered pan, cover the bottom with frozen hash browns in a thin layer. In microwave, zap for 5 minutes. In a bowl, mix your eggs with water. Add your other ingredients, to taste. Pour over hash browns and zap for 5 minutes on High. Stir once after 2½ minutes, then stir again after the 5 minutes. Zap again for another 1 to 3 minutes. Diced ham could be used instead of the sausage.

Chad Emanuel

Fluffy French Toast

1 C. flour
1 tsp. baking powder
½ tsp. salt
1 C. milk

2 eggs (beaten)
10 slices French bread or
   Texas toast

ORANGE SYRUP:
1 C. orange juice   1 C. sugar

For Orange Syrup: In a small saucepan, mix orange juice and sugar. Boil for 5 minutes and set aside. In a separate bowl, sift flour with baking powder and salt. Stir in eggs and milk. Beat well. Cut bread in thirds. Dip in batter and fry. Serve with orange syrup.

Kim Algreen

Brunch

Southwest Style Quiche

¼ C. butter
½ C. flour
1 C. milk
6 eggs (separated)
¼ C. cilantro
3 scallions (chopped)
1 small red pepper
(chopped)

2 jalapeno peppers
(seeded & chopped)
1½ tsp. ground cumin
1 T. olive oil
1 (7 oz.) can corn
¼ C. pitted black olives
½ lb. grated Jack cheese
⅓ C. salsa

Preheat oven to 375⁰. Coat a 15x10-inch pan with non-stick cooking spray, then line with wax paper, and then coat wax paper. In a saucepan melt butter and stir in flour until smooth and mix begans to boil. Stir in milk until smooth and slightly thick. Remove from heat. In a large bowl beat egg yolks until thick. Stir in cilantro, gradually stir yolks into milk. Beat eggs whites until stiff, but not dry, then fold into egg yolk mixture. Spread into pan and bake for 18 to 22 minutes or until top springs back when touched. Meanwhile saute' other ingredients, except ham, cheese, and salsa until heated through. Immediately after removing dough from oven loosen edges with knife and invert onto clean towel, peeling off wax paper. Layer ham, vegetable mixture, and cheese on warm roulade. Starting at shorter end lift one end of towel. Roll the roulade, raising the towel as you go. Arrange on lettuce leaves and top with salsa. I usually warm the salsa. Serve warm.

Ann Winjum

112

Crepes

4 eggs
1 C. flour
½ C. milk
½ C. water

½ tsp. salt
2 T. melted butter
2 tsp. sugar
1 tsp. vanilla

Measure all ingredients, except flour into large mixing bowl. Beat with electric mixer on medium speed gradually adding flour. Cook in non-stick frying pan. Make very thin, just covering the bottom of the pan. When lightly browned turn and cook other side for a few seconds. Sprinkle with lemon juice and sugar; roll up before eating. (They can also be filled with cherry pie filling, rolled up and served with sour cream or whipped cream. Be creative.)

Serve on Fat Tuesday

Fat Tuesday is the Tuesday before Lent begins. At one time, Lent meant no eggs, fat, meat, or dairy products. Because people did not want their stored food to go to waste during Lent and the coming warm weather, they would eat all they could the Tuesday before Lent. It was a festive occasion, when one could splurge before the fasting of Lent began.

Often pancakes would be made to use up any eggs on hand. This is a recipe for French pancakes, crepes. As a child my mother would serve these crepes with sugar sprinkled on them and fresh lemon juice squeezed over them. I still enjoy eating crepes this way although I haven't converted my family to this method.

The Parish Mardi Gras

Our Parish celebrates the Mardi Gras with a family get-together, much food, karoake, talent show, games, pinata, and all the fun we can think of.

Teresa Hoffelmeyer

113

Norwegian Pancakes

3 eggs

1 C. sugar

¼ tsp. salt

1 tsp. grated lemon rind

1 C. milk or Half & Half

½ C. melted butter

1 C. flour

Beat eggs until light in a large mixer bowl (about 3 minutes). Add remaining ingredients in order given. Heat a non-stick skillet or crepe pan. Pour in ¼ C. batter covering bottom of pan. When pancake begins to lose its gloss and turns light brown on the bottom, loosen sides and turn. When light brown on second side, fold into fourths and serve. (These are very sweet and rich and very much like a crepe. Serve with a little fresh lemon juice squeezed over them.)

Kim Algreen

French Breakfast Puffs

½ C. sugar

⅓ C. shortening

1 egg

1½ C. flour

1½ tsp. baking powder

½ tsp. salt

¼ tsp. nutmeg

½ C. milk

Cream sugar, shortening, and egg. Sift flour, baking powder, salt, and nutmeg. Alternate milk and dry ingredients when adding to the creamed mixture. Spoon into 12 muffin cups. Bake at 350⁰ for 20 to 25 minutes. While baking mix ½ C. sugar and 1 tsp. cinnamon and melt 6 T. margarine. When puffs are done, dip tops in melted butter and then in sugar-cinnamon mixture.

Jill Johnson

Raisin Bran Muffins

5 C. flour
2 tsp. baking soda
2 tsp. salt
3 C. white sugar

15 oz. box Raisin Bran
4 eggs (beaten)
1 qt. buttermilk
1 C. salad oil

Combine the first 5 ingredients together. Add eggs, butter-milk, and salad oil. Mix well. Cover and refrigerate. Will keep in the refrigerator for up to 6 weeks. Fill muffin tins ⅔ full and bake at 400° for 15 minutes.

Nancy M. Corkrean

Mashed Potato Doughnuts

3 eggs
2 C. sugar
1½ C. warm mashed
   potatoes
⅓ C. margarine (melted)
1 C. buttermilk
6 C. flour

4 tsp. baking powder
1½ tsp. soda
1 tsp. salt
1 tsp. nutmeg or vanilla,
   lemon juice or mace
   can be substituted for
   the nutmeg

Mix all the above ingredients in the order given and refrigerate for 1 hour. Roll and cut out for doughnuts. Fry in Crisco or lard. These freeze very well. Roll in sugar as you use them.

"These are a must for our fishing trips to Minnesota. About an hour down the road, someone is sure to say, "How about a cup of coffee and a doughnut?"

Mildred Waltz

115

Light as a Feather Doughnuts

¾ C. milk
¼ C. sugar
1 tsp. salt
¼ C. margarine

¼ C. warm water
1 pkg. yeast
1 egg
3¼ C. flour

Scald milk, then stir in sugar, salt, and margarine. Cool to lukewarm. Measure water into large warm mixing bowl. Sprinkle in yeast and stir until dissolved. Add lukewarm milk mixture, egg, and half the flour, beating until smooth. Stir in enough additional flour to make a soft dough. Turn dough out onto lightly floured board. Knead until smooth and elastic, about 10 minutes. Place in a greased bowl, turning to cover all sides. Cover and let rise until double. Punch down and roll to ½-inch thickness. Cut with 2½-inch doughnut cutter. Place on greased baking sheets, cover, and let rise until doubled (about 1 hour). Handle as little as possible. Fry in deep fat at 375° for 2 to 3 minutes or until brown on both sides. (Fry flat side first.) Drain on absorbent paper towel. While still warm, dip in glaze or cinnamon-sugar mixture.

For Glaze: Blend together 2 C. powdered sugar, ⅓ C. milk, and 1 tsp. vanilla. After dipping warm doughnuts in glaze, drain on rack.

For Cinnamon-Sugar: Combine ½ C. sugar and 2 tsp. cinnamon.

"Occasionally my Grandma Lehn would take care of my brothers, sister, and myself after school. She made these doughnuts on one of those occasions and they are delicious."

Linda Hermanstorfer

Cakes & Frostings

Fresh Apple Cake

2 C. sugar
1 C. shortening
2 eggs
3 C. flour
2 tsp. soda

¼ tsp. salt
1½ tsp. cinnamon
6 C. peeled & sliced apples
¾ C. nuts

Cream sugar, shortening, and eggs. Sift flour, soda, salt, and cinnamon. Add to creamed mixture. Work the apples into the dough (with mixer). I put the nuts into the topping instead of the cake. Spread into greased 9x13-inch pan and bake at 325° for 40 to 50 minutes.

TOPPING:
1 pt. Half & Half
1 C. brown sugar
¾ C. nuts

2 rounding T. cornstarch
Pinch of salt
2 T. butter

Boil until thick. Add 1 tsp. vanilla. Spread over fresh baked apple cake.

Anna King

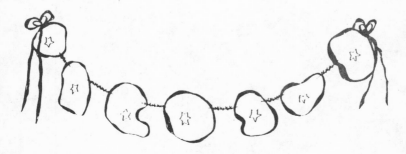

Apple Nut Cake

3 C. flour (sifted)
3 C. chopped apples
2 C. sugar
1 C. Wesson Oil
1 C. nuts

3 eggs
1 tsp. soda
½ tsp. salt
2½ tsp. cinnamon

Sift dry ingredients. Add beaten eggs and the oil. Mix with a spoon. Add nuts and apples. Bake in a tube pan or 2 bread pans. These should either be sprayed or greased and floured. Bake at 350° for 1 hour or until done.

Harriet Nevins

Fresh Apple Cake

3 large apples
  (cut in small pieces)
1 C. chopped nuts
1¼ C. Wesson Oil
2 C. sugar

2 eggs
¼ tsp. salt
1½ tsp. soda
2 T. vanilla
3 C. flour

Mix sugar, oil, and eggs. Add apples, nuts, dry ingredients, and vanilla. Cake will be thick. Bake at 275° for 1¼ hours in greased 9x13-inch pan. Mix following topping to pour over cake:

1 small can Carnation milk
1 C. sugar

1 stick oleo
1 T. vanilla

Bring milk, oleo, and sugar to a boil and boil hard for 3 minutes. Add vanilla. Poke holes in cake and pour over.

Katherine Hartman

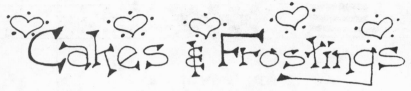

Roman Apple Cake

1 C. shortening
1 C. white sugar
½ C. brown sugar
2 eggs (beaten)
1 C. buttermilk
1 tsp. soda

1 tsp. baking powder
¾ tsp. salt
2 tsp. cinnamon
2 C. flour
2 C. diced apples

TOPPING:
½ C. sugar
½ tsp. cinnamon

½ C. nuts (optional)

Cream shortening and sugars; add beaten eggs. Sift dry ingredients and add buttermilk. Fold in diced apples. Pour into greased and floured 9x13-inch pan. Mix topping ingredients and sprinkle on top of batter. Bake at 350⁰ for 40 minutes.

Marilyn McNamara

Applesauce Cake

1 C. white sugar
½ C. butter
1 egg
1 C. stewed raisins
1½ C. sweetened applesauce

1 C. nuts
2 C. flour
2 tsp. soda
1 tsp. cinnamon
½ tsp. vanilla

Combine first 5 ingredients. Sift flour, soda, and cinnamon; add. Last put in vanilla and nuts. Bake in moderate oven (350⁰) in 9x13-inch pan for approximately 40 minutes or until tests done.

Irenee Tracy

Applesauce Cake

½ C. butter	1 tsp. cinnamon
2 C. sugar	½ tsp. nutmeg
2 eggs	¼ tsp. allspice
2½ C. flour	1½ C. canned applesauce
1½ tsp. soda	½ C. raisins
1 tsp. salt	½ C. black walnuts

(Note: Soak raisins in warm water until plump then drain.) Cream butter, then gradually add sugar, creaming until light. Add eggs, beating well after each. Sift together dry ingredients. Add alternately to creamed mixture with applesauce, ending with applesauce. Stir in raisins and nuts. Pour batter into greased and lightly floured 13x9-inch pan. Bake at 350⁰ for about 45 minutes until done. Cool in pan.

BUTTER FROSTING:

6 T. butter	About ¼ C. cream
1 (1 lb.) pkg. powdered sugar (about 4½ C.)	1½ tsp. vanilla

Cream butter and gradually add about half the sugar, blending well. Beat in 2 T. cream and vanilla. Gradually blend in the rest of the sugar. Beat in enough cream to make it spreading consistency. You may not need all of the cream, however if frosting is too stiff add more cream, a few drops at a time. Be careful, it doesn't take much for it to be too runny.

"I only make this cake twice a year, at Thanksgiving and for my dad's birthday. It's a very heavy and rich cake."

Mary Anne Snyder

Cakes & Frostings

Grandma Lantz's Angel Food Cake

1 C. cake flour (sifted)
¾ C. fine sugar
1½ C. egg whites
1½ tsp. cream of tartar

¼ tsp. salt
1½ tsp. vanilla flavoring
¼ tsp. almond flavoring
¾ C. sugar

Combine sifted flour with ¾ C. sugar and sift four times. Beat together egg whites, cream of tartar, salt, and flavorings until whites hold up in soft peaks, but are not dry. Add remaining ¾ C. of sugar, 2 T. at a time, beating after each addition. Fold in flour and sugar combination very, very gently and carefully, Bake in ungreased 10-inch tube pan in a 375⁰ oven for about 35 to 40 minutes. Invert pan and cool.

Larry Lantz

Blum's Coffee Crunch Cake

1 angel food cake
(baked & cooled)

2 C. whipped cream
for frosting

CRUNCH MIX:
1½ C. sugar
¼ C. strong coffee

¼ C. corn syrup
1 T. sifted baking soda

Boil sugar, coffee, and syrup to 310⁰ on candy thermometer. Remove from heat and stir in soda. Pour into 13x9-inch pan and cool. Break into small pieces. Frost cake with whipped cream and press crunch mix into sides and top of cake. Refrigerate.

Jeanette Neel

122

Carrot Cake

2 C. *flour*
2 C. *sugar*
2 *tsp. soda*
1 *tsp. cinnamon*

1 *tsp. salt*
1½ C. *cooking oil*
4 *eggs*
3 C. *raw carrots (grated)*

Sift dry ingredients into a large bowl. Add oil and beat well. Add eggs, 1 at a time and beat after each addition. Add carrots last and pour into greased and floured Bundt or fluted pan. Bake at 350⁰ for 1 hour. Let cake set for 10 minutes before removing from pan. Frost when cool.

FLUFFY FROSTING:
1 (3 oz.) *pkg. cream cheese*
1½ *tsp. vanilla*
3¼ C. *sifted powdered sugar*

6 T. *butter*
1 T. *cream*

Cream the cheese and butter. Add remaining ingredients, mix well, and frost cake.

Patricia Morris

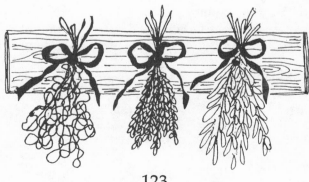

123

Crumb Cake

2 C. flour
2 tsp. baking powder
1½ C. sugar
¾ C. soft butter

2 eggs (beaten well)
¾ C. milk
1 tsp. vanilla

Sift flour and baking powder into mixing bowl. Add sugar and butter. Mix and rub into a crumb like texture. Remove ¾ C. and save. Add eggs and milk to bowl and beat until smooth. Stir in vanilla. Pour into greased 13x9x2 5/8-inch pan and sprinkle reserved crumbs on top. Bake at 350° for 30 to 40 minutes. No frosting is needed.

Mary Lehmer

Lemon Chiffon Cake

2 C. flour
1½ C. sugar
1 tsp. baking powder
1 tsp. salt
½ C. oil

7 eggs (separated)
¾ C. cold water
2 tsp. vanilla
2 tsp. grated lemon rind
½ tsp. cream of tartar

Mix together flour, sugar, baking powder, and salt. Make a well and add oil, egg yolks, water, vanilla, and lemon rind. Beat with spoon until smooth. Beat egg whites and cream of tartar until stiff. Fold egg yolk mixture into egg whites. Bake in tube pan at 350° for 50 minutes. Invert on pop bottle to cool. Frost with lemon frosting.

LEMON FROSTING:
2½ C. powdered sugar
3 T. soft butter

Juice of 1 lemon
¼ tsp. salt

Mix together and spread on cake when cool.

Ruth Eivins

Lemon Cooler Cake

1 pkg. lemon cake mix
1 (3½ oz.) pkg. vanilla
  instant pudding
2 eggs

Juice of 1 orange, plus
  water to make
  1⅓ C. liquid
1 T. grated orange rind

Preheat oven to 350°. Generously grease and flour a 10-inch Bundt pan. Combine in a large bowl the cake mix, dry pudding mix, 2 eggs, 1⅓ C. juice, and water. Mix at medium speed for 2 minutes. Stir in orange rind. Pour into prepared pan. Bake for 45 to 55 minutes. Cake is done when a toothpick inserted in center comes out clean. Cool for 25 minutes.

For Topping: In a small sauce pan bring 3 T. orange juice and ¼ C. sugar to boil. Simmer for 3 minutes. Drizzle over top and sides of cake to glaze.

Rosemary Stuchel

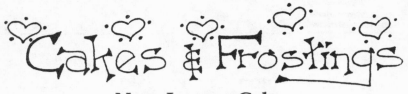

New Lemon Cake

1 box lemon cake mix
1 pkg. lemon instant
  pudding

4 eggs
¾ C. oil
¾ C. water

TOPPING:
⅓ C. orange juice
2 C. sifted powdered sugar

2 T. oil

Mix the cake mix and instant pudding together. Add eggs, oil, and water to cake and pudding mix. Beat for 10 minutes. Bake at 350° for 35 to 40 minutes. This makes a 13x9-inch cake. When done and while hot, prick all over top with sharp fork. Mix topping ingredients together and pour on cake, spreading topping around. Very good served warm!

Harriet Nevins

Brown Mountain Cake

1 C. soft oleo
2 C. sugar
3 eggs
3 C. sifted flour
1 tsp. baking soda
½ tsp. salt

3 T. cocoa
1 C. buttermilk or commercial
  sour cream
1 tsp. vanilla
½ C. warm water

Cream oleo and sugar. Beat in eggs, 1 at a time. Sift dry ingredients together. Add alternately with buttermilk to creamed mixture. Stir in vanilla and warm water. Bake in lightly greased and floured 9x13-inch pan at 350° for about 45 minutes.

Marilyn McNamara

Lemon Jello Cake

1 (3 oz.) pkg. lemon Jello   ¾ C. water
1 pkg. lemon cake mix   ¾ C. oil
4 eggs

Mix all ingredients together in a large mixing bowl and beat for about 4 minutes. Bake in 9x13-inch cake pan at 350⁰ for 35 to 40 minutes. Let the cake cool before putting on glaze.

FROSTING GLAZE:
2 small lemons or   2 C. powdered sugar
   1 large lemon

Squeeze all juice from lemons and pour juice in a small mixing bowl. Add powdered sugar and stir well. Poke holes in cake with fork, about ½-inch apart. Pour lemon glaze over cake. Best when kept refrigerated.

Terri Johnson

Crazy Cake

No eggs   1 tsp. vanilla
3 C. flour   ¾ C. oil (Mazola, Wesson,
2 tsp. soda   or Crisco)
1 tsp. salt   2 tsp. vinegar
½ C. cocoa   2 C. water
2 C. sugar

Sift together flour, soda, salt, cocoa, and sugar. Mix together in a small bowl vanilla, oil, vinegar, and water. Make a hole or well in dry ingredients. Pour in liquid ingredients and beat until smooth. Pour into a 13x9x2 5/8-inch cake pan. Bake at 350⁰ for 40 to 45 minutes. This is a moist cake.

Mary Lehmer

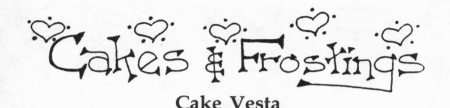

Cakes & Frostings

Cake Vesta

4 level T. cocoa
2 C. sifted flour
1 C. sugar
1½ tsp. baking soda

Pinch of salt
1 C. Miracle Whip
¾ C. cold water
1 tsp. vanilla

FROSTING:
1 stick butter
1 (8 oz.) pkg. cream cheese

1 lb. confectioner's sugar

Sift dry ingredients together, then add remaining ingredients and mix well. Bake in a greased and floured 9x13-inch cake pan at 350° for 30 to 35 minutes. Cool.

For Frosting: Cream butter and cream cheese after softened. Add sugar and mix well.

"This recipe is from Bryan's Great-Grandma, Zilpha Pickens."

Bryan Camp

Easy German Chocolate Cake

1 German chocolate cake mix
1 can sweetened cond. milk
2 crushed Heath bars

12 oz. carton of whipped topping

Bake German chocolate cake according to directions on box. Let cool for 5 to 10 minutes. Poke holes in cake with wooden spoon handle. Pour sweetened condensed milk over cake and let it cool completely. Spread whipped topping over cake and sprinkle Heath bars on top.

Bev Maxwell

Sally's Chocolate Cake

½ C. cocoa	2 eggs
½ C. hot water	¼ tsp. salt
2 tsp. soda	1 C. buttermilk
1¾ C. sugar	2 C. flour
½ C. Crisco	1 tsp. vanilla

Mix together cocoa, soda, and hot water; set aside. Cream, sugar, shortening, eggs, and salt until nice and fluffy (about 10 minutes). Add flour, buttermilk, and vanilla alternately to the creamed mixture ending with flour. Add cocoa mixture last and mix well. Bake at 350° until cake starts to leave sides of pan. This will make one 9x13-inch or two 9-inch layers or 32 cupcakes.

"This recipe was given to me by a friend many years ago and became our traditional birthday cake."

FUDGE FROSTING:

½ oz. chocolate (finely cut)	¼ C. Crisco
1 C. sugar	1/8 tsp. salt
⅓ C. milk	

Bring to a full rolling boil and boil for 3 minutes. Add 1 tsp. vanilla and beat until ready to spread. This recipe will frost two 8-inch layers. If you like a dark chocolate you can use a full ounce of chocolate. I use this frosting for this cake and double the recipe. If the frosting should start to harden on you quickly add a little milk and stir to the spreading consistency.

Mildred Waltz

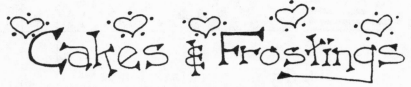

Fruit Cake - Peter's Mother
"Mrs. P.J. Cunningham's Famous Recipe"

1 lb. sugar
1 lb. butter
1 lb. flour or 4 C. sifted
2 lbs. raisins
1 lb. currants
1 C. black walnuts
1 lb. citron
1 lb. red & green candied
  cherries
½ lb. candied red & green pineapple

11 eggs
2 tsp. cinnamon
1 tsp. nutmeg
1 tsp. cloves
1 tsp. soda, dissolved in
  hot water
1 C. wine (Virginia Dare) or
  1 C. apricot brandy or
  1 C. tart fruit juice

Cream butter and sugar. Add well-beaten eggs. Mix 2 C. flour with fruit and the other 2 C. of flour with the spices. Add flour mixture alternately with wine. Add floured fruit last, then last of all the soda, dissolved in small amount of hot water. Use large bowl to mix batter. Makes 6 or 7 small cakes. (Make weeks ahead.) Line pans with wax paper and bake at 350⁰ for 1½ to 2 hours, until toothpick comes out clean.

FRUIT CAKE FROSTING:
2 C. brown sugar
2 C. thick cream
  (preferably sour)

Butter, size of walnut
1 tsp. vanilla

Boil until soft ball. Remove from and add butter and vanilla. Cool, then beat until creamy and spread on cakes.

Ruth Cunningham

Stained Glass Window Fruit Cake

1½ lbs. pitted dates
1 lb. candied pineapple chunks
1 lb. candied cherries (red & green)
2 lb. nuts (English walnuts, pecans, or sliced almonds)
2 tsp. baking powder

2 C. sifted flour
½ tsp. salt
4 eggs (beaten)
½ C. Karo syrup (light or dark or mixed)
¼ C. packed brown sugar
¼ C. cooking oil

Mix fruits and nuts. Sift dry ingredients: flour, baking powder, and salt. Mix eggs, syrup, sugar, and oil. Gradually mix in dry ingredients. Pour over fruit mixture. Firmly pack in greased container with wax paper on the bottom. Bake at 275⁰ for about 1 hour. (I like to use small foil loaf pans, they don't have to bake so long.) Cakes are done when top appears dry. This is a fruit cake that is really eaten.

Mildred Waltz

Hickory Nut Cake

½ C. butter
1½ C. sugar
2½ C. sifted cake flour
3 tsp. baking powder
¼ tsp. salt

1 C. milk
1 tsp. vanilla
1 C. hickory nutmeats
   (can substitute pecans)
5 egg whites

Cream the butter and gradually beat in the sugar. Sift flour, measure, and sift with the baking powder and salt. Add alternately with the milk to which the vanilla has been added. Add the nuts and fold in the stiffly beaten egg whites. Pour into three greased layer pans. Bake in preheated 350⁰ oven for 20 minutes. Note: You can use any white box cake and add nuts. Any favorite frosting may be used.

MARGUERITE'S FROSTING:

1 stick margarine
1 lb. powdered sugar

3 ozs. soft cream cheese
1 tsp. vanilla

Mix well to spreading consistency.

Mildred Waltz

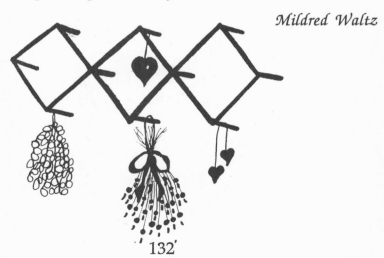

132

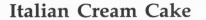

Italian Cream Cake

1 C. buttermilk	2 C. flour
1 tsp. soda	1 tsp. vanilla
2 C. sugar	1 C. chopped nuts
1 stick butter	1 C. coconut
½ C. shortening	5 eggs (separated)

FROSTING:

1 stick oleo (softened)	8 ozs. cream cheese
2 C. powdered sugar	(softened)
1 tsp. vanilla	

Preheat oven to 325⁰ and lightly grease three 8-inch cake pans. Combine buttermilk and soda. Let stand for 4 or 5 minutes. Beat egg whites until stiff and set aside. Cream butter, sugar, and shortening together. Add egg yolks, 1 at a time and beat after each. Add milk, alternately with flour and stir in vanilla. Fold in egg whites, coconut, and nuts. Pour into three 8-inch cake pans. Bake at 325⁰ for 25 minutes.

For Frosting: Mix frosting ingredients together and frost when cool.

Joanne Nichols

133

Cakes & Frostings

Norm's Cake

CAKE:
1 box lemon supreme cake mix   ½ C. salad oil
1 box instant lemon pudding   ½ pt. sour cream
4 eggs   1 tsp. rum extract (optional)
½ C. evaporated milk

FILLING:
1 small pkg. chocolate chips   1 tsp. instant coffee
3 T. brown sugar   2 tsp. cinnamon

Mix filling ingredients and set aside. Mix well the cake mix, pudding mix, and all other cake ingredients. Grease and flour Bundt pan. Cover bottom of pan with some batter and sprinkle with filling mixture. Alternate batter with filling, ending with batter. Bake at 350° for 55 minutes. Cool and remove to plate. Sprinkle top of cake with rum or brandy (if you wish). Dust with powdered sugar.

Jeanette Neel

Oatmeal Cake

1¼ C. boiling water
1 stick margarine
1 C. quick oatmeal
2 eggs
1 C. white sugar
1 C. brown sugar

½ tsp. salt
1 tsp. cinnamon
1 tsp. soda
1⅓ C. flour
1 T. vanilla

TOPPING:
6 T. margarine
½ C. Half & Half
1 C. nuts

1 C. brown sugar
1 C. coconut

Pour boiling water over margarine and oatmeal. Let set a few minutes. In a large bowl beat eggs and sugar. Add flour, salt, cinnamon, and soda. Stir in oatmeal mixture and vanilla; mix well. Bake at 350° for 35 minutes in 9x13-inch greased pan.

For Topping: In a medium saucepan heat margarine and Half & Half. Stir in nuts, brown sugar, and coconut. Spread on top of cake and put back in oven for about 10 minutes or until it starts to bubble.

Katherine Hartman

135

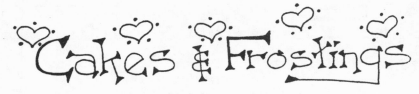
Pumpkin Cake Roll

3 eggs
1 C. granulated sugar
⅔ C. pumpkin (canned)
1 tsp. lemon juice
¾ C. flour

2 tsp. cinnamon
1 tsp. ginger
½ tsp. nutmeg
1 C. finely chopped walnuts
1 tsp. baking powder

FILLING:
1 C. powdered sugar
2 (3 oz.) pkgs. cream cheese

4 T. butter
½ tsp. vanilla

Beat eggs on high speed mixer for 5 minutes. Gradually beat in sugar. Stir in pumpkin and lemon juice. Stir together flour, baking powder, cinnamon, ginger, and nutmeg. Fold into pumpkin mixture and spread into greased and floured 15x10x1-inch pan. Top with walnuts and bake at 375⁰ for 10 to 15 minutes. Turn out on paper towel and sprinkle with powdered sugar. Starting at narrow end, roll towel and cake together. Cool. Unroll to spread filling over the cake. Beat together powdered sugar, cream cheese (softened), softened butter, and vanilla. Roll again from narrow end and chill. Can be frozen.

Kelly Stevens

St. Valentine's Day

Teresa Hoffelmeyer

Who was this saint whose feast day is celebrated with children and adults alike exchanging cards, gifts, and candy?

It is said that he was a priest in the 3rd Century who was imprisoned for refusing to deny his Christian faith. Before he was beheaded, he sent messages to loved ones from his cell which read, "Remember your Valentine."

One family in our parish celebrates this day with a special evening meal eaten in the dining room followed by a small gift exchange. Last year my son was invited to join the fun and as his gift he brought home half a dozen heart shaped sugar cookies to share with his not-so-fortunate family.

The recipe for red cake and red cake icing, which used to be served at our smorgasbord meal long ago, would now be a great cake for St. Valentine's Day. (Red hearts are appropriate symbols for this day. Red symbolizes martrydom and hearts symbolize love.)

Red Cake

½ C. Crisco	2 tsp. cocoa
1½ C. sugar	1 C. buttermilk
2 eggs	2¼ C. cake flour
1 oz. red cake coloring	1 tsp. soda
1 tsp. vanilla	1 T. vinegar

Cream Crisco and sugar. Add eggs, make a paste of cocoa red coloring and vanilla. Blend into mixture of shortening. Add flour and buttermilk. Mix soda and vinegar together. Add this last to the cake and mix well. Bake at 350° for 25 minutes in 3-layer cake pans. When cool slice each layer in half (in other words have six thin layers.)

(Icing on Next Page)

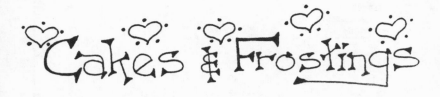

Cakes & Frostings

Red Cake Icing

1½ C. milk
4½ T. flour

1½ C. sugar
2 sticks margarine

Warm milk before adding to flour to keep from lumping. Cook until thick and let cool. Cream sugar and margarine until fluffy, about 20 minutes. Add flour mixture slowly in mixer. Add 1 tsp. vanilla and ice between layers and rest of cake.

Nancy Welch
Katherine Hartman

Seafoam Frosting

1½ C. packed brown sugar
⅓ C. cold water
2 egg whites

2 tsp. light corn syrup
Dash of salt
1 tsp. vanilla

In the top of a double boiler combine sugar, cold water, egg whites, corn syrup, and salt. Beat on low speed of electric mixer for 30 seconds to blend. Place over boiling water, beating constantly on high speed of mixer. Cook for about 7 minutes or until frosting forms stiff peaks. Remove from heat and add vanilla. Beat 2 to 3 minutes longer or until of spreading consistency. Frost tops and sides of two 8 or 9-inch layers or one 10-inch tube cake.

Rosemary Stuchel

Pudding Frosting

1 (3.9 oz.) pkg. chocolate or
vanilla instant pudding
1 C. cold milk

¼ C. powdered sugar
2 C. whipped topping
(Cool Whip)

Combine pudding mix, powdered sugar, and milk in bowl. Beat slowly with a rotary beater or electric mixer on slow speed for about 1 minute. Fold in whipped topping and spread on cake at once. Keep cake refrigerated. Tastes great on marble cake or yellow cake.

Terri Johnson

Frustration
By: Jane Shoemaker
Submitted By: Lucille Russell

The teacher pulled and tugged and pulled;
Tim's overshoes were on at last.
She breathed a sigh of deep relief
when they were finally buckled fast.

But her elation ended soon,
For Timmy raised his tousled head
And eyed her with a gap-toothed smile,
"These ain't my overshoes," he said.

Again she struggled with the boots
Until upon the floor they lay.
"Whose boots are these - do you know, Tim?"
"My sister's - I wore hers today."

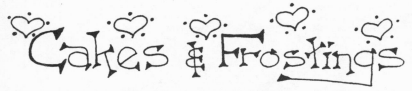

Cakes & Frostings

Our Family's Sacred Celebrations

What is sacred in our lives and how do we celebrate the sacred? There is a book called, *I'm In Charge of Celebrations* by Byrd Baylor. In this book, a young girl tells of experiences, mostly in nature, that so touch her heart she wants to celebrate them. We've all experienced such moments; a sunset, a walk through the woods when new snow is falling, etc. These occasions, which touch not only our senses but our hearts, are worth remembering with celebrations.

As a family, do some sharing about sacred moments and then begin looking for some sacred moments to celebrate and write these down. It should be fun to see how many sacred moments your children can find and in what ways they may choose to celebrate the sacred in their lives.

Candy

Birdies Coated Walnut

¾ C. sugar
⅓ C. sour cream
2 T. milk

¼ tsp. salt
½ tsp. vanilla
3 C. English walnuts

Combine all ingredients, except vanilla and walnuts. Cook to hard ball stage, then let rest in cold water. Add the vanilla and 3 C. of English walnut halves or large pieces. Mix to coat and pour out on wax paper and separate.

Mildred Waltz

Matthew
By: Karen Pommier

At our church, Matthew, who is 27 years old and has Down's Syndrome, is always ready to be an altar server at Mass. His favorite duty is to ring the bell during the consecration when Father elevates the bread and wine.

One time during Mission Week, our visiting priest decided to have Mass at the church hall. We informally sat around a table and Matthew offered to assist Father.

When Father elevated the Blessed Bread, Matthew discovered he had no bell to ring. Rather than leave a job undone, Matthew very reverently spoke, "Ring-a-ling-a-ding-a-ling. Ring-a-ling-a-ding-a-ling." Then, again, he said it aloud, when Father raised the Blessed Cup. At what is usually the most solemn part of the Mass, I overheard many a muffled chuckle.

I'm sure God is pleased with Matthew and his earnest desire to serve the Lord.

Shortcut Caramels

1 C. butter or margarine
1 (16 oz.) pkg. (2¼ C.
*   packed) brown sugar*
1 C. light corn syrup

1 (14 oz.) can (1¼ C.)
*   sweetened cond. milk*
1 tsp. vanilla

Line a 9x9x2-inch baking pan with foil, extending foil over edges of pan. Butter the foil and set pan aside. In a heavy 3-quart saucepan melt the 1 C. of butter or margarine over low heat. Add brown sugar, sweetened condensed milk, and light corn syrup; mix well. Carefully clip candy thermometer to side of pan. Cook over medium heat, stirring frequently, until thermometer registers (242°), firm-ball stage. Mixture should boil at a moderate, steady rate over the entire surface. Reaching firm-ball stage should take 15 to 20 minutes. Remove saucepan from heat and then remove candy theremometer from saucepan. Immediately stir in vanilla. Quickly pour the caramel mixture into prepared baking pan. When caramel is firm, use foil to lift it out of pan. Use a buttered knife to cut candy into 1-inch squares. Wrap each piece in clear plastic wrap. Makes 81 pieces or about 2¾ pounds.

Shortcut: Substituting sweetened condensed milk for cream cuts the cooking time in half.

For Chocolate Shortcut Caramels: Prepare shortcut caramels as directed, except melt 2 sqs. (2 ozs.) unsweetened chocolate with the butter or margarine.

Mary Brayton

Candy

E.B.'s Favorite Baked Caramel Corn

1 C. butter or margarine
2 C. firmly packed brown
   sugar
½ C. light or dark corn syrup

1 tsp. salt
1 tsp. vanilla
½ tsp. baking soda
6 qts. popped corn

Melt butter and stir in brown sugar, corn syrup, and salt. Bring to a boil, stirring constantly, then boil without stirring for 5 minutes. Remove from heat and stir in baking soda and vanilla. Gradually pour over corn and turn onto two large shallow baking pans. Bake at 250° for 1 hour, stirring every 15 minutes. Remove and cool. Makes 5 quarts.

Carl Neal

Christmas Meringues

3 egg whites
¼ tsp. cream of tartar
¾ C. sugar

⅓ C. nuts (optional)
1 to 2 drops green food
   coloring

Heat oven to 250°. Line cookie sheets with foil. In a small bowl, beat egg whites and cream of tartar until foamy. Gradually add sugar, 1 T. at a time, beating 3 to 5 minutes or until stiff peaks form. Fold in nuts and desired amount of food coloring. Spoon 1-inch mounds onto foil-lined cookie sheets. Bake at 250° for 40 to 50 minutes or until crisp and dry. Cool completely and remove from cookie sheets. Makes about 3 dozen pieces of candy.

Shirley Privratsky

Never-Fail Popcorn Balls

1 C. sugar
1 C. white syrup
1 tsp. baking powder

1 tsp. butter
1 tsp. vanilla
5 qts. popped corn

Let syrup come to a boil. Add sugar and let that come to a boil. Remove from heat and add baking powder and butter. Stir until it foams up. Add vanilla and pour over popcorn. From into balls. Makes about 2 dozen medium-sized balls. Can rub hands with butter or margarine for easier handling of popcorn balls.

Variations: Can add a few drops of green food coloring with the vanilla and shape popcorn into cones to make Christmas tree. Use red decorator frosting to drape "garland" around trees and use different colors of frosting for ornaments. Yellow or white decorator "star" can be placed on top of tree. Or use orange food coloring and shape popcorn into pumpkins and decorate like a Jack-o-lantern. A good seller at bake sales!

Teresa Kordick Westphal

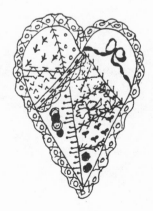

Candy

Divinity

2 stiffly beaten egg
  whites
2½ C. sugar
½ C. white corn syrup

½ C. water
1 tsp. vanilla
Chopped nuts

Boil sugar, syrup, and water to hard ball stage. Pour over the stiffly beaten egg whites and mix. Add vanilla and beat until thick. Add the nuts and pour into a buttered pan to cool.

Mary Lou Foley
Martha Street

Date Loaf

2 pts. sugar
1 pt. milk
Pinch of salt

1 pt. chopped dates
1 pt. nutmeats

Cook sugar and milk together until it forms a softball in cold water. Add dates and cook to softball stage again, then add nuts and a pinch of salt. Beat until stiff. Then roll in a wet cloth and place in refrigerator to set. Slice and serve as desired.

"When my aunt moved to the South many years ago, this recipe was given to her by the woman who cooked for her. She sent it to my mother, and it has been a Christmas MUST ever since."

Wanda Martin

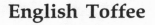

English Toffee

¾ C. butter (melted) ¼ tsp. salt
1 C. sugar 6 ozs. chocolate chips
¾ C. blanched slivered 1 C. chopped pecans
  almonds

Combine all ingredients, except pecans and chocolate chips in a large buttered saucepan. Cook using medium-high heat until mixture changes to a deep caramel color. (It is very important to use a high heat so the mixture will cook quickly.) Stir constantly. Pour onto a buttered cookie sheet, rotating to spread evenly. Spread chocolate chips over the hot candy. Spread smooth when melted. Sprinkle pecans over top and press while chocolate is still warm. Cool and break into pieces.

Teresa Pearson

Toffee Candy

¼ lb. butter 4½ oz. milk chocolate
¼ lb. margarine   candy bar
1 C. sugar Finely chopped nuts
3 T. water   (English walnuts)
  (approx. ½ C.)

Combine butter, margarine, sugar, and water in a saucepan. Cook over high heat until butter melts, then on medium heat until mixture turns to a muddy toffee color, about 20 minutes, stirring constantly. When ready, mixture makes a "crackly" hard sound in cold water. Pour onto cookie sheet or aluminum foil. Let harden. Pour melted candy bar over top.

Elizabeth M. Edwards

Fudge Candy

4½ C. sugar
½ tsp. salt
2 T. butter
1 can evaporated Pet milk
1 (12 oz.) pkg. semi-sweet
   chocolate pieces

1 (12 oz.) pkg. Baker's
   German sweet chocolate
1 pt. marshmallow creme
2 C. nuts (walnuts)

Have ready in a large bowl the semi-sweet chocolate, German sweet chocolate, marshmallow creme, and nuts. Bring to a boil the sugar, salt, butter, and milk. Pour this mixture over the ingredients in the bowl. Beat until the chocolate is melted. Pour into buttered pan and let stand for 2 hours before cutting.

Dorothy Hochstetler

Cheese Fudge

1 lb. oleo
1 lb. Velveeta cheese

4 lbs. powdered sugar
1 C. cocoa

Butter 12x18-inch pan well. In a large heavy saucepan melt cheese and oleo together. Sift cocoa into sugar and stir into melted cheese and oleo. Gets pretty stiff by the end. Press into greased pan and let cool. Always smooth and creamy.

Shirley Bittinger

Fantasy Fudge

3 C. sugar
¾ C. Parkay margarine
⅔ C. (5⅓ oz. can)
  evaporated milk
1 (12 oz.) pkg. semi-
  sweet chocolate chips

1 (7 oz.) jar Kraft
  marshmallow creme
  or 160 small
  marshmallows
1 C. chopped nuts
1 tsp. vanilla

Combine sugar, margarine, and milk in a heavy 2½-quart saucepan. Bring to a full rolling boil, stirring constantly. Continue boiling for 5 minutes over medium heat, stirring constantly to prevent scorching. Remove from heat and stir in chocolate chips until melted. Add marshmallow creme or 160 small marshmallows, nuts, and vanilla. Beat until well blended. Pour into greased 13x9-inch pan. Cool at room temperature, then cut into squares. Makes 3 pounds.

Kay Johnson

Marvelous Marble Fudge

½ C. Karo light or dark
corn syrup
⅓ C. evaporated milk
2 (8 oz.) pkgs. Baker's semi-
sweet chocolate chips

2 tsp. vanilla
¾ C. confectioner's sugar
(sifted)
⅓ C. peanut butter

Line a 8x8x2-inch pan with plastic wrap. In a 2-quart saucepan stir corn syrup and milk. Add chocolate, stirring constantly. Cook over medium-low heat until chocolate is melted. Remove from heat and stir in vanilla, then add sugar. With wooden spoon beat until smooth. Spread in pan and drop peanut butter by spoonfuls on fudge. With knife, swirl peanut butter thru fudge to marbleize. Chill for 2 hours or until firm. Invert onto cutting board. Peel off plastic wrap. Makes about 25 (1½-inch) squares.

For Microwave: In a 3-quart micro-proof bowl stir corn syrup and milk. Stir in chocolate and microwave at High (100%), stirring once for 6 minutes or until chocolate is completely melted and almost entire surface is bubbly. Continue as above.

Elizabeth M. Edwards

Nutmello Goodies

1 pkg. (1 C.) Nestle's
semi-sweet chocolate
chips
1 pkg. (1 C.) Nestle's
butterscotch chips

½ C. peanut butter
3 C. miniature
marshmallows
1 C. salted peanuts

Combine over hot (not boiling) water the first 3
ingredients until melted and mixture is blended and
smooth. Remove from heat, then add marshmallows
and peanuts; mix well. Spread in aluminum foil lined 8-inch square pan. Chill until firm, then cut into
1-inch squares. Makes 64 squares.

Josephine Sitkiewicz

Microwave Peanut Brittle

1 C. roasted &
unsalted peanuts
1 C. sugar
½ C. corn syrup

½ tsp. salt
1 tsp. butter
1 tsp. vanilla
1 tsp. baking soda

Stir together peanuts, sugar, syrup, and salt.
Microwave on High for 4 minutes. Stir and
microwave for an additional 4 minutes. Add butter
and vanilla. Microwave for 2 minutes. Add teaspoon
of soda and stir vigorously until light and foamy.
Pour immediately. Cool and break into chunks.
Warning: This mix becomes very hot and needs to
be watched so as not to scorch or burn.

Margaret Tiernan

Candy

Peanut Clusters

1 (12 oz.) pkg. chocolate chips
1 lb. white almond bark
1 tsp. vanilla
2 (12 oz.) pkgs. salted peanuts

Melt chocolate chips and almond bark. Add vanilla and then the peanuts. Drop by teaspoonfuls onto waxed paper.

Sue Finnell

Peanut Clusters

1½ lbs. almond bark (white)
1 (12 oz.) pkg. chocolate chips
4 C. roasted & unsalted peanuts

Melt bark and chips together in top half of double boiler over water. When melted and thoroughly mixed, stir in peanuts. Drop by spoonful onto waxed paper. Cool and store in cool place.

Margaret Tiernan

Peanut Butter Fudge

2 C. sugar
½ C. dark Karo corn syrup
¾ C. milk
2 T. cocoa
1 T. vanilla
⅓ C. peanut butter
2 T. margarine
6 marshmallows

Cook sugar, corn syrup, milk, and cocoa to softball stage, using a large heavy saucepan. Add vanilla, peanut butter, margarine, and marshmallows. Beat well, then turn onto a buttered platter.

"Grandma always made this fudge for Christmas."

In Memory of Margaret Stuchel
Submitted by Sue Stuchel

Cookies & Bars

Cookies & Bars

Bacon and Egg Cookies

2 blocks of almond bark
1 bag pretzel sticks

1 large bag M & M candies

Work in small amounts. Place foil over a cookie sheet or tray. Melt almond bark in microwave or over low heat. Place 2 sticks together in various areas of cookie sheet. Leave about ¼ to ½-inch between the sticks to represent bacon strips. With a spoon, place a circle of almond bark in the middle of the strip. Press a yellow M & M in the middle of the almond bark. Push to flatten slightly. Let them cool until firm or refrigerate. Peel off foil.

Sharon Johnson

Celebrating the "Easter Bunny"

Sharon Johnson and her daughter, Jill, have started a tradition in Winterset playing the "Easter Bunny" very early each Easter morning. Every year they choose a family with young children and before sunrise they sprinkle the family's lawn with brightly colored eggs and candies. Elderly neighbors, special friends, and even our priest have been visited by this bunny.

Cookies

Beacon Hill Cookies

1 C. chocolate chips (6 ozs.)
2 egg whites
½ tsp. vanilla
½ tsp. vinegar

¾ C. chopped English walnuts
Dash of salt
½ C. sugar

Melt chips over hot water. Beat egg whites with a dash of salt, then gradually add the sugar until stiff peaks form. Beat in vanilla and vinegar. Fold in chocolate and nuts. Drop by teaspoon on a greased cookie sheet. Can decorate with a large chunk of nut in center. Bake at 350⁰ for about 10 minutes. Remove immediately from pan. Do not overbake. Will make about 36 cookies. They are fragile. They make their own crunchy bottoms.

"Father Schulte really liked these."

Mildred Waltz

Cookie Walk

The annual St. Joseph's Christmas-Cookie Walk is held the second Saturday in December. Parishioners are asked to donate Christmas cookies and candies in any amount they choose. The cookies and candies are then sold by the pound to the public. The community eagerly awaits this event each year, as our parish members continue to donate superior quality goodies!

In this section, you will find some of our favorite cookie walk cookies as well as other family favorites.

Butterhorn Cookies

CRUST:

4 C. flour

1½ C. butter

Dash of salt

1 pkg. yeast, mixed with
3 egg yolks

1 C. sour cream

FILLING:

3 egg whites (beaten stiff)

1 C. sugar

¼ C. nuts (chopped)

½ tsp. vanilla

Mix all the crust ingredients. Roll out and cut into pie shapes. Spread with the filling, which has been all mixed together. Roll up beginning with wide end. Bake at 350° for 10 to 15 minutes or until lightly browned. Remove from pans and roll in powdered sugar.

Shirley Privratsky

We always used to celebrate our "Nameday." A nameday is the feast of the saint for whom a person is named. The person celebrating their nameday (or saint's day) would be honored by a visit from friends and relatives. The hostess would serve a large meal late in the day. It was difficult to know how many to plan for, as there were never any invitations sent. The evening was usually spent playing cards and visiting.

The entire family would come for this special occasion, and by the end of the evening, all available space was occupied by the little ones who could no longer stay awake.

This tradition is still carried on by some of the younger generation.

Shirley Privratsky

Cookies

Cherry Bon-Bons

24 maraschino cherries
(drained & save the juice)
½ C. soft butter
¾ C. powdered sugar
1½ C. flour

1/8 tsp. salt
2 T. Half & Half
1 tsp. vanilla
Powdered sugar & cherry
glaze (recipe below)

Beat butter until creamy and add ¾ C. sugar, beating well. Stir in flour, salt, Half & Half, and vanilla. Shape into balls. Press around 1 cherry, covering completely, and place on ungreased cookie sheet. Bake at 350⁰ for 18 to 20 minutes. Transfer to wire rack and cool. Sprinkle with powdered sugar and then drizzle with glaze.

GLAZE:
2 T. melted butter
1 C. sifted powdered sugar

¼ C. cherry juice

Combine these ingredients, adding food coloring, if desired. Place glaze in small plastic bag, snip off corner, and gently squeeze over cookies.

Margaret Tiernan

Cookies & Bars

Chocolate Chip Cookies

1 C. margarine (softened)
¾ C. sugar
¾ C. brown sugar
2 eggs
2½ C. flour

1 tsp. soda
1 tsp. salt
1 (12 oz.) pkg. chocolate chips
½ C. walnuts

Cream margarine and sugar together. Add eggs, soda, and salt; mix well. Stir in flour, chocolate chips, and nuts. Refrigerate, covered overnight (THIS IS IMPORTANT). The next day, drop them by the teaspoonful onto cookie sheets. Bake at 350° for 10 minutes, no longer. Yield: 6 dozen.

Jill Johnson

Mom's Favorite
By: Karen Pommier

The subject of "Mom's favorite child" arose in conversation with my six sisters one day. (Our four brothers were in a different room playing cards.) Of course, I thought, they must be referring to me because Mom always made me feel so special, especially when she allowed me to secretly accompany her every Saturday to the grocery store while everyone else stayed home and cleaned.

Then, one by one, each sister very convincingly related how each of them got to do or have special things with Mom that no one else was aware of. Truly, each of us was "Mom's Favorite."

Cookies

Chocolate Cornflake Cookies

4 large (8 oz. each) Hershey
   chocolate bars with almonds
2 (1 oz.) env. Choco-Bake

Kelloggs cornflakes
   (approx. 13 handfuls)

Melt Hershey bars in a bowl placed in a pan of hot water. Add Choco-Bake and stir in cornflakes. Drop by teaspoonful on a cookie sheet. Makes approximately 4 dozen cookies. Note: Choco-Bake is unsweetened pre-melted chocolate flavor made by Nestle.)

Karen Pommier

Chocolate Cream Cookies

2½ C. flour
½ tsp. salt
½ tsp. baking powder
1 tsp. soda
½ C. butter
1½ C. dark brown sugar

2 eggs
1 tsp. vanilla
1 C. sour cream
1 C. chopped nuts
1 (12 oz.) pkg. chocolate chips
   (bits)

Sift dry ingredients together. Cream butter and sugar. Add eggs and vanilla, mixing well. Add sifted dry ingredients alternately with sour cream. Add chopped nuts and chocolate bits; blend. Drop on greased sheet and bake at 375⁰ for 10 minutes or until brown.

"This is one of my very favorites. Took them to parish council one night and they went over big with the men."

Anna King

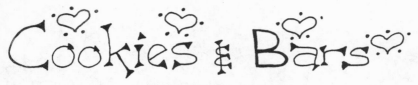

Christmas Cookies

10 T. granulated sugar
2 C. margarine & butter
  (mixed)

4 C. flour
1 tsp. vanilla
1 tsp. rum flavoring

Cream butter and margarine; add sugar, rum, and vanilla flavoring. Add flour and mix well. Roll in balls the size of marbles. Place on cookie sheet. Dip fork in flour and press criss-cross on ball of dough to flatten. Place pecan or cherry on cookies. Bake at 350⁰ until lightly brown on edges. May sprinkle powder sugar over when baked.

Josephine Sitkiewicz

Cornflake and Oatmeal Cookies

½ C. brown sugar
½ C. sugar
½ C. shortening
1 unbeaten egg
½ tsp. vanilla

1 C. flour
½ tsp. baking soda
¼ tsp. salt
1 C. crushed cornflakes
1 C. oatmeal

Cream together brown sugar, sugar, shortening, egg, and vanilla. Add flour, baking soda, salt, cornflakes, and oatmeal. Put heaping teaspoonful of mixture on greased cookie sheet and bake at 350⁰ until done, approximately 10 minutes.

"This is the recipe that I used when I was in 4-H in Jr. High. I won 2 blue ribbons with this."

Margo Camp

Cookies

Cornmeal Cookies

¾ C. fat (margarine or butter)
¾ C. sugar
1 egg
1½ C. flour

½ C. cornmeal
1 tsp. baking powder
¼ tsp. vanilla
½ C. raisins (if desired)

Mix fat and sugar in a large bowl. Add egg and beat well. Add rest of the ingredients and mix well. Drop dough from a teaspoon on a greased baking pan. Bake at 350⁰ (moderate oven) for about 15 minutes until lightly browned. Makes about 3 dozen cookies.

Kristi Hill

Cream Cheese Cookies

2 sticks margarine
1 (3 oz.) pkg. cream cheese
1 C. sugar
1 tsp. vanilla

2 C. flour
Pinch of salt
1 C. nuts

Cream margarine and cream cheese together. Beat in sugar, vanilla, flour, salt, and nuts. Chill dough in bowl, roll in waxed paper, and slice. Or you can drop by spoonfuls onto greased cookie sheet. Bake at 375⁰ for 8 to 10 minutes.

Cindy Watson Pottebaum

Danish Brune Kager
(Brown Christmas Cookie)

1 C. butter or lard
1 C. brown sugar
1 C. dark corn syrup
1 tsp. baking soda
1 tsp. cardamon
1 T. grated orange rind
1 tsp. cloves

½ tsp. salt
½ tsp. allspice
1 tsp. cinnamon
4 to 5 C. flour
¼ C. finely chopped almonds
Oiled cookie sheets

Place butter or lard, sugar, and syrup on burner to heat. When melted remove from burner and add the rest of the ingredients. Mix well and form into rolls as for refrigerator cookies. The dough improves if it is allowed to remain in refrigerator for 3 weeks before baking. These cookies are sliced very thin and decorated with ½ of an almond. Bake at 375° until crisp, about 9 minutes on oiled cookie sheet. These were traditionally mixed up the first week of December, aged, then baked up for holiday company. Note: This is egg free for the allergic family.

Georgia Ryan

Cookies

Flying Saucers

½ C. soft margarine
1 C. sugar
1 egg
1 tsp. vanilla
2 C. flour

½ C. cocoa
1 tsp. baking soda
½ tsp. baking powder
1 C. milk

FILLING:
1 C. margarine
2 C. powdered sugar

2 C. marshmallow creme
1 tsp. vanilla

Cream butter and sugar; beat in egg and vanilla. Add dry ingredients alternately with milk. Beat until smooth. Drop on greased cookie sheet and bake for 7 minutes at 400°. Cool and fill. To fill, frost one cookie with filling mixture and place another cookie on top.

For Filling: Cream margarine and powdered sugar. Add marshmallow creme and vanilla. After filling, place in a baggie and freeze.

"A cool treat for kids on a hot summer day."

Kelly Stevens

Chocolate Topped
Oatmeal Cookies

1 C. soft margarine or butter
½ C. granulated sugar
½ C. brown sugar
1 egg
1 tsp. vanilla
2 C. sifted flour

½ tsp. salt
1 tsp. soda
1½ C. quick oatmeal
1 C. coconut
5 thin Hershey bars

Beat margarine or butter until creamy. Add sugar and beat until fluffy. Beat in egg and vanilla. Sift together flour, salt, and soda. Add to creamed mixture a little at a time. Beat well after each addition. Stir in oatmeal and coconut. Shape dough into small balls. Place on ungreased cookie sheet and flatten slightly. Bake at 350⁰ for about 10 to 12 minutes. Place chocolate pieces on top of each cookie while hot.

Delores Nicholson

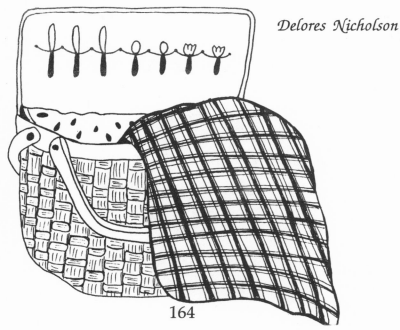

164

Cookies

Giant Oatmeal Slice Cookies

1½ C. flour
½ tsp. salt
½ tsp. baking soda
5 tsp. pumpkin pie spice
1 C. margarine
1 C. sugar

1 C. brown sugar
2 eggs
1 tsp. vanilla
3 C. oats
1 C. nuts or raisins (optional)

Combine flour, salt, baking soda, and spices. Cream margarine and sugars. Add eggs and vanilla. Beat in flour, then add oats, 1 C. at a time, then add nuts or raisins. Drop by ¼ cupfuls, about 5-inch apart on ungreased cookie sheet and bake at 350⁰ for 12 to 14 minutes. For chewy cookies, do not overbake. Remove from oven before they look completely done.

"These are the best ever oatmeal cookies. This is our type of Christmas cookie!"

Joy Drury

Frosted Cream Cookies

¾ C. lard
½ C. sugar
½ C. dark molasses
½ C. sour milk + 1 tsp. soda
2 C. flour

2 eggs
1 tsp. cinnamon
1 tsp. cloves
Pinch of salt
1 tsp. ginger

Cream lard, sugar, and molasses. Sift dry ingredients together and add to creamed mixture alternately with the milk. Drop by spoonfuls and bake at 350⁰ for 5 to 10 minutes.

Mary Lehmer

Grandma King's Oatmeal Cookies

½ C. oleo
1½ C. brown sugar
4 eggs (beaten)
7/8 C. sour cream
1 C. raisins
2 C. oatmeal
1½ C. flour

1 tsp. cinnamon
1 tsp. salt
1 tsp. soda
1 tsp. baking powder
½ tsp. ground cloves
½ C. nuts

Cream oleo, brown sugar, and beaten eggs; until smooth. Sift 1½ C. flour and 1 tsp. each - cinnamon, salt, soda, baking powder, and ½ tsp. cloves. Sift into creamed mixture along with 7/8 C. thick sour cream, 1 C. raisins, 2 C. oatmeal, and ½ C. nuts. Bake at 350° for about 10 minutes.

Luella Fairholm

Holiday Shortbread Drops

1 C. butter or margarine
½ C. sugar
1 egg yolk
¼ tsp. salt

2 C. flour
1 C. raisins
1 C. chopped English walnuts
2 tsp. vanilla

Cream shortening and sugar well. Blend in egg yolk, vanilla, flour, and salt. Mix well. Mix in raisins and walnuts. Drop by teaspoon onto greased baking sheets and bake at 375° to 400° (depends on your oven) for 10 to 12 minutes or until delicately browned. Makes about 4 dozen cookies.

Mildred Waltz

166

Cookies

Grandma Roach's Rocks

1 C. shortening
1½ C. brown sugar
3 eggs (unbeaten)
3 C. sifted all-purpose flour
½ tsp. baking soda
2 tsp. baking powder
1 tsp. cinnamon

1 tsp. nutmeg
1 tsp. mace
1 tsp. vanilla
1 (7¼ oz.) pkg. pitted dates
  (finely chopped)
½ C. chopped nuts

Let shortening stand at room temperature until softened. Cream with sugar in a large mixing bowl. Add eggs, 1 at a time and beat for 1 minute after each addition. Add the vanilla. Sift together all dry ingredients and add ½ C. of this mixture to the dates and nuts. Add the remaining dry mixture to the creamed mixture and mix on a low speed just until thoroughly blended. Add the floured dates and nuts; mix on a low speed also. Drop by teaspoonful onto a greased baking sheet and bake at 375⁰ for 10 minutes.

Maureen Roach

167

Gingerbread Cookies

5 C. flour
2 tsp. ground ginger
1½ tsp. baking soda
1 tsp. ground cinnamon
1 tsp. ground cloves
½ tsp. salt

1 C. shortening
1 C. sugar
1 egg
1 C. molasses
2 tsp. vinegar

Sift together flour, ginger, baking soda, cinnamon, cloves, and salt; set aside. Cream together shortening and sugar in bowl until light and fluffy, using electric mixer at medium speed. Add egg, molasses, and vinegar, beating well. Gradually stir dry ingredients into creamed mixture, mixing well. Cover and chill in refrigerator at least 3 hours. Divide dough into fourths. Use ¼ of dough at a time and roll out on a floured surface, 1/8-inch thick. Cut into shapes with cookie cutters and bake at 375° for 5 to 6 minutes.

Nancy M. Corkrean

Holiday Wreaths

¼ C. butter or margarine
4 C. miniature marshmallows
¼ tsp. green food coloring

½ tsp. vanilla
4½ to 5½ C. cornflakes
Candy red hots

Melt butter in microwave for 30 seconds. Add marshmallows and coat with butter. Microwave for 1 minute, stir, and microwave for 1 minute longer. Add coloring and vanilla; stir. Fold in cornflakes and blend well. Drop from teaspoon onto waxed paper on cookie sheet. Shape into wreaths with fingers. Decorate with red hots. Refrigerate until set.

Joan Hilton

Cookies

Fresh Orange Cookies

1½ C. sugar
1 C. margarine (softened)
1 C. sour cream or
   plain yogurt
2 eggs
4 C. flour

1 tsp. soda
1 tsp. baking powder
½ tsp. salt
⅔ C. orange juice
Grated peel of 1 orange

FROSTING:
¼ C. margarine (melted)
2 C. powdered sugar

1 T. grated orange peel
2 to 3 T. orange juice

Heat oven to 375°. In a large bowl, cream sugar and margarine until light and fluffy. Add sour cream and eggs; blend well. Lightly spoon flour into measuring cup and level off. Add flour, soda, baking powder, salt, orange juice, and peel; mix well. Drop by rounded teaspoonfuls onto ungreased cookie sheets and bake at 375° for 8 to 11 minutes or until edges are light golden brown. Remove from sheets immediately. In a small bowl, combine all frosting ingredients and beat until smooth. Frost warm cookies. Makes about 6 dozen.

Joanne Gasiel

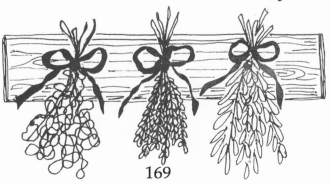

Cookies & Bars

Jumbo Raisin Cookies

2 C. raisins
1 C. water
1 tsp. soda
1 C. shortening
2 C. white sugar
1½ tsp. cinnamon
¼ tsp. each nutmeg & allspice

3 eggs (unbeaten)
1 tsp. vanilla
4 C. sifted flour
2 tsp. salt
1 tsp. baking powder
1 C. chopped walnuts

Boil raisins in water for 5 minutes, then drain, reserving the liquid. Measure ½ C. of liquid. (If needed, add water to liquid to make ½ cup.) Cool and stir in soda. Cream shortening, sugar, and spices. Beat in eggs, 1 at a time. Add vanilla and raisin liquid to sifted flour, salt, and baking powder. Add raisins and walnuts. Chill dough until stiff. Drop by teaspoon 1-inch apart on greased cookie sheet and bake at 375° for 12 to 15 minutes.

Anna King

Kringlas
(Norwegian & Scandinavian)

1½ C. sugar
1 T. butter
2 C. sour cream

Flour to stiffen
2 tsp. baking powder
½ tsp. salt

Cream sugar and butter in a large bowl, then add sour cream. Sift together flour, baking powder, and salt. Add to first mixture. Take about 1 tsp. batter and make a figure 8. Bake at 350° for 8 to 10 minutes. These were holiday cookies and favorites of my father and grandfather. Note: Kringla are to be eaten with butter.

Stephen Weltha

170

Cookies

Lady Fingers

8 eggs
2 C. sugar
12 T. cold water
2 C. flour
2 tsp. baking powder

2 tsp. vanilla
¼ tsp. salt
1 C. powdered sugar
3 T. water (more if needed)
Unsalted peanuts

Start beating eggs and when foamy add sugar. Beat until lemon yellow and fluffy. Add vanilla and water, then the dry ingredients, folding these into egg mixture. Bake at 350⁰ in a greased 9½ x14½ -inch pan. Test with a toothpick to see when done. Cool and cut into squares. Makes about 2 dozen, depending how large you want the squares. Mix powdered sugar and enough water to make a thin frosting. Dip lady finger cookies into powdered sugar frosting, coating all sides and then dip into crushed unsalted peanuts.

"These are sort of messy, gets all over your fingers but they are so good. A must for Christmas at our house. The whole family can help shell the peanuts."

Martha Street

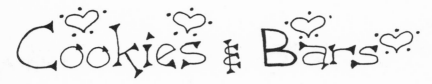

Cookies & Bars

Never Fail Cookies

3 C. flour
1 C. shortening
1 tsp. soda
2 tsp. baking powder

2 beaten eggs
4 T. milk
1 C. sugar

Put the 3 C. of flour, 1 C. shortening, 1 tsp. soda, and 2 tsp. baking powder in a large bowl and mix as for pie crust. Add the 2 beaten eggs, 4 T. milk, and 1 C. sugar. Roll thin and cut into desired shapes. Bake at 350⁰ for 10 to 12 minutes.

Cheryl Emanuel

Favorite Cookies

4 sqs. unsweeetened chocolate
½ C. butter or salad oil
2 C. sugar
4 eggs

2 tsp. vanilla
2 C. flour
2 tsp. baking powder

Melt chocolate in a pan and cool. Add butter or oil and sugar. Cream well. Beat in eggs, 1 at a time. Add vanilla, flour, and baking powder. Chill overnight. Make into balls, about 1-inch in diameter. Roll in powdered sugar. Bake at 375⁰ for 10 to 15 minutes.

Sue Finnell

Cookies

No-Bake Cookies

1 stick margarine
2 C. sugar
½ C. cocoa
¼ C. water or ½ C. milk

½ C. peanut butter
1 tsp. vanilla
3 C. oatmeal
1 C. nuts

Boil margarine, sugar, cocoa, and water. Cook until the temperature reaches soft ball on candy thermomter. Add peanut butter, vanilla, oatmeal, and nuts. Mix thoroughly. Drop by teaspoonful onto waxed paper layed on your counter top and let cool before storing.

Barb Schmitz

Peanut Blossoms

1 C. shortening or margarine
1 C. peanut butter
1 C. sugar
1 C. brown sugar
2 eggs
4 T. milk

1 tsp. vanilla
3½ C. flour
2 tsp. baking soda
1 tsp. salt
Chocolate star or kisses

Cream shortening, peanut butter, and sugars. Add eggs, milk, and vanilla; mix well. Add dry ingredients and mix thoroughly, then shape into balls. Roll balls in sugar. Place on greased cookie sheet and bake at 375° for 8 minutes. Place chocolate stars or kisses on cookie and return to oven for a few minutes. Press the chocolate pieces firmly down so cookie cracks around edge.

Frances Stevens

173

Cookies & Bars

Peanut Butter Chip Cookies

1 C. shortening	2 eggs
1 C. sugar	2 C. flour
1 C. brown sugar	1 tsp. soda
1 tsp. vanilla	2 C. peanut butter chips

Cream shortening, sugar, brown sugar, and vanilla until light and fluffy. Add eggs and beat mixture. Add flour and soda. Mix well and stir in peanut butter chips. Drop by teaspoonful onto ungreased cookie sheet. Bake at 350⁰ for 10 to 12 minutes, until light brown. Cool slightly before removing from cookie sheet. This makes about 5 dozen 2½-inch cookies.

Mary Dooley

Prize of Iowa

1 C. white sugar	1 tsp. soda
1 C. brown sugar	1 tsp. vanilla
1 C. solid shortening	¼ tsp. cream of tartar
2 eggs	2 C. flour
1 tsp. baking powder	2 C. oatmeal (quick or reg.)

Beat first 4 ingredients. Add remaining ingredients and mix well. May bake immediately by teaspoonfuls pressed flat or form into three loaves. Chill and slice. Bake at 350⁰ for 10 to 12 minutes. Raisins or butterscotch chips may be added for variation.

Ruth Cunningham

Cookies

Peanut Butter Temptations

½ C. butter
½ C. peanut butter
½ C. brown sugar
½ C. sugar
1 egg
½ tsp. vanilla

1¼ C. flour
¾ tsp. baking soda
½ tsp. salt
1 bag Reese's mini peanut
    butter cups

Cream butter, peanut butter, sugar, and brown sugar. Beat in egg and vanilla. Sift flour, baking soda, and salt; blend into creamed mixture. Shape dough into 1-inch balls and place in ungreased 1½-inch muffin tins (not regular size). Bake at 375° for 8 to 10 minutes until lightly browned. Immediately after removing cookies from oven, press a peanut butter cup into the center of the dough. Cool for 10 minutes, then remove cookies from tins.

"These cookies are great for holiday giving!"

Cindy Watson Pottebaum
Cathy Bowman

Cookies & Bars

Snickerdoodles

1 C. shortening
1½ C. sugar
2 eggs
1 tsp. vanilla
½ tsp. salt

⅓ tsp. maple flavoring
2¾ C. flour
2 tsp. cream of tartar
1 tsp. soda

COATING:
2 T. of sugar

2 T. of cinnamon

Preheat oven to 400°. Blend and cream well the shortening, sugar, eggs, and flavorings. Sift together flour, cream of tartar, soda, and salt. Mix both together. Roll into balls and roll each in mixture of sugar and cinnamon. Bake for 5 to 8 minutes.

Marie White

At St. Joseph Church in Winterset, we have two buildings - the church and the parish hall. After services on Sunday, we have coffee and rolls for everyone at the hall. For our family, it's a favorite thing to go to the hall after Sunday Mass.

One Sunday our three-year-old son Sam was resisting going to church so we told him that we would have donuts after Mass. That seemed to brighten his spirits and he got ready faster than ever.

As we got out of the car and started walking toward the church, he started crying and screamed, "No, No! Not that church! The donut church! I want to go to the donut church!"

Cindy Watson Pottebaum

176

Cookies

Sour Cream Sugar Cookies

3¼ C. sifted flour
1 tsp. soda
½ tsp. salt
½ C. soft butter or margarine
1 C. sugar

1 egg (unbeaten)
1½ tsp. vanilla
1 tsp. nutmeg
½ C. thick sour cream

Sift together flour, soda, and salt. Combine in a large bowl the butter, sugar, egg, and flavoring. Beat for 2 minutes. Add sour cream and then the flour mixture gradually. Set oven at 400° to preheat. Roll on lightly floured surface to ¼-inch thickness. Sprinkle with sugar and roll in lightly. Cut with floured cutters and place on cookie sheet. Bake for about 12 minutes until golden brown. Makes about 2½ dozen.

"I don't mind the flour sifting as I have a battery flour sifter. Just couldn't get along without it."

Anna King

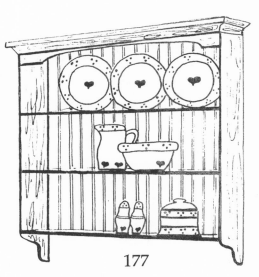

Cookies & Bars

Snowball Surprise

¾ C. butter or margarine
½ C. sugar
¼ tsp. salt
1 egg
½ tsp. vanilla

1¾ C. flour
Jellied fruit candy, such as
gum drops or orange slices
(cut into small pieces)
¾ C. sifted powdered sugar

Heat oven to 350°. Beat butter or margarine until softened. Add sugar and salt; beat until fluffy. Add egg and vanilla; beat well. Gradually add flour until well mixed. Shape dough into 1-inch balls, pressing a candy into center and shaping dough around candy. Place balls about 2-inches apart on ungreased cookie sheet. Bake for about 15 minutes or until edges are golden. With a pancake turner, transfer 2 or 3 cookies at a time into a bag with powdered sugar. Shake until coated. Cool on rack. When cool, gently shake once more in powdered sugar. Makes about 36.

Margaret Tiernan

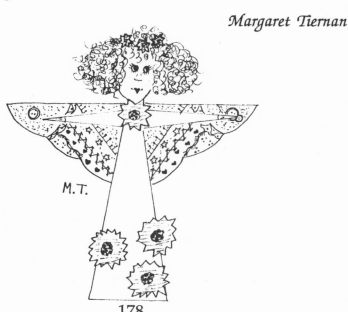

M.T.

Cookies

Starlight Sugar Crisps or Friendship Knots

3½ C. flour
1¼ tsp. salt
1 C. oleo
⅓ C. water
1 tsp. sugar
1 pkg. dry yeast

2 eggs (well-beaten)
½ C. sour cream
1 tsp. vanilla
1½ C. white sugar
2 tsp. vanilla

Sift together in a large bowl the flour and salt. Cut oleo in until like pie crust. Soften dry yeast in ⅓ C. water and 1 tsp. sugar. Blend together eggs, sour cream, and vanilla with the yeast mixture and dry ingredients. Mix well and chill at least 2 hours. Combine sugar sugar and vanilla. On a cloth covered board, sprinkle ¼ C. vanilla sugar and roll out ½ of dough to about 10x16-inch size. Sprinkle more of sugar on top, then fold one end to middle, then other end over this so you have 3 layers. Turn dough ¼ turn and roll out again to 10x16-inch size and sprinkle with 2 T. sugar. Fold to 3 layers, then turn ¼ turn, and roll this time to 12x18-inch. Cut down center, then in ½ to ¾ inch strips. On well greased cookie sheet place twisted strips and loop ends over so looks like knot. Place 1-inch apart on cookie sheet and bake at 350⁰ for 15 to 18 minutes, until light brown. Remove while warm to wax paper to cool. Repeat to 2nd half of dough.

"I made these a lot for friends when illness or death visits their home. That's why I call them my friendship knots."

Shirley A. Bittinger

St. Nicholas Celebration
By: Teresa Hoffelmeyer

On the first Sunday in December, we have our St. Nicholas celebration. The parishioners make the following cookies in the shape of St. Nicholas. Placed under a Christmas tree at the front of the church, these cookies make the entire church smell of cinnamon and spice.

At the end of Mass, it is our custom that all children who have not yet received their first communion come forward to receive a blessing from Father. On this particular day, they come forward, sit down, and listen to stories about the life of St. Nicholas, Bishop of Myra. Then St. Nicholas, dressed as a Bishop, enters the church. He thanks the children for keeping the memory of St. Nicholas alive and encourages them to be generous just as St. Nicholas was. He then passes out the St. Nicholas cookies.

After mass we gather at the Parish Hall for a special brunch. We have an assortment of coffee cakes, rolls, sausage casseroles, and hot spiced cider. The Hall is decorated with folk art Santas and a sign that says, WE BELIEVE IN ST. NICHOLAS. The high school students serve and clean up after this brunch.

Although we celebrate the feast day of St. Nicholas December 6th as a parish family, this day could be celebrated in the home with your own family adapting some of the ideas above.

St. Nicholas Cookies

1 C. shortening
2 C. sugar
4 eggs
¾ tsp. salt
2 tsp. baking powder
4 C. flour

4 tsp. cinnamon
2 tsp. allspice
1½ tsp. ginger
2 tsp. nutmeg
1½ tsp. cloves

(Continued on Next Page)

Cookies

(St. Nicholas Cookies - Continued)

Cream shortening and sugar; add eggs. Sift together remaining ingredients and gradually stir into creamed mixture. Turn out onto a floured board. Knead in additional flour until dough is no longer sticky, about 1 cup. Chill and then roll dough to about ¼-inch thickness and cut around paper St. Nick pattern (below). Place on greased cookie sheet and decorate as you desire. Bake at 350⁰ until golden brown.

Mayme's Sugar Cookies

"As a young child I spent a lot of time with my Grandma, Mayme Dermody. She used to make wonderful sugar cookies and send them home in a little brown paper bag. Her sugar cookies, as I remember, were the best. I often helped her make these cookies but there was never a recipe. After her death, I often thought of those little brown bags with those crispy, sugary cookies inside. Since there was no recipe, I tried different recipes and finally combined several. I added the milk (she had always added milk to the dough) and came up with Mayme's cookies. I sometimes put a couple in a paper bag so they'll be just like Grandma's."

1 C. margarine	2½ tsp. baking powder
1 C. sugar	¾ tsp. soda
1 egg	¼ tsp. salt
1 T. vanilla	⅓ C. milk
3½ C. flour	

Mix margarine, sugar, and egg. Add vanilla. Add flour, baking powder, soda, salt, and milk. Chill dough. Roll out and cut with biscuit cutter. Sprinkle with sugar and bake at 350⁰ for 10 to 12 minutes.

Linda Hermanstorfer

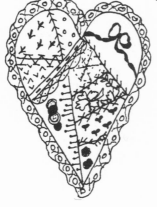

Mom's Sugar Cookies

4½ C. sugar
4 eggs
1 C. butter or lard
1⅓ C. whole milk
2 tsp. vinegar

2 tsp. soda
½ tsp. salt
2 tsp. lemon or vanilla
9⅓ C. flour &
    2 tsp. baking powder,
    sifted together

Combine the first 5 ingredients in mixer and blend. Then add soda, salt, and flavoring. Last add flour and baking powder, a cup at a time using the dough blades or hooks. Roll out and cut into desired shapes. Bake at 375° for 6 to 8 minutes.

"These are our most used cookies. We cut animal shapes and frost at Christmas with colored icing to use as ornaments on the Christmas tree. Also stars, santas, angels, canes, and stockings are nice."

Elma Tracy

Fr. Hahessy Remembered
By: Elma Tracy

When we first moved to Winterset, Fr. William Hahessy was our priest at St. Joseph's and we liked him very much. I was working in a home in town in early 1941. Fr. called for someone to go with him to a basketball game in Stuart one Saturday night. He liked to go to ball games very much. When we got there, the line to enter the building was about half a block long. While we were waiting in the line, Fr. said, "I wonder if I couldn't shorten this line if I went up there and said, 'Confessions will be heard from this window from now on'." To me, that was Fr. Hahessy.

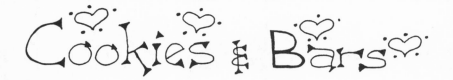

Cookies & Bars

Sugar Cut-Out Cookies

1¼ C. soft butter
2 eggs
5 C. flour
1 tsp. salt

2 C. sugar
½ C. milk
4 tsp. baking powder
1 tsp. nutmeg

Cream butter and sugar. Add eggs and beat until fluffy. Stir together dry ingredients and add alternately with milk. If dough is sticky, add flour to handle. Roll ¼-inch thick on floured surface. Cut out with your favorite cookie cutters. Bake on ungreased cookie sheet at 375⁰ for 8 minutes. Makes about 100 cookies.

Terri Johnson

Swedish Toast

1 C. sugar
1 C. oleo
2 eggs

4 C. flour
½ tsp. baking powder
2 tsp. almond extract

Mix dough together. Form 4 long strips, slightly flattened on 12x18-inch cookie sheet. Bake at 350⁰ for 20 to 25 minutes. Remove from oven and while still hot cut into ½-inch thick slices and roll in cinnamon-sugar mixture. Place on greased cookie sheet and return to oven. Bake for 15 minutes more or until slightly brown.

Shirley Bittinger

Cookies

Favorite Sugar Cookies

1 C. white sugar
1 C. powdered sugar
1 C. real butter (2 sticks)
  (no substitutes)
1 C. oil
2 eggs

1 tsp. vanilla
4 C. flour + 2 T.
1 tsp. soda
1 tsp. cream of tartar
½ tsp. salt

In a large bowl, cream butter, sugar (both white and powdered), and eggs. Beat in oil and vanilla. Combine flour, soda, cream of tartar, and salt. Gradually add flour mixture, beating until well combine. Chill dough, (I usually refrigerate overnight). With hands roll dough into small ball (the size of a walnut). Place on cookie sheet. Press dough with a flat-bottom glass that has been dipped in sugar. Bake at 350⁰ until lightly brown.

Note: Wanda takes only enough dough out of the refrigerator for about one pan of cookies at a time, so that it doesn't get too warm to roll into balls.

Wanda Martin
Carl Neal
Loretta Lehmer
Bev Maxwell
Barb Corkrean
Lois Pettit

Cookies & Bars

Danish Apple Bars

2½ C. flour	1 C. cornflakes
1 tsp. salt	4 large apples
1 C. shortening	1 C. sugar
1 egg yolk (beaten)	1 tsp. cinnamon
Milk	1 egg white (beaten)

ICING:
1 C. powdered sugar   1 tsp. vanilla
1 T. water

Sift together dry ingredients. Add shortening and cut in until crumbly. Beat egg yolk and add enough milk to egg yolk to equal ⅔ C. liquid. Add slowly to flour and blend (do not over blend). Divide dough in half. Roll out half and put in jelly roll pan (15½ x 10½ -inch), pressing up on sides of pan. Sprinkle crushed corn-flakes over bars. Peel and slice apples and spread over cornflakes. Sprinkle with sugar and cinnamon. Roll out remaining dough and put over top and seal (do not vent top dough). Brush with beaten egg white. Bake at 375⁰ for 1 hour. Spread icing on while still warm.

Patricia Morris

Banana Bars

2 C. flour
1⅓ C. sugar
2 tsp. baking soda
½ tsp. salt

1 C. ripe bananas (mashed)
¾ C. vegetable oil
4 eggs
2 tsp. vanilla

FROSTING:
½ C. butter
1 (3 oz.) pkg. cream cheese

1 T. vanilla
3 C. powdered sugar

Combine dry ingredients. Add the mashed bananas, oil, eggs, and vanilla. Beat until blended. Bake in a 10x15-inch greased pan for 20 to 25 minutes at 350°. Cool. Sprinkle with powdered sugar or frost with cream cheese frosting.

For Frosting: Beat softened butter and cream cheese together. Beat in vanilla. Add powdered sugar, ½ C. at a time and beat well.

"My daughter Katie and Fr. Maurice Schulte shared the same birthday, December 27th. Every year without fail, Fr. Schulte would come to our house to celebrate his birthday with Katie. Even when weather conditions prevented relatives from attending, Fr. Schulte was there. (Fr. Schulte died in 1988 but Mike Brown who used to go fishing with him, and Katie Corkrean and many other kids still remember the special times they shared with him.")

Debby Corkrean

Cookies & Bars

Butterfinger Bars

1 C. brown sugar
½ C. white sugar
1 C. margarine
4 C. quick oatmeal

6 ozs. chocolate chips
¾ C. creamy peanut butter
1 tsp. vanilla or burnt
    sugar extract

Mix together first 4 ingredients and press into 9x13-inch pan. Bake at 350⁰ for 15 minutes. Melt chocolate chips, then add peanut butter and flavoring. Spread over the bars when done and let cool.

Cheryl Emanuel

Applesauce Brownies

½ C. shortening
1 C. sugar
2 eggs
½ C. applesauce
1 tsp. vanilla
2 sqs. baking chocolate

1 C. flour
½ tsp. baking powder
¼ tsp. soda
¼ tsp. salt
½ C. chopped nuts

In a saucepan melt shortening and chocolate. Cool slightly. Stir in sugar, applesauce, and vanilla. Beat eggs and stir into mixture. Sift dry ingredients and stir into mixture. Add chopped nuts. Pour into greased and floured 9x9-inch pan. Bake at 350⁰ for 35 to 40 minutes. Cut into bars when cool.

Jean Gillespie

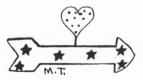

Blonde Brownies

4 C. brown sugar   1 tsp. salt
4 T. vanilla   1 tsp. soda
4 eggs (well-beaten)   3 C. sifted flour

Blend well and add nuts, if desired. Spread about ½-inch deep in 9x13-inch pan and bake at 325° until light touch doesn't leave a dent. Cut in squares before they are cool.

Irenee S. Tracy

Caramel Brownies

1 German chocolate cake mix   1 large can evaporated milk
1 stick margarine or butter   1 (14 oz.) pkg. Kraft cararmels
  (melted)   1½ C. chocolate chips

Mix cake mix with 1 stick melted butter/margarine and ½ C. + 2 T. evaporated milk. Pat ½ of mixture into lightly greased 9x13-inch cake pan. Bake at 350° for 7 minutes. While baking this, melt caramels with ⅓ C. evaporated milk (on stove or in microwave). Take brownies from oven and pour caramel mixture over layer of brownies and sprinkle with chocolate chips. Place remaining batter on top by dropping by spoonfuls. Bake an additional 15 to 20 minutes at 350°.

Variation: Mix cake mix with ¾ C. melted butter, ⅓ C. evaporated milk, and ½ C. nuts.

Cheryl Emanuel
Kelli Homerwold

22 Minute Cake Brownie

2 C. flour
2 C. sugar
1 tsp. soda
1 stick oleo
½ C. oil
1 C. water

3 T. cocoa
½ C. buttermilk
2 eggs
1 tsp. almond extract
1 tsp. vanilla

FROSTING:
1 stick butter
⅓ C. milk
3 T. cocoa
4 C. powdered sugar

1 tsp. vanilla flavoring
1 tsp. almond flavoring
1 C. nuts (if desired)

In a large bowl mix first 3 ingredients. In a saucepan add the next 4 ingredients and bring to a boil. Add to first 3 and add last 4, mixing well. Pour into a 12x18-inch pan. Bake at 350⁰ for 30 minutes or until done.

For Frosting: In a saucepan melt 1 stick butter, ⅓ C. milk, and 3 T. cocoa. Bring to a boil, then add the powdered sugar. Beat until smooth. Add vanilla flavoring, almond flavoring, and nuts if desired. Spread evenly over brownies while warm.

Brownie Variation: No almond extract.

Frosting Variation: 1 stick margarine, ¼ tsp. vanilla, ¼ C. cocoa, Pinch of salt, ⅓ C. buttermilk, 1 C. nuts, and 2½ C. powdered sugar

Anna King
Barb Schmitz
Veronica Klug

Chocolate Brownies and Chocolate Frosting

1 stick of margarine
4 eggs
1 C. sugar

1 C. flour + *1 T. flour*
1 lb. can Hershey syrup

FROSTING:
6 T. milk
6 T. margarine

1 C. sugar
½ C. chocolate chips

Beat together eggs and margarine, add sugar and continue to beat. Add flour and can of Hershey syrup. Bake at 350⁰ for only 20 minutes in 9x13-inch pan. Don't overbake.

For Frosting: Boil milk, margarine, and sugar for 1 minute. Add chocolate chips until smooth. Pour this on while still warm.

Variation: Use 1 C. white corn syrup in place of 1 C. sugar in brownie recipe.

Elizabeth M. Edwards
Eileen Moore
Sue Finnell

Creme-de-Menthe Brownies

2 C. *flour*
2 C. *sugar*
2 *tsp. soda*
½ *tsp. salt*
2 *sticks margarine*

1 C. *water*
4 T. *cocoa*
¾ C. *buttermilk*
2 *eggs*
1 *tsp. vanilla*

FILLING:
½ C. *butter*
3 T. *creme-de-menthe*
3 *ozs. cream cheese*

2 T. *instant vanilla pudding*
2 C. *powdered sugar*

Stir first 4 ingredients with spoon. In saucepan, bring to a boil the margarine, water, and cocoa. Add this to flour mixture and beat with electric mixer for 5 minutes. Add buttermilk, eggs, and vanilla, mixing well. Bake on large sheet cake pan at 350° for 20 minutes.

For Filling: Cream butter, cream cheese, and pudding. Add sugar and creme-de-menthe. Stir until smooth, then spread on cooled brownies. Top with a can of chocolate frosting.

Phyllis Patrick

Mom's Brownies

2 C. flour
2 C. sugar
½ tsp. salt
2 sticks margarine
1 C. water

3 T. cocoa
2 well-beaten eggs
1 tsp. soda
½ C. sour milk
1 tsp. vanilla

FROSTING:
1 stick margarine
3 T. cocoa
4 T. milk

4¾ C. powdered sugar
1 tsp. vanilla

Mix flour, 2 C. sugar, and ½ tsp. salt. Melt 2 sticks margarine, 1 C. water, and 3 T. cocoa. Add these three to first three. Add 2 well beaten eggs, 1 tsp. soda, ½ C. sour milk, and 1 tsp. vanilla. Bake at 350⁰ for 20 minutes in a greased and floured 17x11x1-inch pan.

For Frosting: Heat in pan (don't boil) the margarine, cocoa, and milk. Add powdered sugar and vanilla.

Karen Gronemyer
Delores Nicholson

Zucchini Brownies

2 C. shredded zucchini
2 C. flour
2 tsp. vanilla
3 T. cocoa
½ C. oil

½ tsp. salt
1½ C. white sugar
1½ tsp. soda
½ C. nuts (optional)

Mix all together and pour into a 9x13-inch pan which has been greased and floured. Bake at 350⁰ for 25 to 30 minutes. When cool frost with fudge frosting.

Harriet Nevins

Carrot Bars

4 eggs
2 C. sugar
1 C. oil
½ tsp. salt
2 tsp. soda

2 tsp. cinnamon
½ C. nuts
3 small jars baby food carrots
    or 1½ C. mashed carrots
2 C. flour

Mix all ingredients together well. Pour into 12x18-inch greased cookie pan with edge. Bake at 350⁰ for 25 minutes.

FROSTING:
1 (8 oz.) pkg. cream cheese
1 tsp. vanilla

¼ lb. oleo (soft)
1 lb. powdered sugar

Mix well and spread on cooled bars.

Shirley Bittinger

Cherry Walnut Bars

CRUST:

2 C. flour   1 C. butter
1 C. powdered sugar

Combine and pat into greased jelly roll pan. Bake at 350° for 12 minutes.

FILLING:

4 beaten eggs   ½ C. nuts (chopped)
¼ C. flour   1 C. coconut
2 C. brown sugar   2 tsp. cherry juice
½ C. maraschino cherries

Spread the filling mixture over baked crust and bake for 20 to 25 minutes.

Shirley Privratsky

Cookies & Bars

Chocolate Caramel Bars

1 pkg. German chocolate
  cake mix
¾ C. melted margarine
⅓ C. evaporated milk
1 C. chopped walnuts

1 (14 oz.) pkg. caramels
½ C. evaporated milk
1 C. chocolate chips
1 C. coconut (optional)

Mix the first 4 ingredients with spoon. Press half of mixture into greased 9x13-inch pan and bake at 350° for 7 minutes. On stove, melt caramels, and evaporated milk. Stir until smooth and creamy. Put chocolate chips and coconut on top of baked mixture. Pour melted caramels over chips, then place remaining dough mixture over caramels. Bake at 350° for 15 minutes. Cool thoroughly before cutting into bars.

Kelly Stevens

Choconut Mound Bars

4 C. graham cracker crumbs
¾ C. margarine (melted)
½ C. sugar
1 pkg. flaked coconut
1 (15 oz.) can sweetened
  condensed milk

1 (12 oz.) pkg. milk chocolate
  chips
1 (12 oz.) pkg. butterscotch
  chips
1½ C. chopped walnuts

Mix together the first 3 ingredients and pat into a 10x15-inch greased pan. Sprinkle coconut, chocolate chips, butterscotch chips, and nuts on top. Dribble the sweetened condensed milk over the top and bake at 350° for about 15 to 20 minutes.

Debby Corkrean

Chocolate Revel Bars

1 C. margarine
2 C. brown sugar
2 eggs
2 tsp. vanilla
2½ C. flour
1 tsp. soda
1 tsp. salt
3 C. quick cooked oats

1 (14 oz.) can sweetened
condensed milk
1 (12 oz.) pkg. milk chocolate
chips
2 T. margarine
½ tsp. salt
2 tsp. vanilla

In a large bowl cream 1 C. margarine and brown sugar. Beat in eggs and 2 tsp. vanilla. Sift flour, soda, and 1 tsp. salt. Stir in oats. Stir dry ingredients into creamed mixture until blended and set aside. In microwave melt condensed milk, chips, remaining margarine, salt, and vanilla. Stir until smooth, 2 minutes at a time. Pat ⅔ of oat mixture in bottom of 9x13-inch baking dish. Spread chocolate mixture over dough. Dot with remaining oat mixture and bake at 350° for 25 to 30 minutes. Cool and cut into bars.

Nancy T. Emmert

Frosted Creams

1½ C. sugar
1 C. shortening
2 eggs
½ C. dark Karo syrup
2½ C. flour

¼ tsp. salt
2 tsp. cinnamon
1 tsp. soda
½ C. black coffee

Mix all ingredients together and pour into a 13x9-inch pan. Bake at 350⁰ for 35 minutes. Frost with a basic powdered sugar frosting.

"This is a recipe that was passed down from Dan's Grandmother Stella Olga Graeve. We hope you'll enjoy it."

Dorothy J. Kellogg

Festive Caramel Bars

32 individually wrapped
   caramels
⅔ C. (5⅓ oz.) can evap. milk
1 C. flour
1 C. quick oats
1½ C. plain M & M's

½ C. brown sugar
   (firmly packed)
½ tsp. soda
¼ tsp. salt
½ C. oleo
½ C. chopped walnuts

Combine caramels and milk in a heavy saucepan. Cook over low heat, stirring constantly until caramels are melted and mixture is well blended. Combine flour, oats, nuts, sugar, soda, and salt. Add oleo, mixing until mixture resembles coarse crumbs. Reserve 1 C. and press remaining mixture into bottom of greased 9x13-inch cake pan. Bake at 375⁰ for 10 minutes. Sprinkle M & M's over mixture and drizzle melted caramel mixture over candies, then add the 1 C. crumbs that were held back. Bake for 20 to 25 minutes until golden brown. Cool slightly. Chill for 30 minutes. Cut into bars.

Cheryl Emanuel

Fudge Nut Bars

1 (12 oz.) pkg. chocolate chips
1 (15 oz.) can Eagle Brand
  milk

3 T. margarine
¾ C. chopped nuts
2 tsp. vanilla

Melt chips, then remove from heat. Add milk, margarine, nuts, and vanilla; set aside to cool. May need to melt a little more if sets too long.

1 C. margarine
2 C. brown sugar
2 eggs
1 tsp. vanilla
2½ C. flour

1 tsp. salt
1 tsp. soda
3 C. oatmeal
½ C. nuts (optional)

Cream margarine, brown sugar, eggs, and vanilla. Add flour, salt, soda, oatmeal, and nuts, if desired. Put ⅔ into large greased 11x15-inch pan. Spread chocolate mix over this. Crumble the last ⅓ of mixture over filling. Bake at 350° for 20 minutes.

Angela Hill

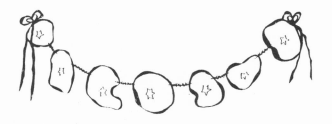

Cookies & Bars

Gingersnap Ice Cream Sandwiches

¾ C. margarine
1 C. plus 3 T. sugar
¼ C. molasses
1 large egg
2 C. flour

2 tsp. baking soda
¼ tsp. ground ginger
¼ tsp. ground cloves
¼ tsp. cinnamon
1¼ qt. vanilla ice cream

In a large bowl beat margarine and 1 C. sugar until blended. Beat in molasses and egg. In a small bowl, mix flour, baking soda, salt, ginger, cinnamon, and cloves. Gradually add to butter mixture, beating until blended. Roll dough into 1½-inch balls and coat in remaining sugar. Place 3-inches apart on greased 12x15-inch baking sheets. Bake in 350⁰ oven until light golden, about 12 minutes. Cool on pan for 2 minutes, then transfer to racks. For each sandwich, place a ¼ C. scoop of ice cream on cookie, gently press another cookie over ice cream. Serve or wrap in foil and freeze up to 2 weeks. Makes 18 to 24 servings.

Rita Drysdale

Heath Bars

1 C. brown sugar
½ C. white syrup
1 C. chocolate chips

1 C. shortening
4 C. oatmeal
½ C. peanut butter

Mix together sugar and shortening. Blend in white syrup and add oatmeal. Bake at 350° for 15 minutes (it will be bubbly) in an ungreased jelly roll pan. Cool until almost cold and cut. Melt chocolate chips and peanut butter. Spread and cut. Refrigerate until cold and recut. Remove from pan.

"These were a favorite bar cookie while I was growing up and still a favorite of my children."

Carita Kelleher

Mixed Nut Bars

1½ C. all-purpose flour
¾ C. powdered sugar
½ C. margarine (softened)
1¼ C. mixed salted nuts

¾ C. light corn syrup
3 T. margarine
½ C. chocolate chips
½ C. peanut butter chips

Heat oven to 350°. Combine the flour and sugar; using a pastry blender, cut in ½ C. margarine thoroughly. Press into 13x9x2-inch pan and bake for 15 minutes. Sprinkle mixed nuts (cut up large nuts) evenly over partially baked crust. In a heavy saucepan over low heat, combine corn syrup, 3 T. margarine, and chips. Stir until chips are melted. Pour mixture evenly over nuts and bake for 5 minutes longer. Cut into bars when slightly warm. Makes 30 to 40 bars.

Sharon Johnson

Cookies & Bars

Oatmeal Bars with Raisin Topping

1¼ C. boiling water
1 C. quick oatmeal
1 stick margarine
1 C. brown sugar
1 C. white sugar

1 tsp. cinnamon
2 eggs
1 tsp. salt
1½ C. flour
1 tsp. soda

TOPPING:
1½ C. raisins
1 C. sugar
⅓ C. milk
2 T. flour

1 C. powdered sugar
2 T. butter
2 tsp. vanilla

Pour boiling water over oatmeal and margarine. Let stand for 20 minutes. Mix flour, soda, white sugar, brown sugar, cinnamon, and salt. When hot mixture has cooled, add eggs and flour mixture, mix well and put in 9x13-inch pan. Bake at 350° for 25 minutes. Cool.

For Topping: Mix and boil for 3 minutes the topping ingredients: Raisins, sugar, milk, flour, and butter. Cool and then add powdered sugar and vanilla. Spread on cake and cut into bars.

Margaret Tiernan

202

Oatmeal Carmelitas Bars

2 C. flour
2 C. quick-cooking oatmeal
1½ C. firmly packed
    brown sugar
1 tsp. soda
½ tsp. salt

1½ C. melted margarine
2 C. chocolate chips
1 C. chopped nuts
1½ C. caramel ice cream
    topping
6 T. flour

Combine flour, oats, brown sugar, soda, salt, and margarine to form crumbs. Press half of crumbs into bottom of greased 10x15-inch pan. Bake at 350⁰ for 10 to 15 minutes. Sprinkle chocolate chips and nuts over baked crust. Mix caramel topping and 6 T. flour well. Drizzle over chocolate chips and nuts. Sprinkle remaining crumbs over top.

Fonda Bass

Pan Magic Cookie Bars

½ C. margarine or butter
1½ C. graham cracker crumbs
1 can condensed milk

1 pkg. shredded coconut
1 C. nuts
1 (12 oz.) pkg. chocolate chips

In a 9x13-inch pan melt butter. Sprinkle graham cracker crumbs over butter. Pour condensed milk over crumbs. Top with chocolate chips, coconut, and nuts. Press evenly in pan and bake at 350⁰ for 25 minutes. Cool and cut into squares.

Barb Schmitz

Oh Henry Bars

4 C. oatmeal
½ C. sugar
⅔ C. melted butter

1 tsp. vanilla
1 C. brown sugar

FROSTING:
1 C. chocolate chips

⅔ C. peanut butter

Mix oatmeal, sugar, butter, vanilla, and brown sugar. Pat into a 9x13-inch pan and bake at 350⁰ for 20 minutes. Frost while still warm with chocolate chips and peanut butter melted together in microwave.

Patricia Morris

Peanut Butter Bars

⅓ lb. finely crushed graham
  crackers
3½ C. powdered sugar
2 C. peanut butter

1 stick oleo
1 (12 oz.) pkg. chocolate chips
½ stick margarine

Mix together graham crackers and powdered sugar. Melt peanut butter and 1 stick oleo together. Add graham cracker mixture and mix well. Press into cookie sheet (I use rolling pin to press it down even.) Melt together in microwave chocolate chips and ½ stick margarine. Spread over first layer. Cool and cut into bars.

Kelli Homewold

Peanut Bars

1 C. white sugar
½ C. shortening
  (butter is best)
1 tsp. vanilla

3 eggs (separated)
½ C. milk
1¾ C. flour

Cream sugar, shortening or butter, egg yolks, and milk. Add the flour and vanilla. Beat 3 egg whites and fold into mixture. Line a cookie sheet with wax paper. Grease pan and paper well. Bake at 350⁰ for 25 to 30 minutes. Remove from pan on wax paper, remove paper from cake, and cool. Cut into bars or squares and frost with a powdered sugar frosting. Roll in chopped salted peanuts.

Shirley Privratsky

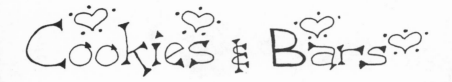

Cookies & Bars

Scotch Bars

1 C. sifted flour
½ tsp. baking powder
1/8 tsp. baking soda
½ tsp. salt
½ C. chopped nuts
   (pecans or other)
1 tsp. vanilla

⅓ C. shortening (vegetable
   oil or oleo)
1 T. hot water
1 C. firmly packed brown
   sugar
1 egg (lightly beaten)
1 C. semi-sweet chocolate chips

Butter baking pan (9x9x2-inch). Sift flour, baking powder, soda, and salt together. Add nuts and mix well. In another bowl put shortening, brown sugar, and water. Mix well. Add egg and vanilla; blend. Then add your flour mixture a small amount at a time, mixing well after each addition. Pour into your greased pan and sprinkle chips over top. Bake in moderate oven (325°) for 20 to 25 minutes (do not overbake). Cool in pan and then cut into bars.

Dorothy Hochstetler

Pumpkin Bars

2 C. sugar	2 tsp. soda
1 C. salad oil	¼ tsp. salt
4 eggs	½ tsp. cinnamon
2 C. flour	1 small can pumpkin

FROSTING:

½ pkg. cream cheese	1 stick margarine
3 C. powdered sugar	Milk

Heat oven to 350°. In a large bowl blend all ingredients at low speed with mixer until moist. Beat for about 2 minutes at medium speed. Pour into greased 15x10-inch jelly roll pan and bake for 25 to 30 minutes.

For Frosting: Mix cream cheese, margarine, and powdered sugar together. Add enough milk to make spreadable.

Patricia Morris
Lois Pettit

Salted Nut Roll Bars

1 pkg. yellow cake mix
⅓ c. butter

1 egg
Miniature marshmallows

TOPPING:
⅔ C. corn syrup
¼ C. margarine (butter)
1 (12 oz.) pkg. peanut
   butter chips

2 tsp. vanilla
2 C. Rice Krispies
2 C. salted peanuts

Mix together cake mix, butter, and egg. Press into a 9x13-inch pan and bake at 350° for 12 to 18 minutes. Remove from oven and sprinkle with marshmallows. Return to oven for 1 to 2 minutes. Cool while preparing topping.

For Topping: In pan heat syrup, margarine, vanilla, and chips until melted and smooth. Stir in cereal and nuts. Immediately spoon warm topping over marshmallows and spread.

Jana Corkrean

Sliced Almond Bars

PASTRY:

½ C. butter

1¼ C. flour

¼ C. sugar

1 egg yolk (beaten)

½ tsp. vanilla

FILLING:

3 T. butter

2 T. milk

½ C. sugar

1 T. honey

1 C. (4 ozs.) sliced almonds

For Pastry: In a large bowl cut butter into flour and sugar, using pastry cutter, until mixture is coarse crumbs. Stir in egg yolk and vanilla. With hands work into a ball. Wrap and refrigerate dough 1 to 2 hours. Preheat oven to 325⁰. Press evenly onto bottom and sides of 9-inch pan, forming ¼-inch ridge. Bake until golden brown, 30 to 35 minutes.

For Filling: Meanwhile, in a small saucepan heat butter and milk until butter is melted. Add sugar, honey, and almonds. Stir well and spread filling over warm pastry. Return to oven and bake another 20 to 30 minutes. Cut into 1½-inch squares. Makes 36 bars. Cool completely.

Kelly Stevens

Cookies & Bars

Sour Cream Raisin Bars

2 C. raisins
1 C. butter or margarine
  (softened)
1 C. packed brown sugar
1¾ C. quick-cooking oats
1¾ C. all-purpose flour

1 tsp. soda
1 C. granulated sugar
2½ tsp. cornstarch
1½ C. dairy sour cream
3 egg yolks
1 tsp. vanilla

Place raisins in heavy saucepan, cover with water, and simmer for 10 minutes. Drain and set aside to cool. Heat oven to 350⁰. Cream butter and brown sugar. Stir in oats, flour, and soda. Press half of mixture into greased 13x9x2-inch pan and bake for 7 minutes. In a heavy saucepan, combine granulated sugar and cornstarch. Stir in sour cream and egg yolks. Over medium heat, cook and stir until mixture thickens. Add vanilla and raisins. Pour over partially baked crust. Crumble remaining oat mixture on top and bake for 30 minutes. Cool and cut into bars or squares. Makes 48 bars, 15 to 16 dessert squares.

Sharon Johnson

Sour Cream Raisin Bars

1½ C. oatmeal   1 C. brown sugar
1½ C. flour   1 C. margarine
1 tsp. soda ·

Mix like pie crust and put 1½ C. in bottom of 9x13-inch pan. Bake at 350⁰ for 15 minutes.

FILLING:
4 egg yolks   3 T. cornstarch
1½ C. sugar   2 C. raisins
2 C. sour cream

Cook over low heat, stirring constantly until thick. Pour over baked crust and top with remainder of first mixture. Bake at 350⁰ for 20 minutes.

Barbara Corkrean

Cookies & Bars

Sugar Kuchen

2 C. sugar
12 egg yolks
1 qt. sour cream
2 tsp. soda
½ C. margarine

½ C. shortening
1 tsp. salt
2 tsp. baking powder
1 tsp. anise (powdered)

CRUMB TOPPING:

2 sticks soft margarine
¾ C. sugar
1 T. cinnamon

1 tsp. anise (powdered)
About 1 C. flour

Melt the margarine and shortening. Put the soda in with the cream. Beat egg yolks until light in color, then add the sugar and beat well. Add the margarine-shortening and the cream. Add baking powder, anise, and salt. Add enough flour to make a firm dough. Chill overnight. In the morning, roll out dough quite thin, place in cookie sheets, brush with cream, sprinkle with desired amount of crumbs, and cut into squares. Bake at 350⁰ until lightly browned.

For Crumb Topping: Mix all the ingredients by hand and work until you have a fine crumbly mixture. Add more flour if you need it to make the mixture fine and absorb the margarine. I usually taste it to see if it is sweet enough.

"My mother made Sugar Kuchen often, but it was a must at Christmas time. I have made it for my own family and still do to carry on the tradition."

Shirley Privratsky

Tangy Lemon Squares

1 C. margarine
½ C. unsifted powdered sugar
2⅓ C. unsifted flour
4 eggs

2 C. sugar
⅓ C. lemon juice
1 tsp. baking powder
Powdered sugar for topping

Melt margarine and mix with powdered sugar. Add 2 C. of the flour, beating until blended. Spread evenly over bottom of a greased 11¾ x7½ x1¾ -inch pan. Bake at 350° for 20 minutes. In a small bowl beat eggs until light and foamy. Gradually add sugar, beating until thick and blended. Add lemon juice, remaining ⅓ C. flour, and baking powder; beat until well blended. Pour lemon mixture over baked crust and bake for 25 minutes. Remove from oven and sprinkle evenly with powdered sugar.

Kay Johnson

Celebrating Candlemas

We think of February 2nd as Groundhog Day, but in our church it is also the day we celebrate the presentation of the infant Jesus at the Temple in Jerusalem, 40 days after Christmas.

For many years, the Church also celebrated this day with a ritual blessing of candles to be used by the Church and Church community. This was called Candlemas.

You may want to celebrate this day as a family. Place one large candle in the center of the table, then gather as many candles as you can find that you will use throughout the year: birthday candles, jack-o-lantern candles, candles stored away in case the electricity goes out, Advent candles, etc.

Discuss Jesus as the "Light of the World." Talk about days gone by, when there was no electricity and how dark it would be when the sun set. Candles were important. Then say some prayers thanking God for the gift of light. Bless the different kinds of candles as family members hold them up. Flashlights and other kinds of lights could also be blessed.

214

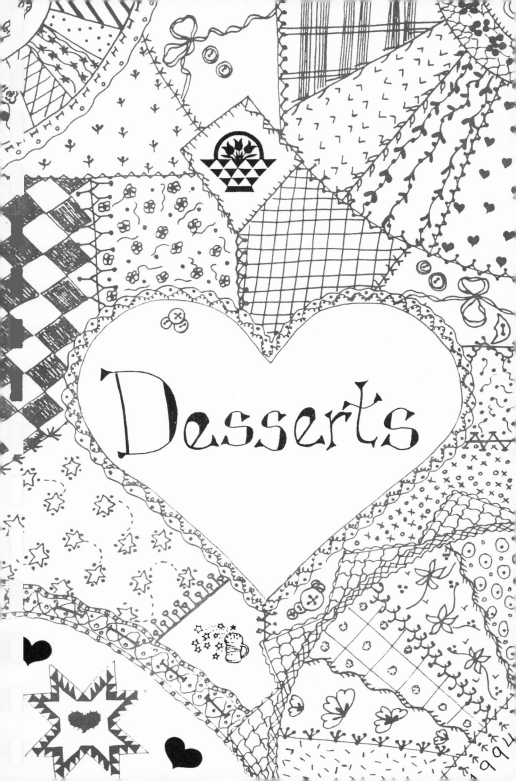

Desserts

Apple Crisp

8 apples (thinly sliced)
1 tsp. cinnamon
1 tsp. lemon juice
½ C. water

1 C. sugar
¾ C. flour
4 T. butter
¼ tsp. cinnamon

Butter 8½ x8½ -inch baking dish. Fill with apple slices, then add 1 tsp. lemon juice and 1 tsp. cinnamon. Pour water over this. In separate bowl mix remaining ingredients until crumbly. Spread over top of apples and bake at 375° for 45 minutes. Test with fork for doneness.

Dorothy Hochstetler

Apple Crisp or Cherry Crisp

½ C. butter
1 C. light brown sugar
¾ C. flour

4 C. sliced apples
½ C. water

Variation for Cherry Crisp: Don't add the water and use a can of cherry pie filling instead of apples.

Blend the first 3 ingredients and put half of apples in greased baking dish (8x8x2-inch) and add half of the dry mix. Add remainder of the apples, water, and cover with remainder of dry mixture. Bake at 350° for 40 minutes.

Mary Lehmer

Baked Apples

6 apples
1 C. brown sugar
1 C. water
2 T. butter

½ tsp. cinnamon
½ tsp. ground nutmeg
A little salt

Place washed, cored, and unpeeled apples in 10x6-inch baking dish. Sprinkle with salt to bring out the flavor. Combine sugar, water, butter, and spices in saucepan. Bring to boil and pour over and around apples. Bake at 350° for about 1 hour, until skin of apple can be pierced with a fork.

Mildred Hoffelmeyer

Stewed Apples

3 lb. bag of Jonathan apples
1 C. sugar

½ tsp. cinnamon

Peel and quarter apples and place in 6 to 8 quart pan. Add 1½ inches of water to cover the bottom of the pan and a pinch of salt. Cover and bring to a boil. Add sugar to taste and a sprinkling of cinnamon. Continue cooking over low heat until apples are soft but not mushy.

Mildred Hoffelmeyer

Fried Apples

3 lb. bag Jonathan or
   Delicious apples
½ C. white or brown sugar

Pinch of salt
1 to 2 T. margarine

Melt margarine in a large deep skillet. Slice the washed, cored, and unpeeled apples into skillet. Fill skillet heaping full as apples will cook down. Sprinkle with salt. Add ½ C. or more of sugar. Cover and cook on a low heat until apples begin to get soft. Remove lid and allow apples to cook down. Serve hot. Good with vanilla ice cream.

"These apple recipes come from my mother-in-law. Because their family has a large apple orchard in Missouri, we receive 4 or 5 bushels of apples each fall. In addition to making applesauce, pies, and drying apples, I make these recipes to help use up all our apples." By: Teresa Hoffelmeyer

Mildred Hoffelmeyer

Blueberry Cream Cheese Squares

1½ C. graham cracker crumbs
½ C. powdered sugar
1 stick oleo (melted)
1 C. sugar
1 (8 oz.) pkg. cream cheese
   (room temp.)

2 eggs (beaten)
2½ T. lemon juice
1 (21 oz.) can blueberry pie
   filling

Preheat oven to 350⁰. Butter a 9x13-inch pan. Mix crumbs, powdered sugar, and margarine. Press in bottom of pan, using a fork. Mix sugar, cream cheese, and eggs. Spread over the crust and bake for 20 minutes. Cool. Stir lemon juice into pie filling and spread over cream cheese mixture. Cover tightly and refrigerate. Variation: May use cherry pie filling instead of blueberry, if desired.

Rosemary Gronstal

Banana Split Dessert

2 C. crushed vanilla wafers
(crumbs)
1 stick melted margarine
3 to 4 bananas (sliced)
2 (10 oz.) pkgs. frozen
strawberries
(thawed & drained)
1 can Eagle Brand milk
¼ C. lemon juice

1 (20 oz.) can crushed
pineapple (drained)
1 (8 oz.) carton Cool Whip
½ C. coconut
¼ C. chopped nuts
¼ C. maraschino cherries
(halved)
Chocolate syrup

Combine crumbs with margarine. Press into 9x13-inch pan. Chill for 1 to 2 hours. Slice bananas on top and spoon on drained strawberries. Combine milk (Eagle Brand) with lemon juice. Spoon over strawberries. Spread pineapple over it and spread on Cool Whip. Sprinkle on coconut, then sprinkle on nuts. Put on cherries and refrigerate overnight. Cut into squares. Drizzle on syrup and serve.

Joan Hilton

The Best Cheese Cake

3 well-beaten eggs
2 (8 oz.) pkgs. cream cheese
(softened)
1 C. sugar
¼ tsp. salt

2 tsp. vanilla
½ tsp. almond extract
(optional)
2 C. sour cream
Graham Crust recipe

Combine eggs, cheese, sugar, salt, and extracts. Beat until smooth. Blend in sour cream and pour into graham crust. Bake at 375⁰ for 35 minutes or until set. Chill for about 4 to 5 hours. Serves about 10. For Crust: Mix 1¾ C. graham cracker crumbs, ½ tsp. cinnamon, and ½ C. melted butter.

Mary Anne Roby

Bread Pudding

¾ C. butter
20 slices white bread
1¾ C. sugar + 2 T. sugar
½ tsp. cinnamon
½ tsp. nutmeg

1 T. vanilla
¼ tsp. salt
6 C. milk
8 eggs
¾ C. raisins

Preheat oven broiler. Butter one side of each slice of bread and place buttered side up under broiler and toast - watch carefully. Cool on wire rack. Cut bread into triangles and arrange in two 8x8-inch pans. Sprinkle with 2 T. sugar and set aside. In a large bowl beat eggs, remaining sugar, spices, salt, and vanilla until smooth, about 3 minutes. Scald milk and with mixer on low add the milk in a steady stream. When blended, add raisins and pour over bread, allowing time for bread to soak up milk mixture. Bake in hot water bath for 40 minutes at 400⁰. (I take a large 12x18-inch pan and put about ¼ -inch of water in it and then put my 8x8-inch pan inside this and cook 1 pan at a time.)

BRANDY SAUCE:
2 eggs
1 C. confectioner's sugar

1 C. whipping cream
½ tsp. brandy

Beat eggs until light in color. Slowly add sugar and set aside. Whip cream and add ½ tsp. brandy and fold this into egg mixture. Refrigerate.

AMARETTO SAUCE:
1 C. sugar
1 stick butter
¼ tsp. cinnamon

1/8 tsp. nutmeg
¼ C. amaretto

Heat sugar and butter in a heavy saucepan over medium heat to softball stage (235⁰), stirring constantly. Remove from heat and add cinnamon, nutmeg, and amaretto.

Teresa Hoffelmeyer

Buster Bar Pie

1 (15 oz.) pkg. Oreos
1 stick margarine
½ gallon ice cream
1 (8 oz.) can Hershey's
    fudge sauce

1 can salted peanuts
    (about 2 C.)
1 jar butterscotch-caramel ice
    cream topping
    (Mrs. Richard's)
1 (12 oz.) carton Cool Whip

Crush Oreos with rolling pin (in heavy bag) and reserve ½ C. crushed Oreos for topping. Melt margarine and pour over crushed Oreos. Press into 9x13-inch pan and bake at 350⁰ for 3 minutes. Let cool. Slice ice cream and layer on top. Put in freezer until hard. Spread chocolate fudge on ice cream and sprinkle with peanuts to cover. Drizzle butterscotch caramel over nuts. Spread Cool Whip on top then sprinkle with reserved crushed Oreos. Put in freezer for several hours or overnight. Before serving let stand at room temperature for 10 to 15 minutes until easy to slice.

Nancy T. Emmert

Cheesecake Fruit Cups

8 ozs. cream cheese
¼ C. sugar
2 eggs

Vanilla wafers
Fruit filling

Beat first three ingredients well and set aside. Place 1 vanilla wafer in foil cupcake liner - prepare 12. Pour 2 or 3 T. of cream cheese mixture over wafer and bake at 350⁰ for 10 to 12 minutes. Cool and top with fruit filling. Cherry, peach, or blueberry. Let set at least 2 hours before serving.

Marilyn McNamara

Chocolate Cheese Cake

1½ sticks melted butter
1½ C. flour
¾ C. chopped pecans
1 (8 oz.) pkg. cream cheese

1 large carton Cool Whip
1 C. sugar
1 box (large) instant chocolate
 pudding mix

For 1st Layer: Combine, butter, flour, and ½ C. nuts and mix with a fork until crumbly. Press into a 9x13-inch pan and bake at 375° for 25 minutes. Let cool.

For 2nd Layer: Combine ½ of Cool Whip with cream cheese and add sugar and blend with mixer. Spread over cooled crust.

For 3rd Layer: Prepare instant pudding according to box and spread over 2nd layer.

For 4th Layer: Spread remaining Cool Whip over all and sprinkle with remaining nuts. Refrigerate for 3 hours or longer and cut into squares.

Barb Schmitz

Cherry Cobbler

1½ C. flour
½ tsp. salt
2 tsp. baking powder
1 C. sugar
½ C. shortening
1 egg

⅓ C. milk
2 C. cherries (seeded)
1 T. tapioca
1 T. lemon juice
2 T. butter

Sift flour and measure. Sift flour, baking powder, salt, and sugar together. Cut shortening into dry ingredients. Beat egg and add milk and combine with flour mixture. Stir until flour is damp (set this batter aside). Pour cherries into greased shallow baking dish. Sprinkle with tapioca and add lemon juice and butter. Drop batter in 6 mounds on top of cherries. Bake at 400° for 30 minutes. Serves 6. Serve with vanilla ice cream. Can also use pineapple, blackberries, or blueberries.

Doris "Dee" Dolton

Cherry Dessert

6 egg whites
¾ tsp. cream of tartar
2 C. sugar
2 tsp. vanilla
1 can cherry pie filling

¾ C. chopped nuts
2 C. soda crackers (broken into small pieces)
1 carton Cool Whip

Add cream of tartar to egg whites. Beat until foamy. Gradually add sugar and beat until it peaks. Fold in vanilla, chopped nuts, and soda crackers. Spread in 9x13-inch pan and bake at 350° for 20 to 25 minutes. Cool, spread on Cool Whip, and top with cherry pie filling.

Ruth Eivins

Desserts

Cherry Delight Dessert

Graham cracker crust
1 pkg. Dream Whip or
  8 oz. carton Cool Whip

1 C. powdered sugar
1 (8 oz.) pkg. cream cheese
1 can cherry pie filling

Prepare Dream Whip as on package. Beat cream cheese, Dream Whip, and powdered sugar thoroughly. Spread onto graham cracker crust. Put 1 can cherry pie filling on top and chill overnight.

Variation: Instead of a graham cracker crust, combine the following: 2 C. flour, 2 sticks softened butter, and 1 C. finely chopped pecans. Spread in 10x13-inch pan and bake at 325° for approximately 10 to 12 minutes or until golden brown. When cool add topping and cherry pie filling.

Joe Barker
Kelly Stevens

Dirt Cups

2 C. cold milk
1 pkg. (4 serving size) instant
  chocolate pudding

1 (8 oz.) carton whipped
  topping
16 ozs. crushed chocolate
  sandwich cookies

Beat milk and pudding with wire whisk, 1 to 2 minutes. Let stand for 5 minutes. Stir in whipped topping and half of the crumbs. Fill 8 oz. cups ¾ full. Top with remaining crumbs and refrigerate for 1 hour. Decorate with gummy worms, malted milk balls, gum drop flowers or anything creative to resemble flower pots. Makes 8 to 10 servings.

Mary Brayton

Cherry Refrigerator Dessert

1½ C. graham cracker crumbs
3 T. melted butter
¼ C. sugar
½ C. milk

3 C. miniature marshmallows
1 C. whipped cream
½ tsp. vanilla
1 can cherry pie filling

Combine crumbs with butter and sugar. Press half of mixture in buttered 9x9-inch dish. Combine marshmallows and milk. Cook in double boiler until marshmallows melt. Let cool. Fold whipped cream into marshmallows and milk; add vanilla. Spoon half of this mixture over crumb mixture. Spoon cherry pie filling over this and top with remaining marshmallow mixture, then remaining crumb mixture. Refrigerate until firm.

"This recipe is from my Great Grandmother, Dorothy Camp, who is 101 years old."

Linnea Camp

Frozen Lemonade Dessert

CRUST:
40 Ritz crackers
¼ C. powdered sugar

1 stick oleo

FILLING:
1 can Eagle Brand milk
1 (6 oz.) can lemonade

9 ozs. Cool Whip

For Crust: Crush Ritz crackers coarsely, then add powdered sugar and oleo (melted). Reserve ¾ C. of mixture for topping. Press rest into a 9x13-inch pan. For Filling: Blend Eagle Brand milk, lemonade, and thawed Cool Whip with a mixer until frothy white. Pour into pan and top with remaining crumbs and freeze.

Kelly Stevens

Chocolate Dessert

1 C. flour
½ C. margarine
½ C. chopped pecans
8 ozs. cream cheese
1 C. powdered sugar

1 C. Cool Whip (8 ozs.)
2 (3½ oz.) pkgs. instant
    chocolate pudding
3 C. milk

For Crust: Blend flour, melted margarine, and pecans until crumbly. Press into a 9x13-inch baking pan and bake at 350⁰ for 15 minutes. Let cool.

For 2nd Layer: Mix cream cheese, powdered sugar, and Cool Whip. Spread on top of crust.

For 3rd Layer: Whip chocolate pudding and milk. Put on top of layer two. Cover with Cool Whip and shaved chocolate.

Nancy Welch
Sue Finnell
Terri Johnson
Margaret Tiernan

Heath Bar Dessert

20 graham crackres
10 soda crackers
6 T. melted butter
2 pkgs. vanilla instant pudding

2 C. vanilla ice cream
2 C. milk
2 tsp. burnt sugar flavoring

Crush all 30 crackers very fine. Add butter and mix well. Pat into 9x13-inch pan. Beat together pudding, ice cream, milk, and flavoring. Pour over cracker crust.

TOPPING:
2 pkgs. Dream Whip
1 C. milk

4 Heath bars

Whip Dream Whip and milk until fluffy. Grate in Heath bars and pour over pudding mixture. Garnish with shaved Heath bars.

Nancy T. Emmert

Caramel Ice Cream Topping

3 C. brown sugar
1⅓ C. light corn syrup
8 large marshmallows

⅔ C. water
¾ C. butter
1⅓ C. evaporated milk

Combine sugar, syrup, and water in a heavy saucepan. Cook to soft-ball stage. Add butter and marshmallows. Stir until melted. Cool and add milk, stirring well. Makes 1½ quarts.

Rosemary Stuchel

227

Homemade Vanilla Ice Cream

3 C. sugar
4 tsp. flour
6 eggs (beaten)
½ gallon milk

1 pt. whipping cream
Half & Half
3 T. vanilla

Mix sugar and flour. Add eggs and milk. Stir and cook just to boiling. Cool slightly. Add whipping cream and enough Half & Half to make 1½ gallon. Add vanilla. Freeze accordingly to your freezer's directions.

Carl Neal

In 1993, we had our first parish Ice Cream Social. It was a great success thanks to the help and advice we received from several churches in our community who do this each year. Homemade ice cream, pies, and brownies were donated by parishioners. Jr. High and High School students, with the help of adults, were in charge of this fund raiser. The money earned from the Social went toward sending nine youths and three adults to World Youth Day in Denver!

Cider Honey Sauce

2 T. lemon juice
1 C. apple cider
⅓ C. honey
½ tsp. grated lemon peel

1 T. cornstarch
2 T. butter or margarine
Several dashes of nutmeg

In a saucepan combine juice, cider, honey, lemon peel, and nutmeg. Stir in cornstarch. Cook and stir until bubbly. Stir in butter until melted. Serve warm. Makes 1 cup. Good over ice cream, pie or bread pudding.

Anna King

Hot Fudge Sauce

½ C. butter
1 C. chocolate chips

2 C. powdered sugar
1 (12 oz.) can evaporated milk

Bring to boil over medium heat, stirring constantly. Cook and stir for 8 to 10 minutes more. Let cool and pour over your favorite ice cream or dessert.

Cindy Watson Pottebaum

Lemon Delight

1 C. flour
½ C. chopped pecans
1 stick margarine
1 (8 oz.) pkg. cream
  cheese

2½ C. Cool Whip
2 (3.4 oz.) pkgs. instant lemon
  pudding
3 C. milk
1 C. powdered sugar

For First Layer: Mix flour, pecans, and margarine. Press into 9x13-inch pan and bake at 350⁰ for 10 minutes and then let cool.

For Second Layer: Blend together the cream cheese and powdered sugar. Fold in 1 C. Cool Whip and spread on crust.

For Third Layer: Mix instant puddings with milk and spread on top of second layer.

For Fourth Layer: Spread 1½ C. Cool Whip on top and garnish with minced pecans, if desired.

Variation: May also be made with chocolate or butterscotch puddings.

Karen Pommier

Lazy Peach Pie

½ C. oleo
1 C. flour
1 C. sugar
2 tsp. baking powder

½ tsp. salt
¾ C. milk
1 large can sliced peaches
    with juice

Melt ½ C. oleo in bottom of oblong pan (9x13-inch). Sift together flour, sugar, baking powder, and salt. Add milk to flour mixture. Pour over oleo in pan. Pour peaches with juice over top of cake mixture. Bake at 350⁰ for about an hour. This is fast and easy. Delicious served warm with a scoop of ice cream.

Berta Kordick

Wash-Day Peach Cobbler

1 (16 oz.) can peach fruit or
    your choice
1 C. flour
1 C. sugar + ¼ C. sugar

1 C. milk
2 tsp. baking powder
Dash of salt
1 stick margarine

Preheat oven to 400⁰. In a medium saucepan over medium heat, cook fruit until boiling. Set aside. In a medium mixing bowl, combine flour, 1 C. sugar, milk, baking powder, and salt. In a 2-quart casserole dish, melt margarine. Pour batter over butter. Add hot fruit - do not stir. Sprinkle ¼ C. sugar over entire casserole. Bake at 400⁰ for 20 to 30 minutes. Serve warm with ice cream, if desired. Makes 4 to 6 servings.

Mary Lehmer

Pudding Cream Coffee Cake

CRUST:
2¼ C. flour
1 C. margarine

½ C. chopped nuts

FILLING:
1 (8 oz.) pkg. cream cheese
2 small pkgs. chocolate
   pudding

3 C. milk
¾ C. powdered sugar
1 large carton Cool Whip

For Crust: Melt margarine in a 9x13-inch pan. Add flour and nuts; mix well. Press firmly into pan and bake at 350° for 25 minutes. Cool.

For Filling: Beat together cream cheese, powdered sugar, and ½ the carton of Cool Whip. Spread over cooled crust. Prepare the 2 pkgs. of chocolate pudding with the 3 C. of milk and cool. Spread over cream cheese mixture. Let cool, then top with remaining Cool Whip. Chill, cut into squares, and serve.

Margaret Tiernan

Pumpkin Dessert

1 (16 oz.) can pumpkin
1 C. sugar
4 beaten eggs
1 can sweetened cond. milk

½ tsp. cinnamon
½ tsp. allspice
1 tsp. vanilla

TOPPING:
1 box carrot cake mix
1¾ sticks oleo (melted)

1-1½ C. chopped pecans

Mix together pumpkin, sugar, eggs, spices, and milk. Pour into 9x12-inch greased pan. Sprinkle dry cake mix over pumpkin mix, then drizzle oleo over dry mix. Bake at 350⁰ for 45 minutes. Sprinkle chopped pecans over top and press lightly into cake. Bake for 15 minutes more. Serve with whipped cream. Very rich!

Shirley Bittinger

Sweetened Condensed Milk

1 C. powdered milk
⅔ C. sugar

⅓ C. boiling water
3 T. melted butter

Put all ingredients into blender and mix at high speed until smooth. Use this in any recipe that calls for Eagle Brand condensed milk. Makes 14 ozs. and cost is only about 25 cents compared to the store-bought product at about $1.45 a can!

Teresa Pearson

Desserts

Pumpkin Roll

3 eggs
1 C. sugar
⅔ C. pumpkin (canned)
1 tsp. lemon juice
¾ C. flour
1 tsp. baking powder
2 tsp. cinnamon
1 tsp. ginger

½ tsp. nutmeg
½ tsp. salt
1 C. finely chopped walnuts
1¼ C. powdered sugar
1 (8 oz.) pkg. cream cheese
5½ T. butter
¾ tsp. vanilla

Beat eggs on high speed for 5 minutes. Gradually beat in sugar. Stir in pumpkin and lemon juice. In a separate bowl, mix flour, baking powder, cinnamon, ginger, nutmeg, and salt. Fold into pumpkin mixture and spread into greased and floured 15x10x1-inch pan. Top with walnuts and bake at 375⁰ for 15 minutes. Turn out on towel sprinkled generously with powdered sugar. Starting at narrow end, roll towel and cake together. Cool. Unroll for filling.

For Filling: Combine powdered sugar, cream cheese, butter, and vanilla. Beat until smooth. Spread over cake and roll up.

Karen Pommier

Grandma Lee's Pumpkin Dessert Squares

CRUST:
1 pkg. yellow cake mix
   (minus 1 C.)

½ C. oleo
1 beaten egg

FILLING:
2 eggs
⅔ C. canned milk

2 C. pumpkin
¾ C. sugar

TOPPING:
1 C. cake mix
1 tsp. cinnamon

¼ C. sugar
¼ C. oleo

For Crust: Mix crust ingredients together, then press into a 9x13-inch pan.

For Filling: Beat eggs, add milk, then remaining ingredients. Pour over crust.

For Topping: Cut oleo into other ingredients. Sprinkle over top of dessert and bake at 350⁰ until inserted knife comes out clean.

Larry Lantz

Desserts

Rainbow Tart

8 ozs. cream cheese
½ C. margarine
1¼ C. flour
¼ tsp. salt
⅓ C. sugar

1 T. lemon juice
1 C. heavy cream
Assorted fresh fruits
¼ C. apricot preserves

Mix 4 ozs. of cream cheese and ½ C. margarine until well blended. Add 1¼ C. flour and ¼ tsp. salt. Mix well and form into a ball. Chill until stiff. On lightly floured surface roll into a 14-inch circle. Place in 12-inch tart or pizza pan. Bake at 425⁰ for 12 to 15 minutes or until golden brown; cool. Combine 4 ozs. cream cheese, ⅓ C. sugar, and 1 T. of lemon juice; mix well. Fold in 1 C. of heavy cream (whipped). Spoon onto crust. Arrange top with assorted fruit and brush with glaze of ¼ C. apricot preserves and 1 T. water. Chill before serving. Suggested Fruits: Peaches, kiwi, grapes, strawberries, raspberries, blackberries.

Maureen Roach

Rhubarb Butter Crunch

3 C. diced rhubarb
1 C. sugar
3 T. flour
1 C. brown sugar
1 C. uncooked oatmeal

1½ C. flour
½ C. margarine &
  ½ C. shortening
  (I use 1 C. margarine)

Combine the first 3 ingredients and place in 8x8-inch greased baking dish. Combine brown sugar, oatmeal, and flour. Cut in margarine with pastry cutter. Sprinkle over rhubarb mixture and bake at 375⁰ for 40 minutes.

Debby Corkrean

Rhubarb Cobbler

1 pkg. frozen rhubarb or
   4 C. of fresh (chopped)
1½ C. sugar
2 tsp. cinnamon
1 T. margarine or butter
1½ C. flour

¼ C. margarine
¾ C. sugar
¼ tsp. salt (optional)
3 tsp. baking powder
1 egg (beaten)
½ C. milk

In a greased 9x13-inch pan spread frozen or fresh rhubarb. Sprinkle with 1½ C. sugar, mixed with 2 tsp. cinnamon. Dot top with 1 T. margarine. Put pan in oven at 350° while you prepare the following topping.

For Topping: Place flour in large bowl and cut in margarine. Add the sugar, salt, and baking powder. Next blend in the egg and milk. Remove the rhubarb pan from oven and spread the topping over the hot rhubarb. Return to oven and bake for 30 more minutes.

Joanne Gasiel

Easy Rhubarb Dessert

4 C. rhubarb (cut-up)
1 C. sugar
1 box white cake mix

1 (3 oz.) box strawberry
   gelatin
1 C. water
⅓ C. butter (melted)

Place ingredients in a 9x13-inch pan in the order given. The cake mix and gelatin goes on dry. Water and butter on top. Bake at 350° for 45 to 60 minutes.

Veronica Klug

Strawberry Pizza

1 tube sugar cookie dough
⅓ C. sugar
1 tsp. vanilla
Fresh strawberries

1 (8 oz.) pkg. cream cheese
(softened)
1 jar strawberry glaze

Pat cookie dough into small jelly roll pan. Bake until done and watch closely so you don't get it too brown. Mix together ⅓ C. sugar, 1 tsp. vanilla, and 8 ozs. cream cheese. Spread over cooled cookie dough. Put fresh strawberries on top and then put a jar of strawberry glaze over it. The strawberry glaze is usually found by the canned fruit in the grocery store.

Berta Kordick

Leta's Forgotten Dessert

5 egg whites
1 tsp. cream of tartar
¼ tsp. salt
1½ C. sugar

½ pt. whipping cream
(whipped) or Cool Whip
Fresh strawberries

Your eggs should be at room temperature. Beat 5 egg whites until frothy - not very hard. Add 1 tsp. cream of tartar and ¼ tsp. salt. Beat until peaks form. Gradually add 1½ C. of sugar and beat for 5 minutes more. Place in a 9x9-inch pan and put in a 425° preheated oven. After you put it in the oven, shut the oven off. Leave overnight or for several hours. Remove from oven and top with ½ pint whipping cream. Cover and put in the refrigerator for 3 hours. Top with fresh strawberries or other fruit.

"This is one of my favorite things Mom makes!"

Pam Palmer

Strawberries in The Snow

1 pkg. graham cracker mix or
   make your own graham
   cracker crust
1 (3 oz.) pkg. cream cheese
   (softened)
½ C. sugar

½ tsp. vanilla
1 C. whipping cream
   (whipped)
1 C. miniature marshmallows
Enough strawberries to pour
   over top of each serving

Press graham cracker crust into bottom of square pan (8x8x2-inch). Beat cream cheese and sugar until fluffy. Add vanilla. Fold in whipped cream and marshmallows. Spread into pan and refrigerate for several hours or overnight. Serve topped with strawberries. Yield: 9 servings.

Luella Fairholm

Turtle Cake Dessert

1 chocolate cake mix
1 (14 oz.) pkg. vanilla
   caramel candy
½ C. evaporated milk

½ C. margarine
1 C. chocolate chips
1 C. chopped pecans

Prepare cake mix according to package. Pour half of batter into greased and floured 9x13-inch pan. Bake at 350⁰ for 15 minutes. Unwrap caramels and melt with evaporated milk and margarine in saucepan over low heat. Pour mixture over hot cake, spreading evenly. Sprinkle chocolate chips and pecans on top of caramel mixture. Top with remaining cake batter and bake for 25 minutes. Serve plain or with whipped cream or ice cream.

Cheryl Emanuel

Mocha Walnut Torte

1 box brownie mix
½ C. coarsely chopped
   walnuts
2 C. whipping cream

½ C. brown sugar
   (firmly packed)
2 T. instant coffee
Walnut halves for garnish

Follow cake method for brownies as on package, then add walnuts. Spoon into two greased 9-inch layer cake pans. Bake for 20 to 25 minutes in a 350⁰ oven. Cool. Whip cream until it begins to thicken. Gradually add brown sugar and instant coffee. Spread between layers and over top and sides. Garnish with walnut halves. Chill overnight. Serves 10 to 12.

Rosemary Gronstal

240

As for me
and my house,
we will serve
the Lord

Herbs

Chives

Oregano

Basil

Sage

Thyme

Herb Gardening

SOIL PREPARATION:

Whether your garden is for artistic self-expression or just a place where a few plants are grown to enliven your cooking, you will want to pay careful attention to the soil in which your herb plants will grow. A soil test is a good idea so that pH and fertility can be determined and corrected, if necessary. Deep spading to a depth of 18 inches is advised so that compacted soil is loosened. Enrich the soil with plenty of compost or well-rotted manure. Rotted leaves or sphagnum peat moss are good alternatives. As much as six inches of this material should be worked into the top 12-inches of the planting area in localities where soil is very sandy or mostly heavy clay.

TRANSPLANTING TIPS:

• Don't yank the transplant from its pot by the stem. Loosen the root ball by squeezing plastic pots. Then turn the pot upside-down and rap the edge on your open hand. It should gently tumble into your hand.

• Spread the roots so they do not continue to circle the rootball as they did in the pot. This can usually be accomplished by pushing your thumbs into the rootball's center and then gently pulling outwards. Root-bound plants may have to have rootballs cut. If necessary use a knife and slit the rootball lengthwise in three places.

• Place transplants in planting holes and water well with a solution of liquid fertilizer at half the recommended strength. Backfill and firm the soil.

THE HARVEST

• Always cut stems. This will promote branching, vigorous new growth and strong roots and will increase the plant's future productivity.

• Cut often. This procedure improves air circulation and it helps to create neat, more compact plants that are less woody.

• No major cutting of winter hardy perennial plants should be performed 40 days prior to, the first expected frost in your area. This will give soft, new growth a chance to mature and prepare for winter.

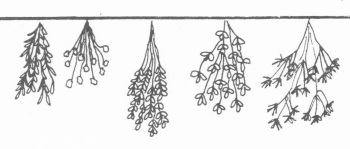
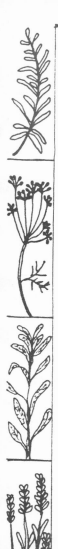

Herb Uses

Here are some common foods and some of the herbs that go well with them. Use sparingly, not all the listed herbs at one time and be creative.

ASPARAGUS — lemon balm, oregano, savory, lemon verbena, parsley, tarragon, lovage.

BEANS — basil, marjoram, oregano, sage, savory, spearmint, thyme, bay, coriander, dill, fennel, garlic, mint, rosemary, tarragon, lovage.

BEETS — basil, savory, thyme, bay, caraway, dill, sage, tarragon.

BROCCOLI — basil, rosemary, lovage.

CABBAGE — marjoram, mint, savory, caraway, dill, fennel, oregano, lovage, borage.

CARROTS — lovage, applemint, basil, marjoram, mint, orange-mint, oregano, thyme, tarragon, anise, bay, caraway.

CAULIFLOWER — marjoram, savory, rosemary, lovage, dill.

EGGPLANT — basil, lovage, marjoram, mint, oregano, sage, thyme, chervil, chives, fennel, garlic.

(Continued on Next Page)

243

Herbs

PEAS — applemint, basil, orangemint, rosemary, sage, savory, spearmint, tarragon, thyme, parsley, lovage, fennel, dill.

POTATOES — basil, marjoram, mint, rosemary, savory, spearmint, thyme, bay, caraway, fennel, garlic, parsley.

SPINACH — lovage, sorrel, basil, mint, rosemary, tarragon, thyme, sage, marjoram, chervil, borage.

TOMATOES — basil, marjoram, oregano, sage, thyme, fennel, dill, chervil.

BEEF — basil, lemon thyme, marjoram, mint, rosemary, savory, thyme, anise, borage, dill, fennel, garlic, lovage, parsley, tarragon.

CHICKEN — lemon balm, basil, lemon thyme, rosemary spearmint, thyme, tarragon, savory, sage, oregano, lovage, marjoram, garlic, fennel, coriander, chives, chervil.

EGGS — lemon balm, basil, marjoram, sage, savory, thyme, tarragon, fennel, dill, bay, parsley, chervil, chives.

FISH — lemon balm, lemon verbena, basil, clary, hyssop, lemon thyme, mint, oregano, rosemary, sage, savory, thyme, bay, caraway, chervil, chives, dill, fennel, garlic, tarragon.

GOOSE — clary, marjoram, sage, thyme, rosemary, tarragon, parsley, chervil, garlic.

LAMB — lemon balm, basil, lavender, marjoram, mint, rosemary, sage, savory, thyme, chervil, dill, fennel, garlic.

PORK — lemon balm, basil, clary, marjoram, pennyroyal, rosemary, sage, savory, thyme, chives, fennel, anise.

RABBIT — basil, lemon thyme, rosemary, sage, thyme.

TURKEY — basil, lavender, lemon thyme, sage, thyme, tarragon, savory, oregano, lovage, garlic, fennel, bay, chervil, chives.

Preserving the Bounty of Your Herb Garden

The joy of an herb garden partially comes from being able to snip off a few leaves to use for lunch or dinner. You can do this anytime after the plants are established and growing. Most plants will grow bushier for having been snipped back at regular intervals.

For most herbs, the main harvest to dry for winter or other purposes, should come just before blossoming because that is when they are most flavorful. Pick them in the morning, if possible, just after the dew has disappeared.

If you cut back only a half to two-thirds of the plants, most will produce a second and third harvest. Don't however, cut perennials later than six weeks before an expected frost so they can rejuvenate before winter.

Harvest the herbs into a paper bag or an open basket, not in plastic, which could cause overheating and deterioration or possibly cause them to mildew. After harvesting, immediately start the washing and drying process to keep top quality.

WASHING

Washing herbs is more important than most people suspect. Herbs can carry quantities of grit and foreign matter into your food.

Use two tubs with a large quantity of herbs and lift from one tube to the other after swishing them clean. Use three or four washings, starting with lukewarm water and ending with cool. Never use water that is ice cold and never let herbs stand in water. Dry small quantities in paper towels or a salad spinner.

Herbs

STRIPPING

Herbs tied in bunches may decorate the kitchen, but they will not be very good to use in cooking. Besides the dirt and grease that can accumulate in a kitchen, most herbs with heavy stems dry better if the leaves are removed first. Lemon balm and the mints are exceptions. They will dry well in bunches, but slip them, stem-end first, into a paper bag to protect them from dust and then tie them in the attic or other warm dry room.

Tarragon and savory leaves will strip easily from the branches if you run the stem between your fingers. For others it is probably easier to use scissors. Savory can be dried on the stems, but if it is convenient do it before drying. Lavender blossoms, marjoram, mint, oregano, balm, rosemary, and thyme are better stripped after drying.

DRYING

It is better not to use an oven for drying herbs because most ovens will not maintain a temperature less than the 100 degrees over which herbs lose quality.

Dry on screening in a well-ventilated attic, over a refrigerator or freezer, or in a warm, dry room. It is better to have it dark, if possible.

Herbs will take two to seven days to dry, depending on the humidity and temperature.

STORING

Store in airtight glass containers. Strip any that were not stripped before drying. The leaves will retain more flavor if left whole. They are most practical to use if crushed. Store crushed herbs in the dark or place in colored glass containers. Use them within a year for maximum flavor.

FREEZING

All herbs can be frozen. Package small quantities in moisture-vapor proof containers.

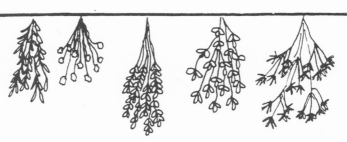

Iced Mint Tea

4 to 5 tea bags   ½ to 1 C. sugar
8 to 10 fresh mint leaves

Put tea bags, mint, and sugar in a china or Corning Ware tea pot. Pour boiling water over and let steep for 10 minutes, stirring once or twice. Pour into a large 4-quart pitcher which is half full of cold water. Add ice cubes.

Variations: Add orange or lemon peel or add lemon balm leaves.

Linda Hermanstorfer

Herbal Teas

Use your favorite herb for an herbal tea. Some popular herbs to use are chamomile, mint, lemon balm, and scented geraniums. Place the herbal leaves or flowers into a warm teapot. Pour boiling water over the herbs and brew the tea for 3 to 5 minutes. Strain the tea and enjoy!

Cindy Watson Pottebaum

Dill Vegetable Dip

1 C. sour cream or
   plain yogurt
1 C. mayonnaise
1 T. dill weed

1 T. minced onion or
   dry flakes
1 T. parsley flakes

Mix all together and chill.

Linda Hermanstorfer

Herbal Vinegars

HERBS TO TRY: Basil, bay, fennel, lemon balm, tarragon, thyme, mint, rosemary, and garlic.

Loosely fill a clean jar with freshly picked herbs, crushing slightly. Warm the vinegar (wine or cider) and pour over the herbs to fill the jar. Cap the jar with an acid-proof lid. Set in a sunny windowsill for 2 weeks, shaking daily. Strain through a cheesecloth and use in salads, marinades, and sauces.

Cindy Watson Pottebaum

Herbal Vinegars

Herb vinegars can be created by bringing white vinegar to a boil. Fill jars or bottles with fresh herbs and pour the hot vinegar into the jars/bottles and seal. (Tarragon, chives, basil, and rosemary make wonderful vinegars. Expermint with combination of herbs - e.g. tarragon and rosemary.)

Linda Hermanstorfer

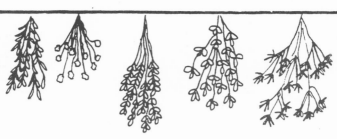

Gourmet Vinegar

¼ C. chopped fresh
  marjoram
¼ C. chopped fresh basil
1 tsp. fresh rosemary
  leaves
¼ C. chopped fresh mint
¼ C. chopped fresh dill

1 bay leaf (crumbled)
¼ tsp. whole allspice
¼ tsp. whole black
  pepper
3 whole cloves
3 C. red wine vinegar

Combine all herbs and spices in a quart jar and fill jar
with vinegar. Cover and let stand in a cool, dark place
for 4 to 6 weeks. Strain or filter through coffee filter
papers. Bottle. Makes about 3 cups.

Teresa Pearson

Pasta Oil

3 sprigs sage
2 garlic cloves
1 small bunch parsley
1 small hot red pepper

5 ozs. Parmesan cheese
  (cut in small chunks)
1 qt. extra-virgin olive
  oil

Use this for pasta salads or add a few fresh herbs or
tomatoes for a quick pasta sauce.

Nancy M. Corkrean

Herbs

Herbal Oils

HERBS TO TRY:
Savory — basil, fennel, rosemary, tarragon, thyme, savory
Sweet — lavender, lemon verbena

Herbal oils add a special flavor to old and new recipes. Use a clear jar and fill loosely with freshly picked herbs. Pour unheated oil over the top to fill the jar. (Use a mild flavored oil like sunflower or safflower oil.) Cover with cheesecloth and place on a sunny windowsill. Let steep for 2 weeks, stirring daily. Strain through the cloth and label. Use the herbal oils as you would regular oil in recipes.

Cindy Watson Pottebaum

Vegetable Consomme′

2 medium leeks
   (white part, diced)
2 celery stalks
4 shallots (chopped)
1 large tomato
3 medium carrots (diced)
3 garlic cloves
   (coarsely chopped)

3 sprigs parsley
8 to 10 basil leaves
10 white mushrooms (diced)
1 sprig thyme
2 bay leaves
2 sprigs cilantro
Freshly ground pepper

Combine all the ingredients in a stockpot and cover with 2-quarts cold water. Bring to a boil, then turn the heat down to a light simmer. Simmer for about 20 minutes. Turn off the heat, keep covered, and set aside to infuse for 20 minutes. Strain the broth through a fine strainer. Use the consomme′ in soups, cooking vegetables, etc.

Italian-Style Vegetables with Pasta

2 T. vegetable consomme'
1 red bell pepper (chopped)
1 yellow bell pepper (chopped)
1 green bell pepper (chopped)
2 small zucchini (sliced)
½ sweet onion
1 (14 oz.) can peeled tomatoes in sauce

4 lg. sun dried tomatoes (softened & chopped)
2 T. chopped, fresh oregano
2 T. chopped fresh basil
Salt & pepper, to taste
1 garlic clove (minced)
4 (2½ oz.) servings of pasta (cooked)

Heat a large skillet. Add the stock and all the ingredients, except the pasta. Cover and cook over medium-low heat for 15 to 20 minutes. Serve over cooked pasta. Serves 4.

Cindy Watson Pottebaum

251

❦Herbs❦

Snow Peas a L'Herbe

½ lb. snow peas
2½ T. oil
1 tsp. fresh tarragon (snipped)

1 T. fresh mint (snipped)
A pinch of cayenne pepper

Wash, drain, and de-vain the peas. Heat oil in pan over high heat.
Quickly stir-fry the peas and herbs for 1 minute. Serves 4.

Teresa Pearson

Split Pea and Basil Soup

1 T. herbal oil
1 large onion
1 clove of garlic (crushed)
1 C. split peas
  (soaked overnight)
1 tsp. tomato paste

1 T. or cube bouillon
1 large potato (diced)
2 qts. water
3 T. basil leaves
Salt & pepper, to taste

Heat oil in a large saucepan and saute' onion and garlic for 5 minutes.
Add drained split peas, tomato paste, bouillon, potato, and water.
Bring to a boil and add the basil, salt, and pepper. Cover and simmer for 40 minutes, until peas are tender. Allow to cool slightly,
then puree' if you wish in a blender. Serve with a basil leaf garnish.

Cindy Watson Pottebaum

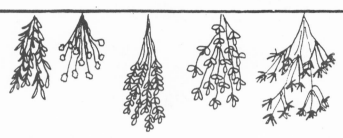

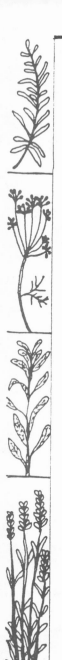

Broiled Zucchini

4 small zucchini
1 T. salad or melted
   butter
½ tsp. fresh snipped
   marjoram

½ tsp. garlic powder
Dash of pepper
½ C. grated Parmesan
   cheese

Cut squash lengthwise into halves. Place cut sides up on broiler pan. Mix seasonings with oil and brush on squash. Broil on top shelf for 5 minutes. Sprinkle cheese evenly over all and broil for 5 more minutes.

Linda Hermanstorfer

Herb Butter

2-3 T. fresh finely diced
   herbs (dill weed,
   lemon balm, chives, etc.)

½ C. unsalted butter
1 tsp. lemon juice

Soften butter and cream with remaining ingredients. Refrigerate in sealed container. If using dried herbs, reduce herb amounts by one-third.

Teresa Hoffelmeyer

Herbs

Herb Cream Cheese Spread

3 ozs. cream cheese (softened) 1 tsp. dill leaves (chopped)
1 tsp. chives (chopped)

Mix ingredients together and let stand, covered in refrigerator for a day to let the flavors mingle.

Cindy Watson Pottebaum

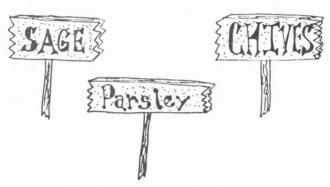

Herb Flavored Honey

6-7 sprigs of fresh herbs, like 2 C. honey
 lavender, mint, thyme or
 rosemary

Heat and stir the honey over medium heat until warm. Place herbs in bottom of heat-proof jar. Pour warm honey over them. Cool at room temperature. Cover and seal tightly and let the flavors mingle for 2 days before serving.

Cindy Watson Pottebaum

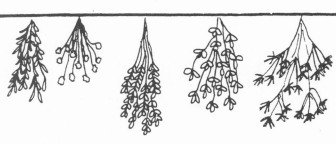

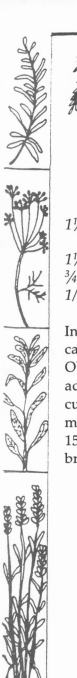

Herb Popovers

1¼ C. milk
  (room temp.)
1¼ C. flour
¾ tsp. salt
1/8 tsp. cayenne pepper

3 large eggs
  (room temp.)
2 T. minced fresh parsley
⅓ tsp. dried thyme

In a medium bowl combine milk, flour, salt, and cayenne. Beat with mixer until blended - DON'T OVERBEAT. Add eggs, 1 at a time, beating after each addition. Stir in parsley and thyme. Grease 6 popover cups and fill ¾ full with batter. Bake at 425° for 20 minutes. Reduce oven temperature to 325° and bake for 15 to 20 minutes longer or until popovers are golden brown. Serve immediately for they fall quickly.

Nancy M. Corkrean

Herbs

Herb Dumplings

1½ C. all-purpose flour
1 T. baking powder
½ tsp. dried thyme
  (crushed)

¾ tsp. salt
¾ C. sour cream
¾ C. milk
2 T. oil

In a mixing bowl stir together dry ingredients. In another bowl combine the sour cream, milk, and oil. Combine the flour mixture with the sour cream mixture. Stir just until all the dry ingredients are thoroughly moistened. Drop the dumplings from a tablespoon to make 8 mounds atop the bubbling soup or stew. Reduce the heat, cover, and simmer the dumplings for about 15 minutes. Do not lift cover. Makes 8 dumplings.

Teresa Pearson

Buttermint Cookies

1½ C. margarine or
  butter
⅔ C. sugar
1 egg

½ tsp. vanilla
½ tsp. peppermint extract
2 C. flour
1 T. crushed mint

Cream butter and sugar. Beat in egg and extracts. Add flour and mint leaves. Dough will be soft, divide into 3 parts. Shape into cylinders 1¼-inch in diameter in plastic wrap. Chill for 1 to 2 hours. Slice ¼-inch thick and place on ungreased baking sheet. Bake for 10 minutes in 350⁰ oven until golden brown. Remove immediately to cooling racks.

Cindy Watson Pottebaum

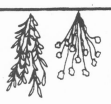

Lemon Tea Bread

¾ C. milk
1 T. finely chopped
  lemon balm
1 T. finely chopped
  lemon thyme
2 C. all-purpose flour

1½ tsp. baking powder
¼ tsp. salt
6 T. butter (room temp.)
1 C. sugar
2 eggs
1 T. grated lemon Zest

GLAZE:
Juice of 2 lemons   Confectioner's sugar

Butter a 9x5x3-inch pan and preheat the oven to 325⁰.
Heat milk with chopped herbs and let steep until cool.
Mix the flour, baking powder, and salt together in a
bowl. Cream the butter and gradually beat in sugar.
Continue beating until light and fluffy. Beat in eggs,
1 at a time. Beat in the lemon Zest. Add the flour mixture alternately with the herbed milk. Mix until the batter is just blended. Put the batter into the prepared pan.
Bake for about 50 minutes or until a toothpick inserted
in the center comes out dry. Remove from the pan onto a wire rack that is set over a sheet of waxed paper.
Pour lemon glaze over the still hot bread. Decorate with
a few sprigs of lemon thyme.

For Lemon Glaze: Put the lemon juice in a bowl and
add the sugar, stirring until thick, but still pourable
paste forms. Pour the glaze over the hot bread.

Sarah Corkrean

Basil Bread

2 C. flour
1 T. baking powder
1 tsp. salt
2 T. fresh basil (chopped)
   (1 T. dry)

½ C. milk
½ C. butter or
   margarine
½ C. sugar
2 eggs

Combine dry ingredients and set aside. In a saucepan, combine milk and sage. Warm over medium heat, then let stand to cool. Cream butter and sugar together and add eggs, 1 at a time. Add flour mixture and mix alternately with milk mixture. Pour into loaf pan and bake at 350⁰ for 50 to 60 minutes. Cool bread on wire rack.

Variation: You can substitute dill or sage for basil.

Cindy Watson Pottebaum

Sage Corn Bread

1 C. flour
¾ C. cornmeal
1½ tsp. baking powder
½ tsp. baking soda
2 T. fresh sage (chopped)
   (1 tsp. dry)

1 C. buttermilk
2 T. honey
2 eggs
3 T. butter or margarine
   (melted)

Sift dry ingredients together and then add sage. Set aside. Beat buttermilk, honey, eggs, and butter together. Add to dry ingredients and stir just enough to moisten. Do not overmix. Pour batter into 9x9-inch greased pan and bake 425⁰ for 25 to 30 minutes or until top is golden. Serve warm with honey.

Cindy Watson Pottehaum

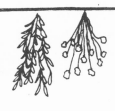

Lemon Thyme Bread

BREAD:

2 C. flour
2 tsp. baking powder
6 T. butter or margarine
  (softened)
1 C. sugar
2 eggs

1 T. lemon Zest
2 T. lemon juice
2 T. lemon thyme
  (chopped)
⅔ C. milk

GLAZE:

2 T. lemon juice   ½ C. powdered sugar

Sift dry ingredients together. Cream sugar and butter, then add eggs. Beat in lemon Zest, lemon juice, and lemon thyme. Add dry ingredients, alternately with the milk. Mix just until blended. Pour into greased and floured loaf pan and bake at 350⁰ for 55 to 60 minutes. Cool bread on wire rack for 10 minutes. Mix lemon juice and sugar for glaze. Turn bread onto wire rack and pour glaze over the top.

Cindy Watson Pottebaum

Herbed Sour Cream Bread

4¾ C. sifted flour
2 T. sugar
2 tsp. salt
2 pkgs. active dry yeast
1 C. warm dairy sour cream
2 eggs

6 T. soft butter
½ tsp. marjoram leaves
½ tsp. oregano leaves
½ tsp. parsley flakes
½ C. very warm water
(120°-130°)

Combine 1 C. flour, sugar, salt, yeast, sour cream, butter, marjoram, oregano, parsley, and water in a bowl. Beat for 2 minutes at medium speed of electric mixer. Add eggs and ½ C. flour; beat for 2 minutes at high speed. Stir in enough remaining flour to make a soft dough. Cover and let rise until doubled, about 35 minutes. Stir down and turn into two well-greased 1-quart casserole dishes. Cover and let rise until doubled, about 50 minutes. Bake at 375⁰ for 35 minutes or until done. Makes 2 loaves.

Jill Kordick

Applesauce & Cinnamon Ornaments

1 (1 lb.) jar sweetened
   applesauce (drained)
8 ozs. ground cinnamon
Wax paper

OPTIONAL:
   1 tsp. ground allspice
   1 tsp. ground cinnamon
   1 tsp. cloves

In mixer bowl combine applesauce with cinnamon, alternately the ingredients until mixture reaches the consistency of cookie dough. Use 1 C. of mixture at a time, patting dough with your hands onto wax paper to about ¼-inch thick. Use decorative cookie cutters to cut out shapes. Make a hole in top of each shape. Dry the ornaments in a warm place for a week, turning them every day.

Nancy M. Corkrean

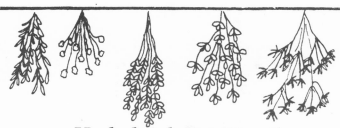

Herbal Advent Wreath

FRESH AND DRIED HERBS AND FLOWERS:
Sage - for immortality
Rosemary - for remembrance
Rue - for repentance and grace
Lavender - for purity and virtue
Thyme - for the bravery of the Holy Child
Costmary - for everlasting life, used by Mary
    Magdalen to make precious ointment
Juniper - for life and hope
Horehound - for good health, a Palestinian herb
TO ADD COLOR:
Yarrow   *Tansy*
Cockscomb   *Sweet annie*
Statice   *Bittersweet*

You will need 3 purple candles and 1 pink candle (blue candles may be used in place of purple). The pink or rose colored candle is lit the third Sunday of Advent to express our joy that Christmas is so near. Arrange herbs, flowers, and 4 candles on circular wreath base. (A white candle may be placed in the center of your wreath at Christmas to symbolize the coming of Christ.)

Teresa Hoffelmeyer

261

Bay Leaf Swag

½ POUND OF ANY OF THE FOLLOWING:

Whole bay leaves
Dried apple slices or
   dried orange slices
Orange peels & lemon peels

Cinnamon sticks
Fresh cranberries
Strawflowers
Baby's breath

String your choice of these or other items on heavy gauge florist wire, cut to the length you need and decorate ends with ribbons.

Teresa Hoffelmeyer

Christmas Potpourri

1½ QUARTS BLENDED:

Bayberry leaves
Spruce needles
Holly leaves
Dried verbena

1 oz. orris root
5 drops pine oil or
   cinnamon oil

½ QUART BLENDED:

Dried orange peel
Dried lemon peel
Whole allspice
Bay or juniper berries

Cloves
Cinnamon sticks
Holly

Gently combine and mix with hands in a ceramic bowl. Place in tightly covered glass jar and store in dry, dark location for about 5 weeks. Shake jar occasionally. Place in decorative containers when ready to use.

Teresa Hoffelmeyer

Meats
&
Main Dishes

J.M.H.

Altar and Rosary Dinners
By: Marie White

In July of 1937, the St. Joseph's Altar and Rosary Society was in charge of serving a fried chicken dinner on the church lawn between the rectory and the church.

The food and chickens were prepared in the homes. However, the rectory kitchen and two kerosene stoves outside were very much needed that day.

The women worked diligently under hardships. They seemed happy though and the men helped by finding, borrowing, and setting up tables. To make it more inviting, tables were covered with tablecloths or, in some cases, nice sheets.

The flies did come for dinner too, which surprised no one.

I was there and collected the small change for the dinner.

Marie White

Barbecue Beef

1 arm or chuck roast (4-5 lbs.)
1 (35 oz.) bottle liquid smoke
2¼ C. smoked barbecue sauce
1 T. onion powder
1½ tsp. garlic powder
1 tsp. celery salt

Salt and season meat. Wrap in foil, sealing edges, and bake in 325° oven for approximately 5 hours or until meat breaks apart with a fork. After breaking meat apart, add 2¼ C. of your favorite smoked barbeque sauce. Return to oven and cook for 1 more hour.

Susie McCauley

Barbecue Beef Brisket

1 brisket (about 4 lbs.)   Onion salt
Celery salt   ½ bottle liquid smoke

BARBEQUE SAUCE:
1 C. chili sauce   1 tsp. pepper
1 C. catsup   ¼ C. wine vinegar
¼ C. Worcestershire sauce   4 T. honey
1 tsp. chili powder   ¼ C. tarragon vinegar
2 dashes Tabasco sauce   ½ C. water
1 tsp. dry mustard   1 tsp. salt

Sprinkle brisket with celery salt, onion salt, and half a bottle of liquid smoke. Marinate for 24 hours. Bake for about 4 to 6 hours at 250⁰. Cool and slice thin. Marinate in barbecue sauce and heat at 350⁰ for 30 to 45 minutes. (Can use gravy from liquid smoke also.)

Patsy Bence

Meats & Main Dishes

Beef and Noodle Casserole

1 lb. hamburger (browned)
3½ C. egg noodles
1 (10 oz.) can cream of chicken
   soup or cream of potato soup

¾ C. cubed Velveeta cheese
½ C. milk
½ C. crushed potato chips

Brown hamburger. Cook egg noodles as directed on package. Mix together the hamburger, noodles, soup, cheese, and milk in 1½-quart or 2-quart casserole dish. Cover with lid and bake at 350° for 40 minutes. Uncover and sprinkle crushed potato chips on top. Bake for 5 minutes longer.

Terri Johnson

Beef Stroganoff

1 T. flour
½ tsp. salt
1 lb. sirloin (cut in strips)
2 T. butter
1 C. thinly sliced mushrooms
½ C. chopped onion
1 clove of garlic (minced)

2 T. butter
3 T. flour
1 T. tomato paste
1¼ C. beef stock or broth
1 C. sour cream
3 T. sherry wine

Combine 1 T. flour and the salt; dredge meat in mixture. Heat skillet and add 2 T. of butter. When melted, add meat and brown. Add mushrooms, onion, and garlic. Cook for 3 to 4 minutes, until onion is barely tender. Remove from skillet. Add 2 T. butter to pan drippings. Blend in 3 T. flour and add tomato paste. Slowly add meat stock and stir until thick. No lumps. Return meat and mushrooms to skillet. Stir in sour cream and sherry. Heat briefly. Serve with rice or noodles.

Mary Anne Roby

Cheeseburger Pie

1 (9-inch) pie crust
1 lb. ground beef
1 tsp. salt
½ tsp. oregano
¼ tsp. pepper

½ C. dry bread crumbs
1 (8 oz.) can tomato sauce
¼ C. chopped onion &
 green pepper
½ C. chili sauce

CHEESE TOPPING:
1 egg
¼ C. milk
½ tsp. salt

½ tsp. dry mustard
½ tsp. Worcestershire sauce
2 C. shredded cheddar cheese

Heat oven to 425°. Bake pie shell for 10 minutes. In medium skillet cook and stir often the meat until brown. Drain off all fat. Return to heat and cook onions and peppers with meat until soft. Stir in salt, oregano, pepper, crumbs, and ½ C. tomato sauce. Mix well and heat until warm. Turn into pie crust and top with cheese topping. Bake for 30 minutes and cut into wedges. Heat remaining tomato sauce with chili sauce and serve with pie. Makes 6 to 8 servings.

For Cheese Topping: Beat egg and milk. Stir in seasonings and cheese; pour over meat mixture.

Barb Schmitz

Meats & Main Dishes

Spicy Chili Mac

1 lb. ground beef
1 onion (chopped)
1 green pepper (chopped)
1 (30 oz.) can chili beans

1 (8 oz.) can tomato sauce
½ C. water
1 C. uncooked elbow macaroni
¼ C. Parmesan cheese

Brown meat and drain fat. Saute' onion and pepper until onion is translucent. Return ground beef to skillet. Add beans, tomato sauce, water, and macaroni. Cover and simmer for 30 minutes. Sprinkle with cheese and serve. Serves 4 to 6.

Rita Drysdale

Curried Beef Roast

1 (2-3 lb.) beef (eye of round)
⅓ C. soy sauce
⅓ C. vinegar
2 T. finely chopped onion

1 T. sugar
2 tsp. curry powder
1 tsp. chili powder
1 tsp. finely shredded
    lemon peel

Place roast in heavy plastic bag. Combine other ingredients and pour marinade over meat. Close bag and marinate in refrigerator for 12 to 24 hours, turning occasionally. Drain roast reserving marinade and place meat in shallow pan. Roast in 325° oven to desired doneness, brushing occasionally with reserved marinade. (Do not brush during the last 5 minutes.) Allow 1½ hours for rare (140°) or 1¾ to 2¼ hours for medium (160°). Let stand for 15 minutes before carving. Cut into thin slices.

Ann Winjum

Hamburger or
Ground Turkey Casserole

1-1½ lbs. hamburger or
   ground turkey (browned)
1 small pkg. noodles
   (cooked & drained)
1 can whole kernel corn
   (drained well)

1 can cream of mushroom
   soup
1 can cream of chicken soup
1 carton sour cream with
   chives or plain sour cream
Salt & pepper, to taste

Mix together browned hamburger or turkey and cooked noodles. Add remaining ingredients and put all in greased casserole dish. Heat all in a low oven (325⁰) until warmed through, about 30 minutes. The amounts can be altered to your taste. Maybe you like lots of hamburger or lots of noodles. This is very flexible and very tasty. Can be made earlier in the day and warmed at serving time. (Using the yolkless noodles, turkey, and low fat sour cream is equally good.)

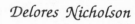

Delores Nicholson

Meats & Main Dishes

Hobo Dinners
"For One or More"

1 lb. hamburger patties
4 C. sliced raw potatoes
1 T. water

4 C. sliced raw carrots
2 C. sliced onions
1 T. margarine

Tear off a piece of foil, about 14-inches long, dull side down. In center of foil, place a hamburger patty the appropriate size for adult or child. Salt and pepper each hamburger, as desired. After meat, pile on sliced raw potatoes, followed by sliced raw carrots, and onions. Add 1 T. water and 1 T. butter or margarine. Roll foil lengthwise down snuggly and roll up ends and place on greased jelly roll pan. Bake at 400° until vegetables are tender and meat is browned. Serve in foil, if desired. Also may be baked 20 minutes or until tender on campfire coals.

Patsy Bence

Meat Loaf

1 lb. hamburger
1 egg
1 pkg. crackers (crushed)

1 can pizza sauce
Salt & pepper, to taste

Crush 1 individual package of crackers. Add 1 egg, and ½ can pizza sauce; mix well. Add 1 lb. of hamburger and salt and pepper; mix well. Shape into loaf and place in a 13x9-inch pan. Pour on remaining pizza sauce and bake at 350° for 1 hour to 1 hour and 15 minutes.

"This is a good meat loaf. My sister Mary Anne gave me this recipe when Dan and I got married and we love it."

Dorothy J. Kellogg

Hungarian Goulash

2 lbs. beef stew meat
  (cut into 1-inch cubes)
1 large onion (sliced)
1 clove of garlic (minced)
½ C. catsup
2 T. Worcestershire sauce

1 T. brown sugar
2 tsp. salt
2 tsp. paprika
½ tsp. dry mustard
1 C. water
¼ C. flour

Place meat in slow-cooking pot and cover with sliced onion. Combine garlic, catsup, Worcestershire sauce, sugar, salt, paprika, and mustard. Stir in water and pour over meat. Cover and cook on low for 9 to 10 hours. Turn control to High. Dissolve flour in small amount of cold water and stir into meat mixture. Cook on High for 10 to 15 minutes or until slightly thickened. Serve goulash over noodles or rice. Makes 5 to 6 servings. Note: I don't use the salt in this recipe.

Rosemary Stuchel

Porcupine Meatballs

2 lbs. hamburger
⅓ C. chopped onions
⅓ C. chopped green pepper
1 (8 oz.) can tomato sauce

2 C. Minute Rice
2 eggs
Salt, pepper, & garlic salt,
  to taste

Shape into 3-inch balls and add to skillet of boiling tomato juice. Boil for 10 minutes. Turn over and simmer for 30 minutes.

Delores Nicholson

"Husband's Delight"

1 lb. ground beef
2 cans tomato sauce
1 large or 2 small onions
1 tsp. salt
Garlic salt, to taste
Pepper, to taste

1 small pkg. cream cheese
1 C. sour cream
½ C. grated Cheddar cheese
1 (8 oz.) pkg. noodles or
    spaghetti

Brown ground beef and onion, then pour off excess grease. Add salt, pepper, and garlic salt. Then add tomato sauce. Simmer for 15 minutes. Cook spaghetti/noodles according to directions on package. Blend sour cream and cream cheese together. Grease a 9x13-inch pan or dish with just a little shortening. Then layer ingredients, spaghetti/noodles first, then meat sauce, cream cheese mixture, and finally sprinkle grated cheese on top. Bake in 350° preheated oven for 20 minutes. Serve this dish with a tossed salad or your favorite vegetable salad and you have a delicious meal.

Wanda Martin

Round Steak and Gravy

2 lbs. round steak
2 T. shortening
Salt & pepper, to taste

2 T. flour
2 C. water
1 T. Kitchen Bouquet

Cut steak in serving size pieces. Brown in shortening. Place pieces in casserole. Brown flour in drippings. Add water and make a thin to medium gravy. Add Kitchen Bouquet and pour gravy over steak pieces and cover. Bake at 350° for 1 hour. Serve with mashed potatoes or rice.

Joanne See

Porcupine Meatballs

1 lb. ground beef
½ lb. ground pork
1 small onion
  (I use instant onion)

½ C. rice
½ C. cracker crumbs
1 egg
Salt & pepper, to taste

SAUCE:
1 can tomato soup

1 can water

Form into balls and place in 9x13-inch pan, sprayed with Pam. Mix sauce ingredients together and pour over meatballs. Cover and bake at 375° for 1 hour.

Rosemary Stuchel

Runza Casserole

1 lb. corned beef
2 C. sauerkraut
1 C. sour cream
Onion, to taste

Garlic, to taste
3 C. Swiss cheese
6 slices rye bread
¾ C. butter

Mix sour cream, sauerkraut, onion, and garlic. Spread it on the bottom of a 9x13-inch pan. Crumble corned beef on top. Put cheese on top of beef. Break bread into pieces and put on top of cheese. Pour melted butter on top and bake at 350° for ½ hour.

Cheryl Emanuel

Meats & Main Dishes

Salisbury Steak

2 lbs. hamburger
6-8 carrots
4 celery stalks
2 onions

1 can tomato juice
Salt & pepper
1 C. peas

Make hamburger, seasoned with salt and pepper, into patties and brown just enough to hold together. Put in baking pan. Slice carrots, onions, and celery. Pour tomato juice over all and bake in 275° oven for 2 hours, then put peas on top and bake a few minutes more, until peas are done.

"This was an old Club Cafe Recipe."

Katherine Hartman

Smorgasbord Meatballs
(For Crowds)

6 lbs. ground beef
¼ C. chopped onion
3 C. oatmeal

4 C. milk
6 tsp. salt
2 tsp. pepper

SAUCE:
¾ C. sugar
1 bottle Worcestershire sauce
6 C. catsup

3 C. water
1 C. + 2 T. vinegar
4 grated onions (2¼ C.)

Brown meatballs and place in baking pans. Mix sauce ingredients together and cook for 10 minutes. Pour over meatballs and bake at 350° for 45 minutes to 1 hour. Feeds 30.

Marilyn McNamara

Sicilian Meat Roll

2 beaten eggs
½ C. tomato juice
¾ C. soft bread crumbs
2 T. snipped parsley
½ tsp. dried oregano (crushed)
¼ tsp. salt

¼ tsp. pepper
2 lbs. extra lean ground beef
4 to 6 ozs. thinly sliced
    boiled ham
1 (6 oz.) pkg. sliced
    mozzarella cheese

In a bowl, combine eggs and tomato juice. Stir in the bread crumbs, parsley, oregano, salt, and pepper. Add ground beef and mix well. On waxed paper or foil, pat meat into a 10x8-inch rectangle. Arrange ham slices on top of meat, leaving a small margin around edges. Reserve 1 slice of cheese and tear up remaining cheese. Sprinkle over ham, starting from short end, carefully roll up meat, using paper to lift. Seal edges and ends. Place roll seam side down in 13x9x2-inch baking dish. Bake at 350⁰ until done, about 1¼ to 1½ hours. (Center of roll will look pink due to ham.) Cut reserved cheese slice into 4 triangles and overlap on top of meat. Return to oven until cheese melts, about 2 minutes. Cool a short time before slicing. Makes 8 servings.

Harriet Nevins

Meats & Main Dishes

Sweet-N-Sour Meatballs

1 lb. ground beef
1 egg
1 C. bread crumbs or oatmeal
2 (8 oz.) cans tomato sauce

2 (16 oz.) cans of cranberry
sauce
1 can chunky pineapple
(optional)

In a large pot put in cranberry and tomato sauce; cook at medium heat. Mix beef, egg, and bread crumbs in a bowl. Make into golf ball sized meatballs and brown in a frying pan. After meatballs are browned, put them into the sauce. After all of the meatballs have been added to the sauce, cover the pot and simmer for 30 minutes. Serve over rice. Add pineapple chunks, if desired. Salt, to taste.

Arlene Werner

Swiss Steak

2 lbs. lean round steak
Pepper
Flour
2 T. corn oil
1¼ C. tomato juice
¼ C. water

1 tsp. cornstarch
½ C. diced carrots
½ C. diced onion
1 C. celery
½ C. diced green pepper
¼ tsp. garlic powder

Season meat with pepper and dust with flour. Brown in oil and drain off excess oil. Place meat in 9x13-inch casserole dish. Combine tomato juice and cornstarch (dissolved in water). Pour over meat and cover with diced carrots, onions, celery, and green pepper. Sprinkle with garlic powder and bake in oven at 325° for 1½ hours or until tender. Yield: 8 servings.

Rosemary Stuchel

Steak Stroganoff

1½ to 2 lbs. round or
   sirloin steak
⅓ C. flour
2 T. fat
½ C. chopped onion
1 clove of garlic (minced)
1 (6 oz.) can broiled
   mushrooms

1 C. sour cream
1 can cond. mushroom soup
1 T. Worcestershire sauce
½ tsp. salt
1/8 tsp. pepper
2 C. cooked hot rice
   (wild rice or combination)

Cut steak into ¾-inch cubes, roll in flour, and brown in hot fat in a large frying pan or Dutch oven. This cooking time should take 10 to 20 minutes. Remove meat. Add onion, garlic, and mushrooms, cooking until onions are golden. Add remaining ingredients, except rice and cook until thickened and bubbly. Return meat and simmer, stirring occasionally, about 1 hour or until the meat is tender. Serve over rice.

Helen Sawyer

277

Meats & Main Dishes

Swiss Steak with Sour Cream and Onions

1½ to 2-inch thick top
   round steak
1 T. shortening
1 clove of garlic
½ C. water

2 sliced medium onions
½ C. sliced mushrooms
1 C. grated American cheese
½ pt. sour cream
Salt, pepper & paprika

Sear steak with shortening and garlic clove in Dutch oven. Remove garlic and add water. Cook, covered over low heat at least 1 hour. Cover with sliced onions, mushrooms, ¾ C. of the cheese, and the sour cream. Salt and pepper, to taste. Cook for ½ to ¾ hour longer. Transfer to serving platter and top with remaining cheese and paprika. Serves 6.

Ruth Cunningham

Tater Tot Bake

¾ lb. lean ground beef or
   ground turkey
1 small onion (chopped)
Salt & pepper, to taste
1 (16 oz.) pkg. tater tot
   potatoes

1 can cream of mushroom
   soup (undiluted)
½ soup can of milk
1 C. (4 ozs.) shredded cheddar
   cheese

Brown meat and onion. Drain any grease. Season with salt and pepper. Place in greased 1½ or 2-quart casserole and top with potatoes. Combine soup with milk and pour over potatoes. Sprinkle with cheese and bake at 350⁰ for 30 to 40 minutes. Makes 2 to 3 servings.

Harriet Nevins

Tater Tot Casserole

2 lbs. ground beef
2 cans cream of mushroom
   soup
2 lb. pkg. Ore Ida tater tots
1 small onion
Salt & pepper, to taste

1 C. milk
1 env. Schilling brown
   gravy mix
2 cans green beans
2 C. grated cheddar cheese

Brown ground beef, onion, salt, and pepper. Drain off excess grease. Add soup, milk, and gravy mix. Place drained green beans on the bottom of a 9x13-inch pan. Pour meat mixture on top of beans. Arrange tater tots on top. Sprinkle cheese on top and bake at 375⁰ for approximately 30 minutes.

Karen Pommier

Elephant Stew

1 elephant
Brown gravy

2 rabbits

Cut elephant into bite-sized pieces (should take about 2 months). Put into a pot(s) with enough brown gravy to cover. Cook on a kerosene stove for 4 weeks. this recipe should serve 3,800 people. If more are expected, add 2 rabbits!

Medical Mission Sisters from Nairobi

Meats & Main Dishes

Bratwurst, Apple and Kraut

4 bratwurst
2 tsp. oil
1 medium tart apple
   (cored & cut in 12 slices)

1 medium onion (sliced)
1 lb. drained sauerkraut
1 C. apple juice
Ground pepper

In a large non-stick skillet, cook bratwurst in oil over medium-low heat until browned on all sides, about 10 minutes. Remove from skillet and set aside. Add apple and onions to skillet; cook over medium heat and stir until lightly browned, about 5 minutes. Stir in apple juice, kraut, and pepper. Add brats to skillet and bring to a boil. Reduce heat and simmer for 20 minutes or until brats are cooked through and the juices run clear.

Clif Neel

Elegant Ham Rolls

2 (10 oz.) pkgs. frozen
   broccoli spears
8 slices Swiss cheese
2 (4 oz.) pkgs. ham (8 slices)

1 can mushroom soup
½ C. dairy sour cream
1 tsp. prepared mustard

Cook broccoli and place cheese on ham and a broccoli spear on top. Roll up and place in 9x13-inch baking dish. Combine soup, sour cream, and mustard. Pour over top and bake, uncovered at 350° for 20 minutes. Delicious!

Berta Kordick

Crunchy Ham Casserole

1 (7 oz.) pkg. elbow macaroni
1½ C. cubed cooked ham
1 (10 oz.) can cream of
  chicken soup
½ C. sour cream
½ C. milk

1 (10 oz.) pkg. frozen broccoli
  spears (cooked & drained)
1 C. Colby cheese (grated)
1 (3 oz.) can French fried
  onions

Prepare macaroni according to package directions. Combine macaroni and ham in 3-quart casserole. Blend soup, sour cream, and milk. Pour half over macaroni and ham. Arrange broccoli spears on top of casserole. Pour on remaining sauce and sprinkle with cheese. Bake at 350⁰ for 20 minutes. Top with French fried onions and bake for 5 minutes longer. Makes 6 servings.

Dorothy J. Kellogg

Glazed Ham Steak

1 C. brown sugar
⅓ C. horseradish sauce
1½ to 2 lbs. ham steak

¼ C. juice (lemon, orange,
  apple or pineapple)

Mix all ingredients in pan and heat to boiling. Place ham steak in 9x13-inch pan. Pour glaze over ham and cook in 350⁰ oven for about 30 to 45 minutes.

Victoria L. Williams

281

Meats & Main Dishes

Easter Ham Balls

2½ lbs. ground cured ham
2 lbs. lean fresh ground pork
1 lb. ground beef
Salt & pepper, to taste

3 beaten eggs
3 C. graham cracker crumbs
2 C. milk

SAUCE:
2 C. tomato soup
2 tsp. dry mustard

⅓ C. vinegar or less
2¼ C. brown sugar

Mix the ham, pork, beef, salt, pepper, eggs, cracker crumbs, and milk together with your hands. Make into ¼ C. balls. Mix your sauce ingredients and baste your meatballs often with this sauce. Bake, uncovered at 325⁰ for 1 hour. Makes 56 ham balls. Use ungreased 9x13-inch pans. Freezes well.

Pam Palmer
Marie White
Shirley Bittinger
Sue Finnell
Katherine Hartman

Blessing of Easter Foods or Easter Baskets

On Holy Saturday, parishioners are encouraged to bring baskets filled with some of the foods they plan to serve Easter Sunday to be blessed by the priest.

Festive Pork Roast

½ C. dry cooking sherry or
   chicken broth
½ c. soy sauce
2 garlic cloves (minced)

2 T. dry mustard
2 tsp. dried thyme
1 tsp. ground ginger
1 boneless pork loin (4-5 lbs.)

APRICOT SAUCE:
1 (8 oz.) jar apricot preserves
1 T. soy sauce

2 T. dry cooking sherry or
   chicken broth

Combine first 6 ingredients and mix well. Add pork loin, turning
to coat all sides. Cover and refrigerate for 3 to 4 hours, turning
occasionally. Remove meat and discard marinade. Place roast, fat
side up on rack in shallow pan, and insert a meat thermometer. Bake,
uncovered for 2-2½ hours or until thermometer registers 160°. The
last 15 minutes of baking, baste with sauce. Cover and let stand for
15 minutes before carving. Serve with remaining sauce.

Fonda Bass

Meats & Main Dishes

Mildred & Marguerite's
Home Canned Meat

1 pork loin
Salt & pepper

Flour
Crisco

Have the meat deparment cut the loin in 2-inch slices. I would bring it home and we would trim and cut into chunks. We rolled the meat chunks in flour and browned it. (Marguerite would brown and pack in jars and I would trim and cut.) We fried the meat in Crisco in cast iron skillets. After frying about 2 batches, we would add water to the skillets and scrape out. We saved this to pour over the packed meat. We liked to use wide-mouthed jars. To each quart add 1 tsp. salt and ¼ tsp. pepper. Pour the liquid over the meat until it is a little below the neck of the jar. Wipe the jar rim well. Put on the hot lids and rings; seal. Process in pressure cooker for 75 minutes at 10 lbs. of pressure.

"This is a big job, but sooo good and quick to prepare for unexpected or expected company. It's a must to take a jar with us when we go up North to fish. Marguerite and I enjoyed working together and we had done this enough that without thought we each knew what our job was."

Mildred Waltz

Komla
"Norwegian"

3 lbs. shank end of ham
   with bone
3 C. raw potatoes
1 C. cooked potatoes

1 egg
1 tsp. salt
¾ tsp. soda
2 C. all-purpose flour

Boil ham in 6-quart heavy pan for 2 hours. Take out ham and reserve broth. Grind raw and cooked potatoes, working quickly, as raw potatoes discolor. Add 1 slightly beaten egg to ground potatoes and mix well. Add salt and soda; mix well. Add 2 C. flour and mix until blended in. Do not overmix. Drop by teaspoonful into hot but not boiling ham broth. (Dip the teaspoon into broth each time before forming the next spoonful of mixture.) Bring to low boil so they don't break apart and cook like this for 1 half hour. Serve Komla with butter, ham, and a salad.

"This is a favorite with us!"

Jeneta Weltha

Marinated Pork Roast

1 (5-6 lb.) pork loin roast   1 tsp. coarse salt

MARINADE:
3 large cloves of garlic   2 tsp. salt
½ tsp. dried rosemary leaves   ½ tsp. thyme
1/8 tsp. powdered allspice   3 T. cooking oil

Rub inside of pork loin with salt. Tie into roll. Mix marinade ingredients and rub into roast. Let marinade for 6 hours or overnight. Bake, covered at 350⁰ for 2 to 2½ hours.

Chris Branstad

Polish Galareia
"Jellied Pigs Feet Delicacy"

4 pigs feet (cut in halves)   6 peppercorns
2 pork shanks   5 whole allspice
1 onion (well-browned)   2 bay leaves
1 stalk of celery (chopped)   ⅓ C. vinegar
1 clove of garlic

Wash pigs feet and skanks thoroughly. Put into large kettle and cover with water. Bring to boiling point and skim. Add onion, garlic, celery, and spices. Simmer, covered very slowly, for about 4 hours or until meat comes off bones very easily. Cool, strain, remove the bones, and spices. Return meat to liquid; add salt, and vinegar. Pour into a loaf pan. Set in refrigerator until firm. Scrape fat from top. Remove loaf from pan onto serving platter and cut with serrated knife. Garnish with cooked carrot slices and hard-boiled eggs.

Mary Grochala

Pansit

"Philippine Pork & Shrimp Noodles"

6 ozs. thin rice noodles
  (rice sticks)
5 T. salad oil
1 small onion (chopped)
1½ C. each small cooked
  shrimp & diced cooked pork
  (such as roast or chops)

1 or 2 garlic cloves
  (minced or pressed)
¼ C. regular strength
  chicken broth
1 green onion (including top)
  (minced)

Soak noodles in warm water to cover for 20 minutes, then drain. Heat 3 T. of the oil in wide frying pan over medium heat. Add noodles and cook, stirring until heated thoroughly (about 1 minute). Transfer to a platter and keep warm. Heat remaining 2 T. of oil in pan over high heat. Add onion, garlic, shrimp, and pork. Cook, stirring for 1 minute. Stir in broth, cover, and cook until well done. Spoon over noodles and top with green onion. Makes 3 or 4 servings.

Marvin & Mira Imes

287

Meats & Main Dishes

Pork Chop Dinner

4 large potatoes (peeled)
1 can mushroom soup
¼ can milk
½ onion (diced)
1 can French style green beans
  (drained well)

4 slices American cheese
4 pork chops
Garlic salt
Salt & pepper, to taste

Reserve 4 T. of soup. Combine remaining soup and milk. Add sliced potatoes, diced onion, salt, and pepper to soup mixture. Put in deep greased casserole dish (9x9-inch). Place cheese slices on top of casserole. Put the green beans on top of cheese slices. Place pork chops on top of beans. Sprinkle chops with garlic salt. Spread remaining soup on chops. Cover and bake at 325° for 1 hour and 30 minutes or longer. Remove cover the last 30 minutes of baking time.

Delores Nicholson

Scalloped Potatoes and Ham

4 lbs. white potatoes
  (peeled & sliced)
¼ tsp. salt
½ tsp. pepper

1 can cream of potato soup
1 lb. shaved ham
½ C. milk
2 T. butter

Chop half of the ham into small pieces. Mix with salt, pepper, potatoes, and soup. Pat down into 13x9-inch pan. Pour milk over this and dot with butter. Cover with remaining ham and bake, covered at 350° until potatoes are tender.

Mary Anne Snyder

288

Pumpkin with Ham, Onions, and Corn
(A Colonial Recipe)

3 C. peeled & diced fresh
  pumpkin (½-inch pieces)
1 C. chicken soup stock
  or broth
2 T. butter or olive oil
2 large yellow onions (sliced)

½ lb. diced ham
  (½-inch pieces)
1 (10 oz.) pkg. frozen corn
Salt & pepper, to taste
Toasted pumpkin seeds for
  garnish

Place the diced pumpkin in a covered 2-quart saucepan. Add the broth and butter or oil; top with the onions. Cover and simmer until the pumpkin is just tender, about 15 minutes. Add the ham and corn; cook until the corn is tender, about 8 minutes. Add salt and pepper, to taste. Top with toasted pumpkin seeds (wash the seeds and dry them first). Place pumpkin seeds in hot frying pan along with some olive oil and toast until brown. Add salt and cool.

Joanne Gasiel

Sauerkraut Balls

8 ozs. sausage
¼ C. finely chopped onion
1 (14 oz.) can sauerkraut
  (drained)
2 T. bread crumbs
3 ozs. softened cream cheese
1 tsp. mustard

¼ tsp. garlic salt
1/8 tsp. pepper
1 (14 oz.) can sauerkraut
  (drained)
2 eggs
¼ C. milk
Bread crumbs

MUSTARD SAUCE:
½ C. mayonnaise

2 T. mustard

Brown sausage and onion. Add sauerkraut and bread crumbs. Combine cheese, mustard, garlic salt, and pepper. Stir into sauerkraut and chill. Shape into ¾-inch ball and roll in flour. Mix 2 eggs and ¼ C. milk. Roll ball in eggs, then in fine bread crumbs. Deep fat fry for 30 to 60 seconds.

Jo Agan

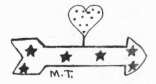

When grilling chicken or ribs, cook them in the crockpot on high for about 3 hours, turning occasionally. This way, when they are grilled, they get the BBQ flavor without the meat having to cook so long that it is dry and tough.

Baked Chicken Breasts Supreme

1½ C. plain yogurt
¼ C. lemon juice
½ tsp. Worcestershire sauce
½ tsp. celery seed
½ tsp. paprika

1 clove of garlic (minced)
¼ tsp. pepper
8 boneless chicken breasts
2 C. fine dry bread crumbs

In a large bowl, combine first 7 ingredients. Place chicken in mixture and turn over a few times to coat. Cover and marinate overnight in the refrigerator. Remove chicken and coat in crumbs. Place in shallow pan and bake, uncovered at 350⁰ for 45 minutes.

Barb Schmitz

Cashew-Chicken Stir-Fry

½ C. water
2 T. soy sauce
4 tsp. cornstarch
½ tsp. minced garlic
¼ tsp. black pepper

2 T. oil
3 C. cubed uncooked chicken
1½ C. sliced celery
1½ C. sliced fresh mushrooms
1⅓ C. cashews

Blend together water, soy sauce, cornstarch, garlic, and pepper; set aside. Heat oil in Wok or skillet over medium-high heat. Add chicken and celery. Stir-fry for 4 minutes or until chicken and celery are tender. Add mushrooms and cashews; stir-fry for 1 minute. Mix in soy mixture; cook and stir until sauce is thickened. Serve with rice. Makes 6 servings.

Cindy Watson Pottebaum

Meats & Main Dishes

California Chicken

4-5 chicken breasts
Salt & pepper
Paprika
Lemon juice

1 C. sour cream
½ env. onion soup mix
Butter or oleo
Seasoned bread crumbs

Skin, bone, and cut in half each chicken breast. Rinse and pat dry. Place chicken pieces on baking dish and sprinkle with lemon juice. Season to taste with salt, pepper, and paprika. Brush with melted butter or oleo. Combine 1 C. sour cream and ½ envelope of onion soup mix. Spread sour cream mixture over chicken pieces. Add bread crumbs, cover, and bake at 350° for 1 hour. Remove cover and bake for ½ hour more (or as needed to brown the chicken pieces). Do not overbake. Serves 8 to 10.

Jean Gillespie

Chicken and Biscuits

1 pkg. sour cream sauce mix
1 can cream of chicken or
    cream of mushroom soup
½ C. wine

1 chicken or chicken parts, like
    breasts (legs or thighs)
2 pkgs. refrigerated biscuits

Mix the sour cream mix as on the package directions. Let set for 10 minutes. Add 1 can of cream of chicken or mushroom soup. Mix well and then add the wine. Put the chicken in a roaster or baking pan. Add salt and pepper, to taste. Put the sour cream mixture over the chicken. Bake at 350° for ½ hour to 45 minutes or until chicken is tender. Put biscuits on top and bake, uncovered for 10 to 15 minutes or until lightly browned. Cover and finish baking until biscuits are done.

Shirley Privratsky

Cheesy Chicken Crescent Dish

1¾ C. cubed chicken
1 C. shredded cheddar cheese
1 (8 oz.) can Pillsbury
   refrigerated crescent rolls

½ can cream of chicken soup
½ can cream of mushroom
   soup
½ C. milk

Preheat to 375⁰. Combine chicken and ½ C. of cheddar cheese. Separate crescent roll dough into 8 triangles. Place about 3 T. chicken mixture on wide end of each triangle and roll to opposite point. In medium saucepan combine soups, milk, and ¼ C. cheddar cheese. Heat until cheese melts. Pour half of soup mixture into greased 8 or 9-inch square baking dish. (Reserve remaining soup mixture for sauce). Arrange filled crescents over hot soup mixture. Bake at 375⁰ for 20 to 25 minutes, until golden brown. During the last 10 minutes, sprinkle with remaining cheese. Serve with remaining sauce poured over top.

Bev Maxwell

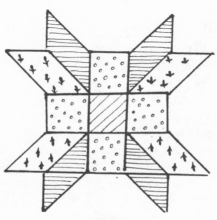

Meats & Main Dishes

Chicken-Vegetable Stir-Fry

2 whole chicken breasts
   (boned & cut in strips)
1 tsp. salt
1 tsp. soy sauce
6 green onions (chopped)
2 T. oil
Broccoli (cut-up)
Mushrooms (sliced)

Carrots (sliced at angle)
Any vegetables can be used
1 (5 oz.) can water chestnuts
   (sliced) (optional)
1 C. chicken bouillon
1 T. cornstarch, dissolved in
   2 T. soy sauce &
   ¼ C. chicken bouillon

Marinate chicken in salt, soy sauce, cornstarch, and green onions. Let stand at least 20 minutes. Add oil to Wok or non-stick pan. Stir-fry chicken, then add vegetables and the chicken bouillon. Stir-fry until crisp. Add cornstarch mixture to thicken. May be served with rice.

Teresa Kordick Westphal

E.B.'s Chicken & Broccoli

6 chicken breasts

2 pkgs. frozen broccoli

SAUCE:
1 can cream of chicken soup
½ C. Hellman's mayonnaise
¼ lb. sharp cheddar cheese

½ tsp. salt
¼ tsp. pepper

Boil chicken until tender. Cool and cut into bite-size pieces. Cook broccoli and drain. Place broccoli in bottom of buttered 9x13-inch pan. For Sauce: Combine soup, real mayonnaise, cheese, salt, and pepper. Cook until smooth. Cover broccoli with chicken then sauce. Bake at 400° for 20 minutes or at 350° for 30 minutes.

Carl Neal

Chicken a la Anna

6 whole large chicken breasts
   (split lengthwise, skinned
   & boned)
¾ C. Italian bread crumbs
¼ C. grated Parmesan cheese
½ C. sliced green onion

2 T. flour
1 C. milk
1 (10 oz.) pkg. frozen chopped
   spinach (thawed & drained)
1 (14 oz.) pkg. boiled ham
   slices

Combine bread crumbs and Parmesan cheese. Dip chicken in mixture to coat lightly. (Set aside any remaining bread crumb mixture.) Arrange in a 9x13-inch baking dish. In saucepan cook onion in butter until tender. Add flour and milk. Cook and stir until slightly thickened. Stir in spinach and ham. Spoon spinach mixture over chicken. Sprinkle with remaining bread crumb mixture. Bake at 350° for 30 minutes or until done. Serves 12. Serve with broccoli casserole.

BROCCOLI CASSEROLE:

2 pkgs. frozen chopped broccoli
1 egg (slightly beaten)
½ C. mayonnaise
2 T. onion

1 can cream of mushroom soup
1 C. grated cheddar cheese
½ pkg. herb stuffing mix
Melted butter, to taste

Cook broccoli slightly less than package instructions, since the dish will be baked. Mix cooked broccoli, egg, mayonnaise, onion, soup, and cheese in greased 2-quart casserole dish. Mix stuffing with melted butter and spread over broccoli. Bake at 350° for 30 minutes.

"This recipe was given to my son, Matthew, at Sec Taylor Stadium by Damon Berryhill's wife Anne. Matt insists I serve him this from time to time. Damon Berryhill was with the Chicago Cubs, but is now with the Atlanta Braves."

George Sexton

Meats & Main Dishes

Chicken Casserole

3 C. cooked chicken (diced)
2 cans cream of mushroom soup
2 cans cream of chicken soup
2 cans chicken with rice soup
1 large can condensed milk
1 (4 oz.) can mushrooms

14 ozs. Chow Mein noodles
1 green pepper (diced)
2 stalks of celery (diced)
¼ C. cooking sherry
2 cans French fried onion
  rings

Mix all ingredients together well. Bake in well greased pan - one 9x12-inch and one 9-inch square at 300⁰ for 1 hour or at 375⁰ for 30 minutes.

Shirley Bittinger

Chicken Casserole

2¾ C. diced chicken
1½ C. chicken broth
1 C. milk
1 can cream of mushroom soup
1 can cream of chicken soup
1½ C. diced Deluxe sliced
  American cheese squares

½ C. diced green pepper
1 small onion (diced)
2 C. large uncooked elbow
  macaroni
Salt & pepper, to taste

Mix all the ingredients together including the uncooked macaroni. Put in a 9x13-inch greased pan and refrigerate overnight. Bake at 350⁰ covered for 50 minutes, then bake uncovered for the final 10 minutes. Serves 10 to 15. (Turkey or ham may be used instead of chicken.)

Pam Palmer
Jeneta Weltha

Chicken and Pork Adobo
(Philippines)

1¼ lbs. lean boneless pork
4 each chicken legs & thighs
1 C. palm vinegar or ½ C.
  each white distilled vinegar
  & water
¼ C. soy sauce

¼ tsp. pepper
1 bay leaf
4 cloves of garlic
  (minced or pressed)
2 T. salad oil
Chopped parsley
Hot cooked rice

Discard fat from pork and cut meat into 1-inch cubes. Place in bowl, then add chicken. Pour in vinegar and soy sauce; add pepper, bay leaf, and garlic. Cover and refrigerate for 1 hour, turning occasionally. Remove meat from marinade and pat dry; reserve marinade. Heat oil in 5 or 6-quart kettle over medium high heat. Add chicken and cook until browned on all sides. Add pork and cook until browned on all sides. Pour in marinade, cover, reduce heat to medium low, and simmer for 15 minutes. Cover, reduce heat to medium-low, and simmer for 15 minutes. Return chicken to kettle, cover, and simmer until chicken is no longer pink and pork is tender. Transfer all meat to platter; cover and keep warm. Skim and discard fat from cooking (liquid). Remove and discard leaf. Boil liquid over high heat until reduced to about 1 cup, then pour over meat. Sprinkle with parsley and serve over rice. Makes about 6 servings.

Marvin and Mira Imes

Meats & Main Dishes

Cranberry and Chicken

1 can jelly or whole cranberries
½ small bottle Catalina salad
  dressing
⅓ pkg. onion soup mix
4 to 6 boned & skinless
  chicken breasts

Mix all ingredients together well. Pour over chicken breasts. Marinate overnight in 9x13-inch pan. Bake in same pan at 350⁰ for 1 hour.

Margaret Roach

Hot Chicken Salad

2½ C. cooked diced chicken
1 C. diced celery
1 C. sliced mushrooms
1 T. minced onion
1 tsp. lemon juice
2 C. cooked rice
¾ C. mayonnaise
1 can cream of chicken soup

TOPPING:
3 T. melted butter
½ C. crushed cornflakes

Mix all ingredients together and place in 2-quart casserole. Top with topping and bake at 350⁰ for 30 minutes.

Mary Brayton

King Ranch Chicken

1 pkg. tortillas
1 cooked boned chicken
1 can mushroom soup
1 can cream of chicken soup

1 C. onion (diced)
1 can Rotel tomatoes
Grated cheese

Place tortillas (which have been broken into bite-sized pieces) in bottom of casserole dish. Combine chicken, mushroom soup, chicken soup, and onion. Then add Rotel tomatoes. Place all of this in casserole dish. Grate cheese on top. Cover and bake at 350° for 1 hour. (Doritos can be used instead of tortillas.)

Maxine Brunsmann

No Peek Chicken

1 C. rice
Chicken pieces or 1 whole
   chicken (cut-up)
1 can cream of celery soup

1 can cream of chicken soup
1 can water
1 pkg. Lipton onion soup mix
1 can mushrooms (optional)

Combine all in a 9x13-inch pan and cover pan with foil tightly. Put in oven at 350° for 2 hours - do not uncover. Take out of oven and let set for 5 minutes. Uncover and serve.

Val Herzog

Meats & Main Dishes

Oven Fried Chicken Breasts

10 half chicken breasts
2 C. sour cream
1 T. Worcestershire sauce
2 T. chopped onion

2 tsp. salt
½ tsp. pepper
1¼ tsp. paprika
Dry bread crumbs

Mix all ingredients together, except chicken and crumbs. Arrange chicken in a shallow 9x13-inch pan, lined with foil. Pour ingredients over chicken, turning each piece to coat. Cover and refrigerate overnight. The next morning dip each piece in bread crumbs. Refrigerate for 1½ hours longer or more. Bake at 325⁰ for 1 hour and 15 minutes or until done. Makes 6 to 10 servings.

Harriet Nevins

Oven-Fried Chicken

1 (3 lb.) chicken
   (cut & skinned)
6 T. flour
1 tsp. salt
Dash of pepper

1 egg (beaten)
2 T. water
1½ ozs. cornflake crumbs
1 oz. Parmesan cheese
8 tsp. margarine (melted)

Mix flour, salt, and pepper; set aside. Blend egg and water; set aside. Mix cornflake crumbs and Parmesan cheese; set aside. Coat the chicken with the flour mixture and roll in the crumb mixture. Place in a glass 9x13-inch baking dish sprayed with Pam. Drizzle with margarine over the top and bake at 375⁰ for 1 hour or until tender.

Rosemary Stuchel

Poppy Seed Chicken Casserole

1 (8 oz.) carton sour cream
1 can cream of chicken soup
½ can water
4 skinned & deboned chicken
   breasts

1½ tubes Ritz crackers
1 heaping T. poppy seeds
1 stick margarine
Salt & pepper, to taste

Boil chicken and cut into bite-sized pieces. Combine soup, water, and sour cream in saucepan. Heat and mix well. Crush crackers, then add poppy seed, salt, and pepper. Mix well and place chicken in 9x13-inch pan. Pour soup and sour cream mixture over top. Cover with cracker mixture. Cut margarine into pats and dab over the top. Bake at 350⁰ for 1 hour.

"This recipe was given to me by my son."

Mildred Waltz

Supreme Chicken Casserole

1 chicken (boned & diced)
2 C. bread crumbs
1 C. Minute Rice
Salt & pepper, to taste

½ C. onion
3 C. chicken broth
4 eggs (beaten)
2 cans mushroom soup

Mix all ingredients together. If too dry add more broth. Bake in a 9x13-inch pan at 350⁰ for 1 hour. Serves 12 to 15.

Luella Fairholm

Meats & Main Dishes

Turkey Burgers

1 lb. ground turkey
½ C. oatmeal
¾ C. diced onion
¾ C. diced green pepper

½ C. shredded carrots
½ C. catsup
½ tsp. salt
¼ tsp. garlic powder (optional)

Mix all together and shape into patties. Grill. Healthy and very good!

Berta Kordick

Sauteed' Turkey Cutlets with Orange Sauce

2 T. flour
4 turkey cutlets
1 T. vegetable oil
½ C. chopped green onions
   (white part only)

1 clove of garlic (thinly sliced)
¾ C. orange juice
1 T. soy sauce
1 T. oriental sesame oil
¼ C. green onion top

Coat cutlets with flour. Shake excess off. Heat oil until hot, then add cutlets. Brown for about 2 minutes on each side. Remove and set aside. Reduce heat, then add white part of onion and garlic; saute' for 2 minutes. Add orange juice and soy sauce. Boil until slightly thickened, stirring occasionally, about 3 minutes. Stir in sesame oil, then add salt and pepper, to taste. Return turkey and accumulated juices to skillet. Simmer until turkey is heated through, 10 to 12 minutes. Can be served with rice or corn bread dressing. Decorate turkey with thin fresh orange slices on the side.

Fonda Bass

Curried Lamb on Rice

1 lb. lean lamb
  (cubed & trimmed of fat)
½ C. chopped onion
1 clove of garlic (minced)
1 T. margarine
2 tsp. curry powder
¾ tsp. salt
¼ tsp. ground ginger

1 medium tomato
  (peeled & chopped)
1½ T. flour
1 cube beef bouillon
1 C. boiling water
2 C. cooked rice
½ C. grated carrot

Brown lamb, onion, and garlic in margarine. Add curry powder, salt, ginger, tomato, and flour. Mix well. Dissolve bouillon cube in water and stir into meat. Cover and simmer for 30 to 40 minutes or until lamb is tender, stirring occasionally. Toss rice with grated carrot. Serve lamb over rice.

Rosemary Stuchel

Mother's Day

For Mother's Day, our parish usually has a mother-daughter banquet. Last year everyone was to wear a hat. It was fun to see the wide variety of hats worn, some very old, some new, and some decorated to be quite unique!

Meats & Main Dishes

Brascioli-Italian Steak Rolls

1½ lbs. breakfast steak or
   minute steak
¼ C. Romano grated cheese
2 hard-boiled eggs
   (finely chopped)
1 slice bacon (chopped fine)
1 egg

1 C. bread crumbs
½ tsp. sweet basil
1 tsp. parsley (dried or fresh)
½ tsp. salt
½ tsp. black pepper
½ tsp. garlic powder

Mix bread crumbs, cheese, chopped boiled eggs, and bacon. Add salt, pepper, basil, parsley, and egg. Mix lightly. Place filling on each steak. Roll and tie loosely with string or secure with toothpicks. Brown in oil. Turn each steak until evenly browned. Cook in spaghetti sauce, about 1½ to 2 hours.

Mary Grochala

Italiano
"Easy and Quick!"

1 lb. ground beef
⅓ C. chopped onion
1 medium garlic (minced)
½ to 1 tsp. oregano
½ tsp. salt

1 can tomato soup
⅓ C. water
2 C. cooked noodles
4 ozs. shredded cheese

Set oven to 350°. Brown beef with onion, garlic, and seasoning. Combine in casserole with soup, water, and noodles. Place cheese around edges on top. Bake at 350° for 30 minutes.

Mary Anne Roby

Memories From Childhood
By: Mary Anne Roby

I often think about how different things in the church are now compared to when I was a child. I can remember the long processions on Holy Days and for First Holy Communion, and how important it was that we fasted after Midnight from both food and water before going to Communion. On that special day, I can remember waking up in the morning and finding dishcloths wrapped around all the water faucets lest I forgot and took a drink. Had that happened I feel quite sure my special day would have been ruined.

Lasagna - Style Casserole

6 ozs. large bow-tie pasta
 (2¼ C.)
1 lb. ground beef
1 (15 oz.) can pizza sauce
1 tsp. minced onion
½ tsp. dry basil

1 egg (beaten)
1 C. Ricotta cheese or
 cottage cheese
¼ C. grated Parmesan cheese
1 C. shredded mozzarella
 cheese

Cook pasta until tender, then drain. Fry meat until browned, then drain off fat. Add pizza sauce, onion, and basil to meat and mix well. In a bowl combine egg and cottage cheese or Ricotta. In a greased 12x9½ x2-inch baking dish, layer half of the pasta. Spoon cheese mixture over pasta. Sprinkle with Parmesan cheese. Layer remaining pasta, meat, and mozzarella cheese. Bake, covered at 425° for 15 minutes, then uncover and bake for 5 to 8 minutes longer or until heated through.

Ann Holtmeyer

Italian Chicken Rolls

2 T. margarine
3 T. olive oil
2 cloves of garlic (pressed)
¼ to ½ tsp. crushed red pepper
¼ C. chopped parsley
6 to 8 anchovies (chopped)
2½ to 3 lbs. chicken breast
  (skinned, boned & cut in 1-inch chunks)

Salt, to taste
2 (2¼ oz.) cans sliced pitted
  ripe olives (drained)
¾ C. dry white wine
¼ tsp. pepper
6 crusty sandwich rolls

Heat margarine and olive oil until hot; add garlic, red pepper, parsley, anchovies, and chicken. Cook, stirring until lightly browned, 5 minutes. Add olives, white wine, and pepper. Simmer, uncovered, stirring occasionally until most of the juices evaporate, about 5 minutes. Add salt, to taste. Split rolls and tear out soft portions. Brush inside with garlic butter. Fill tops equally with chicken mixture, cover with bottoms. Bake, uncovered at 350⁰ until warm, 5 minutes. If made ahead wrap in foil and refrigerate. Heat in 350⁰ for about 15 minutes. Unwrap and bake for 5 minutes or until crisp.

For Garlic Butter: Combine ⅓ C. melted butter or margarine with 1 clove of pressed garlic.

Rita Drysdale

Lasagna

1 lb. Italian sausage
1 lb. ground pork
1 clove of garlic (minced)
1 T. of chopped parsley
  (fresh preferred)
1 T. of basil (fresh preferred)
1½ tsp. salt
1 (1 lb.) can of tomatoes (2 C.)
2 (6 oz.) cans tomato paste
  (1⅓ C.)
1 (16 oz.) pkg. quality lasagna
  noodles (R & F Brand)

*2 (12 oz.) cartons large curd
  cream-style cottage cheese
2 beaten eggs
2 tsp. salt
½ tsp. pepper
2 T. chopped parsley
  (fresh preferred)
¾ C. Parmesan cheese
  (grated)
1½ lbs. mozzarella cheese
  (sliced thin)

Brown meat slowly, then spoon off excess fat. Add salt and the next 6 ingredients to meat. Simmer uncovered until it is a rich thick sauce, 45 minutes to an hour, stirring occasionally. Cook noodles in boiling salted water until tender. Drain and rinse in cold water. Combine cottage cheese with the next five ingredients. Take a 13x9½-inch pan and spray surface lightly with Pam or similar non-sticking spray. Layer noodles in pan. Spread cottage cheese mixture over noodles, followed by the desired amount of meat mixture, followed by the mozzarella cheese. Repeat layers and cover with aluminum foil. Bake in moderate oven (375⁰) for 30 to 40 minutes until slightly bubbling. Let stand for 10 to 15 minutes before cutting in squares. Makes 12 servings. (*Riccota cheese, if available, is preferable.)

Fr. Frank Palmer

Meats & Main Dishes

Lasagna

3 lbs. ground beef
1 lb. ground fresh pork
2 C. chopped onion
2 cloves of garlic (minced)
2 (1 lb. 12 oz.) cans tomatoes
2 (15 oz.) cans tomato sauce
3 T. parsley flakes
3 T. sugar
2 tsp. salt
2 tsp. crushed basil
1 C. grated Parmesan cheese

2 T. parsley flakes
2 tsp. salt
2 tsp. crushed oregano
16 ozs. lasagna noodles
   (cooked & well drained)
1½ lbs. mozzarella cheese
   (shredded)
2 C. grated Parmesan cheese
2 (2 lb.) each cartons cottage
   cheese

Cook and stir beef, pork, onion, and garlic in a heavy saucepan or roaster until meat is browned and onion is tender. Drain off fat. Add tomatoes and break up with a fork. Stir in tomato sauce, 3 T. parsley flakes, 3 T. sugar, 2 tsp. salt, and the basil; simmer, uncovered for 1 hour or until mixture is thick. Heat oven to 350⁰. Mix cottage cheese, 1 C. Parmesan cheese, 2 T. parsley flakes, 2 tsp. salt, and the oregano. In two 9x13-inch pans layer half of each of drained noodles, sauce, mozzarella cheese, and cottage cheese mixture. Repeat, reserving enough sauce for a thin top layer. Spread sauce on top and sprinkle with 1 C. Parmesan cheese. Bake, uncovered for 45 minutes. Let stand for 15 minutes. Serves 24.

Joan Hilton

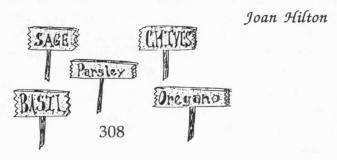

ITALIAN DISHES

Easy Lasagna

1 lb. ground beef
1 (32 oz.) jar prepared
   spaghetti sauce
12 ozs. mozzarella cheese
16 ozs. cottage cheese
1 egg
½ tsp. dried parsley flakes

½ tsp. salt
1/8 tsp. pepper
½ C. water
8 ozs. lasagna noodles
   (uncooked)
½ C. grated Parmesan cheese

Brown ground beef and drain. Add sauce and heat to boiling. Cut 6 slices from mozzarella cheese and reserve for topping. Shred remainder of mozzarella and combine with cottage cheese, egg, parsley, salt, and pepper. Place half of spaghetti sauce and the water in bottom of 13x9x2-inch pan or lasagna pan. Layer half of noodles over sauce and top with half of cheese mixture. Repeat layers and sprinkle with Parmesan cheese. Top with reserved mozzarella slices. (Can be covered and refrigerated at this point. Remove cover before baking.) Bake at 350⁰ for 1 hour or until hot and bubbly around edges. Let stand for 10 minutes before serving. Makes 8 servings.

Sharon Johnson

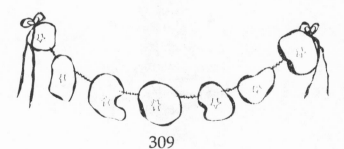

Easy Lasagna

1 to 2 lbs. ground beef
Salt & pepper
1 (30 oz.) jar spaghetti sauce
  (I use Prego with mushrooms)

1 (8 oz.) pkg. lasagna noodles
1 lb. cottage cheese
1 lb. mozzarella cheese (grated)
1 C. grated Parmesan cheese

Brown hamburger in skillet. Drain excess fat and season with salt and pepper. Stir in spaghetti sauce. Cook noodles according to package directions; drain and separate. In a 9x13-inch pan, spread on a thin layer of sauce. Top with ⅓ of noodles, then a layer of ⅓ cottage cheese, then ⅓ of mozzarella cheese and Parmesan cheese. Repeat layers until all is used up. Bake in preheated oven at 350⁰ for 45 minutes. Cool for 10 minutes. Lasagna can be assembled and frozen uncooked - allow 1 hour and 15 minutes baking time. Serves 8 generously.

"This is a meal our family enjoys on Christmas Day. It is our tradition to spend Christmas Eve with Grandparents and family in Carroll. We travel back to Winterset on Christmas Eve so our daughters can wake up in their own beds and enjoy our own Christmas traditions. With all the excitement in our home Christmas Day, surrounded by the love and warmth of each other, the already prepared lasagna becomes a feast fit for a "King".

Jean Pletchette

Mostaccioli Casserole

½ lb. pizza sausage
½ lb. lean ground beef
1 (3 lb.) jar Ragu spaghetti
   sauce

1 small can tomato sauce
1 T. Italian seasoning
1 box Mostaccioli noodles
Mozzarella cheese

Brown meats and drain. Cook noodles and drain. Combine with remaining ingredients, except cheese. Top with grated mozzarella
cheese and bake at 350⁰ for 45 minutes or until done and golden
brown and bubbly. Makes a 9x13-inch dish.

Patricia Morris

Rigatoni Casserole

1 lb. Rigatoni
1 lb. grated mozzarella cheese
Romano cheese
1½ lbs. bulk Italian sausage
2 (12 oz.) cans tomato paste
2 (15 oz.) cans tomato sauce
Salt & pepper, to taste

2 cloves of garlic (chopped)
¼ tsp. oregano
1 tsp. sweet basil
1 bay leaf
2 tsp. sugar
5 to 6 cans of water

Brown sausage with garlic, salt, and pepper. Add tomato paste,
tomato sauce, water, oregano, bay leaf, basil, and sugar. Cook for
about 2 hours. Into 6 quarts of boiling salted water add rigatoni and
cook until almost done; drain. In a casserole dish (3-quart) put a
layer of sauce, a layer of rigatoni, and a layer of mozzarella cheese.
Sprinkle with Romano cheese. Repeat procedure again. Cover and
bake in slow oven (300⁰-325⁰) for about 30 to 45 minutes.

Mary Grochala

Meats & Main Dishes

Pasta Chiena

1 recipe spaghetti sauce
  (next page)
1 recipe Italian meatball
  mixture (below)
4 hard-boiled eggs

1 lb. Mostaccioli macaroni
½ C. Romano cheese
1 lb. shredded mozzarella
  cheese

Roll meatballs to size of a dime. Brown and set aside. In a deep (3-quart) dish put a layer of sauce, a layer of Mostaccioli, a layer of meatballs, sprinkle with 2 chopped eggs, a layer of mozzarella cheese and Romano cheese, and then more sauce. Repeat this procedure once more. Reserve 2 boiled eggs, sliced for topping. Bake at 350⁰ for ½ hour. Do not keep in oven too long for the pasta will absorb the sauce and it will be too dry.

"This entree was traditionally served as the main course (along with chicken, ham, etc.) for our family dinners on holidays and festive occasions; it was the sign that the day was 'special.'"

Mary Grochala

Italian Meatballs

1 lb. ground beef
½ lb. ground pork
2 eggs
1 C. bread crumbs (moistened)
¼ C. Parmesan cheese

1 tsp. dried sweet basil or
  fresh basil
1 T. parsley
1 tsp. garlic powder
Salt & pepper, to taste

Mix all ingredients thoroughly and form into balls. Brown in hot oil. Add to sauce and simmer for at least 2 hours. Should make approximately 10 to 12 meatballs.

Mary Grochala

Spaghetti Sauce

3 (12 oz.) cans tomato paste
6-7 cans water
1 medium onion (chopped)
¼ C. green pepper (chopped)
2 cloves garlic (minced) or
   ½ tsp. garlic powder
¼ C. oil

¼ tsp. oregano
1 tsp. sweet basil
1 small bay leaf
1 T. sugar
½ T. salt
¼ tsp. pepper

In a 8-quart pan saute' onion, green pepper, and garlic in oil. Add tomato paste and water. Stir until smooth, then add rest of the seasonings.

For Meat Sauce: In addition to the above ingredients, brown 1 lb. Italian sausage and 1 lb. of ground beef (chuck) and add to sauce. Simmer uncovered for 1 to 2 hours.

This spaghetti meat sauce recipe has been traditionally used in our family for years. When RAGBRAI came through Winterset in 1991, the parish served 1000 spaghetti dinners under the supervision of Mary Grochala, who added a little of this and a little of that. Over 90 gallons of sauce were made.

A group of cyclists from California, the High-Five Rollers, voted it "the best spaghetti sauce ever tasted" and presented Mary with a spontaneous award.

Fr. Frank Palmer & Mary Grochala (Fr.'s Sister)

Meats & Main Dishes

Spaghetti and Meatballs

1 lb. ground round
1½ cloves of finely chopped
   garlic
1 egg
4 slices bread
1 medium onion (ground fine)
¼ tsp. salt
¼ tsp. dried red peppers
Pinch of oregano
Olive oil

2½ cloves of garlic
   (chopped fine)
1 large can of tomato juice
   (1 qt., 14 ozs.)
3 cans tomato paste
3 cans water (use tomato
   paste cans)
6 bay leaves
1 tsp. salt
½ tsp. red peppers (crushed)
   (NO MORE than ½ tsp.)

Mix ground round, chopped garlic, egg, bread, onion, ¼ tsp. salt, red peppers, and oregano. Let stand at room temperature. Cover the bottom of a 6-quart kettle with olive oil. Brown the chopped garlic in oil over low heat until light brown. Add tomato juice and tomato paste. Add 3 cans of water (use the tomato paste cans to measure). Add 6 bay leaves, the salt, and red peppers. Bring sauce to a boil and then simmer. Cook sauce for about 3 hours. Make about 15 large meatballs from meat mixture. Add them to the sauce for the final 45 minutes of simmering the sauce. Prepare spaghetti and ladle sauce and meatballs over the pasta.

George Sexton

Baked Spaghetti Casserole

2 lbs. ground hamburger
¾ C. finely chopped onion
½ finely chopped green pepper
1 tsp. salt
¾ to 1 lb. spaghetti
2 bay leaves

2 cans tomato soup
1 can mushroom soup
2 cans milk
2 C. sharp cheddar cheese
1 C. mozzarella cheese

Brown hamburger with onion and pepper. Drain and sprinkle with 1 tsp. salt. Break spaghetti into thirds. Cook with a little salt and 2 bay leaves according to package directions; drain. In a large bowl combine hamburger mixture, spaghetti, soups, milk, and 1½ C. cheddar cheese. Put in 9x13-inch baking dish. Sprinkle with remaining cheese and bake at 350° for 1 hour. This may be divided into 2 smaller casseroles and frozen. Works best if you thaw before baking.

Nancy T. Emmert

Meats & Main Dishes

Spaghetti Pizza

2 lbs. hamburger
1 (32 oz.) jar Ragu sauce
1 (3 C.) pkg. mozzarella cheese
Minced onion
1 (7 oz.) pkg. spaghetti (cooked)

Mushrooms, Canadian bacon,
    pepperoni, etc. (your choice)
¾ C. milk with
    1 beaten egg

Fry hamburger with a little minced onion. Grease a 9x13-inch pan. First put all of the spaghetti in bottom of pan, then cover with half of the hamburger mix. Cover that with Ragu sauce. Sprinkle half of cheese on, then other half of hamburger, then pepperoni, and etc. Put the rest of the cheese over that. Last, pour the milk and egg mixture over everything. Bake at 350° for 1 hour, uncovered.

Kathleen Kordick
Jana Corkrean

316

Burritos with Meat Gravy

2 lbs. ground beef
1-2 Jalapeno peppers
  (1 T. approx.)
Salt & pepper, to taste
¼ tsp. garlic powder
1 tsp. chili powder
⅓ C. flour
1 pkg. Schilling brown gravy mix

2 cans refried beans
Water
2 C. grated cheddar cheese
Optional toppings: onion,
  tomatoes, lettuce, taco sauce,
  & sour cream
1 pkg. flour tortillas

Brown ground beef with chopped Jalapeno pepper. Add salt, pepper, garlic powder, and chili powder. Stir flour into mixture and add enough water to make a gravy (approximately 2 C.). Add package of dry gravy mix. In a separate pan heat up the refried beans. For each burrito warm a tortilla by placing on a sheet of aluminum foil on top the stove burner. Place on individual plate. Spoon beans on top of tortilla and wrap up. Pour meat mixture over the burrito Top with cheese and optional toppings as desired.

Karen Pommier

Larry's Enchiladas for Two

¼ stick butter
1 onion (thinly sliced)
¾ C. shredded chicken
    (about ½ large breast)
2T. diced green chilies
3 ozs. cream cheese (diced)
Salt, to taste

4 C. flour tortillas
⅓ C. heavy cream
1 C. grated Monterey Jack
    cheese
Chopped green onion
Sliced black olives

Preheat oven to 375⁰. Grease a 9x13-inch baking dish. Melt butter in large skillet over low heat. Add onion and cook, stirring constantly until onion is limp, but not brown (about 20 minutes). Remove from heat and add chilies and cream cheese. Mix lightly, then add salt. Heat about ¼-inch oil in small skillet. Drop tortillas, 1 at a time into oil and fry for several seconds until they begin to blister. (Do not let them get crisp.) Remove with tongs and drain on paper towels. Spoon about ⅓ C. of filling down center of each tortilla. Roll and set seam side down in baking dish. Moisten top with cream and sprinkle with grated cheese. Bake, uncovered until heated through (20 minutes). Garnish with green onion and olives.

Joan Hilton

Chicken Enchiladas

5 chicken breasts
  (boned & skinned)
1 C. sour cream
2 green onions

10-12 small flour tortillas
1 large can enchilada sauce
½ lb. grated Monterey jack
  cheese

Boil chicken and shred with two forks. Add sour cream, onion, and mix with chicken. Dip tortilla in sauce and lay on cutting board. Add ¼ C. filling, fold ends, and roll tightly. Place seam-side down in greased jelly roll pan or cake pan. When all are rolled, cover with remaining sauce and top with cheese. Bake at 350⁰ for 20 to 30 minutes.

Karen Gronemeyer

Chicken Enchiladas

1 medium onion (chopped)
2 to 3 T. butter
1 can cream of chicken soup
1 can cream of mushroom
  soup
1 lb. longhorn cheese (grated)

1 C. chicken broth
1 small can chopped green
  chilies
1 chicken (cooked & boned)
1 pkg. corn tortillas

Brown onion in butter. Combine with soups, broth, and green chilies. Add pieces of chicken and beat well. In a large 9x13-inch baking dish, place a layer of corn tortillas, layer of chicken sauce, and a layer of grated cheese. Repeat the layers until casserole is filled. Bake at 350⁰ for 30 minutes. Makes 8 servings.

Patsy Bence

Chicken Enchilidas

1½ chickens (boiled &
  deboned)
36 corn shells
2 bricks of cheese
  (shredded, any kind)
2 peppers (chopped)

5 tomatos (chopped)
4 T. cumin, mixed into
  chopped vegetables
3 cans hot enchilada sauce
2 cans chili with no beans
½ onion (chopped)

In a 9x13-inch pan (larger is better), cover bottom of pan with en-chilada sauce. Fry corn shells a few seconds on each side. Dip into enchilada sauce, stuff with chicken, cheese, and vegetables. Roll and stack in pan. Continue to stuff, roll, and stack enchiladas. Save some cheese to sprinkle over top. After all are stacked, spread chili over enchiladas, then sprinkle cheese over the top. Bake at 350° for about 45 minutes or until bubbly. Can use less cumin and mild enchilada sauce for less spicy enchiladas.

Frances Stevens

Mexican Meat Loaf

1 lb. hamburger
1 C. oatmeal
1 egg
1 T. green chilies

1 T. taco sauce
½ onion (chopped)
½ C. ketchup

Combine ingredients and place in loaf pan. Bake at 350° for 1 hour.

Karen Watts

Mexican Lasagna

1 lb. ground beef
1 (12 oz.) jar Ortega mild &
   thick & chunky salsa
6-10 halved hard taco shells

1 C. refried beans
1 C. dairy sour cream
4 ozs. shredded cheddar cheese

Brown beef and drain. Stir in ½ C. salsa. Spread ¼ C. salsa in 10-inch pie plate and top with half of taco shells. Spread in layers half of beans, meat, sour cream, and cheese. Repeat layers and cover with foil. Bake at 350⁰ for 30 minutes. Serve with lettuce, salsa, and sour cream on the side. This can be doubled for a 9x13-inch pan. Allow a little extra baking time.

Frances Stevens

Spanish Rice

1 lb. ground beef
2 (8 oz.) can tomato sauce
3 C. water
1½ C. rice (uncooked)
1 beef bouillon cube

2 T. butter
¼ C. chopped green pepper
Garlic salt, to taste
Onion salt, to taste

Brown ground beef in electric skillet, then add all other ingredients. Stir, bringing to a boil. Cover and reduce heat to simmer and cook until rice is done, 20 to 30 minutes.

Mary Anne Snyder

Meats & Main Dishes

Taco Pie

1 pkg. refrigerated crescent
   rolls
1 lb. ground beef
1 pkg. taco seasonings (I make
   my own using 1 to 2 T.
   chili powder, 1 tsp. oregano,
   ½ tsp. cumin, dash of salt,
   pepper & cayenne)

½ C. sliced green olives
1 C. sour cream
1 C. shredded cheddar cheese
1 small onion (chopped)
1 tomato (chopped)
½ head of lettuce (shredded)
Jar of salsa or picante sauce
1 pkg. corn chips

In a 9-inch greased pie pan make pie crust by pressing crescent rolls to fit. In skillet, cook ground beef until browned and add chili seasonings; drain. Cover pie crust with crushed corn chips (about 1 C.). Spoon meat over corn chips. Spread sour cream over meat, then the olives. Top with shredded cheddar cheese and more crushed corn chips. Bake at 375° for 20 to 25 minutes. Serve with chopped tomatoes, onion, and shredded lettuce and salsa or picante sauce for topping.

Joanne Gasiel

Homemade Taco Shells

1½ C. cold water
1 C. flour

½ C. cornmeal
1 egg

Beat until smooth. Pour ¼ C. batter into hot skillet and rotate until it forms a 6-inch circle. Cook until edges are brown (1 to 2 minutes). Turn and cook other side. Slide tortilla into 350° oil and immediately fold it in half with tongs, keeping halves about 1-inch apart. Fry until crisp. Makes 12 shells.

Mary Brayton

Taco Corn Bread

1½ lbs. ground beef
1 egg
1 T. instant onion
1 (8 oz.) can tomato sauce

1 pkg. taco seasoning mix
1 (8½ oz.) pkg. cornmeal
    muffin mix

Combine ground beef, egg, onion, tomato sauce, and taco seasoning. Spread on bottom of 10-inch baking dish and bake at 350° for 20 minutes. Prepare cornmeal mix according to directions. Spread over top of beef mixture and continue baking in hot oven (450°) for 15 minutes longer.

Berta Kordick

Tijuana Taxi Torte

1 lb. hamburger
½ C. chopped onion
1 pt. whole tomatoes
16 oz. can herbed tomato sauce
1 (4 oz.) can green chilies

1 env. taco seasoning
8 (6-inch) flour tortillas
8 ozs. cheddar cheese (grated)
Salt & pepper, to taste
1 (8 oz.) carton sour cream

Cook meat and onion; drain grease. Mix tomatoes, herbed sauce, chilies, and taco seasoning in with meat and onions. Simmer for 15 minutes. Place one tortilla in bottom of casserole (greased) dish. Top with ¼ C. meat sauce and a little cheese. Keep repeating to make stack 4 tortillas high (2 stacks). Put any leftover meat sauce around stacks. Bake at 350° for 25 to 30 minutes or until cheese melts. Cut each stack into fourths and top with sour cream.

"This casserole was served at my Cursillo which I made in Granger, Iowa in 1976."

Shirley Bittinger

Meats & Main Dishes

B.B.Q. Sauce

½ C. oil
1 C. catsup
2 T. Worcestershire sauce
2 T. mustard
2 tsp. paprika

2 T. liquid smoke
4 tsp. salt
½ C. vinegar
2 C. brown sugar

Combine ingredients and cook in covered skillet or Dutch oven until thick (20 to 25 minutes). Cook and keep refrigerated until needed. Use with chicken, ham, or ribs. Keeps great!

Verlee Gronemeyer

Bohemian Plum Dumplings

4 medium potatoes
   (1½ C. mashed)
½ tsp. salt
2 eggs

¼ C. Farina
1½ C. flour
12 or more plums (pitted)
Sugar & melted butter

Cook potatoes and drain, then mash and let cool. Then add salt, eggs, Farina, and flour. Mix until all flour has been moistened. Roll on a floured (lightly) board to ½-inch thickness. Cut in 3-inch squares. Place (pitted) plum in center of each square and bring dough up over plum. Roll between floured palms of hands and seal edges. Drop into salted (lightly) boiling water. Cover and steam 12 to 15 mintues. Dumplings will float when done. When cooked sprinkle sugar and melted butter over dumplings. (Reserve a small amount of boiled dumpling water for moisture with sugar and butter.)

Josephine Sitkiewicz

Chili Sauce

1½ gallon tomatoes (cut-up)
2 C. sugar
2 C. vinegar
2 C. chopped onion
1 C. chopped green pepper

½ C. chopped red pepper
1 T. salt
1 tsp. cinnamon
½ tsp. cloves
Just chunks of tomatoes, not
    the juice

Bring all ingredients to a boil and simmer until you have half of what you started with. Fill hot jars and seal. Makes about 6 pints.

Veronica Klug

Cranberry Relish

1 bag fresh cranberries
   (cleaned & sorted)
1 C. sugar

1 orange, including peel
   (washed)

Combine all in food processor and grind until coarse. Serve with turkey. Never fails!

Teresa Pearson

Meats & Main Dishes

Norma's Marinade

½ C. soy sauce
½ C. vinegar
½ C. sugar

1 tsp. garlic powder
1 tsp. cloves
1 tsp. ginger

Mix all ingredients together and marinade overnight.

"This is great on Iowa chops. Makes them juicy and really tender. Norma is my niece from Duluth, Minnesota."

Shirley Bittinger

Potsticker Sauce

½ C. Kikoman Soy Sauce
¼ C. rice or distilled vinegar
2 cloves of garlic (grated)

3 tsp. sesame oil
2-4 drops Tabasco sauce

Combine all ingredients and store in airtight container in refrigerator. Mix well prior to serving. Makes about ⅔ cup.

"Once you have tried this on all your favorite Oriental foods, you'll never go back to plain soy sauce!"

Teresa Pearson

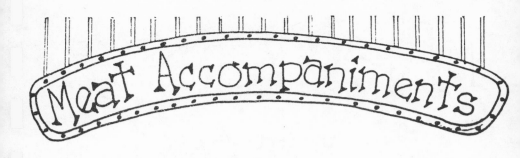

Stuffing

1 (14 oz.) pkg. stuffing cubes
1 lb. sausage (cook & drain)
2 cans chicken broth
 (14½ ozs.)

1 C. chopped onion
1 C. chopped celery
1 stick butter (melted)

Saute' onion and celery in melted butter. Combine all and bake at 350⁰, about 45 minutes. Can be made a day ahead, then baked. May add water chestnuts or walnuts if your kids will eat them.

Teresa Pearson

Instant Stuffing Mix

4 C. large bread crumbs
 or pieces
1 tsp. minced onion
1 tsp. parsley flakes

½ tsp. leaf thyme (crumbled)
¼ tsp. leaf sage (crumbled)
½ tsp. salt
¼ tsp. pepper

Heat bread crumbs in shallow pan in 350⁰ oven for 5 to 10 minutes until dry. Combine balance of ingredients with crumbs. Cover and store at room temperature. This keeps for weeks.

To Use: Melt 3 T. butter or margarine. Stir into crumb mixture. Add ½ to ¾ C. chicken broth, stirring gently. Place in a 1-quart baking dish. Cover and bake at 350⁰ for 30 minutes. Can be varied by adding ¼ C. celery or ¼ C. chopped nuts or 2 T. sesame seeds.

Margaret Tiernan

Meats & Main Dishes

Italian Coating Mix
(For Chicken, Fish & Veal)

4 C. fine bread crumbs
½ C. Romano or Parmesan
  cheese (grated)
½ C. vegetable oil
1 C. chopped parsley

3 small cloves of garlic
  (crushed)
1 tsp. salt
1 tsp. pepper

Combine all ingredients in a large bowl and mix thoroughly. Place in covered container. Keep in refrigerator for 1 week or store in freezer for future use.

To Use: Place 1½ C. in bag, moisten 2½ lbs. cut-up chicken with water. Shake several pieces at a time in bag to coat or dip separately. For chicken, place one layer deep in shallow pan and bake at 400⁰ for 40 minutes until browned and tender.

Margaret Tiernan

Yorkshire Pudding
(Serve with Beef Roast)

1 C. flour
½ tsp. salt

1 C. milk
2 eggs

Beat with rotary beater until just smooth. Bake in a square dish in sizzling hot meat drippings at 450⁰ for 20 minutes. Serve immediately. Serve with beef roast, mashed potatoes and gravy. Pour a little gravy over your Yorkshire pudding. This is actually a "poor man's dish" meant to make a meal that was short on meat go a little further. (This is more like a bread than pudding, as we think of pudding.)

Sheila Algreen

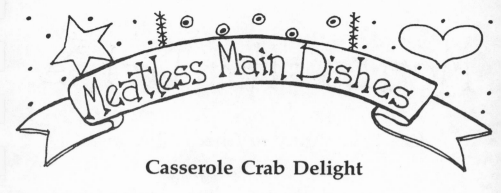

Casserole Crab Delight

1 can King Crab or
   ½ lb. fresh
1 can cream of celery soup
¼ C. milk

1 C. cooked rice
½ C. minced onions
½ C. mayonnaise

Combine all the ingredients together and sprinkle top with crumbs. Bake in a 1½-quart casserole for 40 minutes at 350°. Serves 4. (If recipe is doubled, bake for 1 hour.)

Mary Anne Roby

Chile Relleno Casserole

1 C. Ortega green chiles
   (about 2 (7 oz.) cans)
Jack cheese (grated)
Cheddar cheese (grated)

6 to 8 eggs (beaten)
Cumin
Salt & pepper

Grease or Pam a casserole dish. Layer chiles (split and seeded), handfuls of cheeses, more chiles, ending with cheese. Pour eggs, seasoned with spices, over layered mixture. Bake at 350° for 35 minutes or until set. (If using more chiles, add more cheese and eggs.)

Jeanette Neel

Czech Vareniky or Cheese Buttons

6 C. flour
2 eggs
1 C. warm water

1 C. warm milk
2 tsp. salt
¼ C. Mazola Oil

With fork, beat eggs. Add milk, water, and oil. Add salt to flour and gradually add liquid to flour. Knead on floured surface until smooth. Cover and let stand for at least 15 minutes. While dough is resting, make filling. Can be filled with cottage cheese, fruit or mashed potatoes. Roll dough, cut in squares, and put about a teaspoon of filling in center. Seal edges. Drop in boiling water and cook for about 10 minutes. When done, drain well in strainer. Fry bread crumbs or pieces of the dough in butter. Pour over and serve. Can also be placed in a roaster, put crumbs over, plus a little cream, and heat through. Our favorite is made with cottage cheese.

Shirley Privratsky

Green Rice Casserole

1 C. butter
1 C. onion (chopped)
1 C. celery (chopped)
2 cans cream of mushroom
   soup

1 large jar Cheez Whiz
2 (10 oz.) boxes frozen
   chopped broccoli
3 C. Minute Rice (uncooked)
Salt & pepper

Saute' onion and celery in butter. Mix in soup, Cheez Whiz, and thawed broccoli. Add rice and sauted mixture. Turn into large covered 9x13-inch casserole dish and salt and pepper, to taste. Bake at 375⁰ for 45 minutes.

Nancy T. Emmert

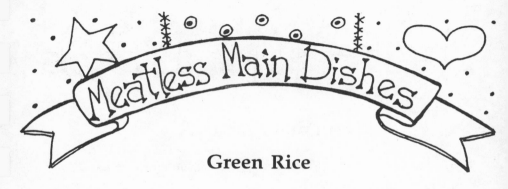

Green Rice

2 C. raw rice
2 C. milk
2 eggs
2 C. shredded cheddar cheese

¾ C. melted butter
1 clove finely chopped garlic
1 C. chopped parsley
1 chopped green pepper

Cook rice and combine all ingredients and mix well. Place in greased casserole and bake for 1 hour at 350°. Serves 10 generously.

Barbara Heck

Ken's Vegetarian Lasagna

14 ozs. cottage cheese
1 C. mozzarella cheese (grated)
1½ C. hard yellow cheese
   (grated)
2 beaten eggs

1 qt. tomatoes
1 can tomato sauce
1 tsp. Italian seasoning
1 pkg. dry onion soup
8 ozs. lasagna noodles.

Mix together cottage cheese, mozzarella cheese, yellow cheese, and eggs. Cook lasagna noodles. Simmer together for 20 minutes the tomatoes, tomato sauce, seasoning, and onion soup. Start layering in a 9x13-inch pan, tomato mixture, noodles, cheese mixture, then repeat. Bake at 350° for 30 minutes.

Sheila Algreen

Meats & Main Dishes

Summer Lasagna

8 ozs. tomato sauce
1 medium onion (chopped)
¼ tsp. basil leaves
¼ tsp. salt (optional)
1/8 tsp. pepper
¼ tsp. oregano leaves
1 C. Ricotta cheese

½ C. shredded mozzarella
  cheese
1 tsp. parsley flakes
3 medium zucchini
  (about 9-inches long)
1 large tomato (sliced)
2 T. grated Parmesan cheese

Combine tomato sauce, onion, basil, salt, pepper, and oregano in a small mixing bowl; set aside. In a medium bowl combine Ricotta, mozzarella, and parsley; set aside. Peel zucchini and cut off ends. Slice zucchini lengthwise into strips. Arrange strips in 8x8-inch baking dish. Cover with wax paper. Microwave at High for 6 to 8 minutes or until fork tender, rearranging after half the time. Drain liquid and place zucchini on paper towel to absorb excess moisture. Let cool slightly. Layer 4 to 6 of the strips in bottom of baking dish. Reserve 6 strips for 2nd layer. Spread Ricotta mixture over zucchini. Layer with sliced tomatoes. Spread half of tomato sauce mixture over tomatoes and top with zucchini slices. Pour remaining sauce over zucchini and sprinkle with Parmesan cheese. Reduce power to 50% (Medium) and microwave, uncovered for 10 to 15 minutes or until zucchini is tender and mixture is hot in center. Let stand for 5 minutes before serving.

Mrs. Albert Hill

Vegetable Lasagna

9 lasagna noodles
1 head of cauliflower
(cut in small pieces)
1 bunch of broccoli
(cut in small pieces)
1 egg
1 (16 oz.) carton small curd
cottage cheese

16 ozs. mozzarella cheese
2 (8 oz.) cans tomato sauce
Garlic
Onion salt
Oregano
Pepper, to taste
1 T. butter

Boil noodles until tender, then drain and rinse. In a small saucepan combine sauce, spices, and butter. Heat until hot and butter is melted. In a bowl beat cottage cheese and egg together. In a 13x9-inch pan place 3 noodles. Sprinkle ⅓ of broccoli and cauliflower. Pour ⅓ of sauce over vegetables. Add ⅓ of cottage cheese mixture over this. Sprinkle ⅓ of mozzarella cheese on top and repeat layers two more times. Cover and bake at 350º for 30 minutes or until vegetables are tender. Uncover and bake for 15 minutes more. Remove from oven and let set for 10 to 15 minutes.

Mary Anne Snyder

Meats & Main Dishes

Oven-Fried Fish

4 fish fillets (1 lb.)
2 C. cornflakes
1 tsp. salt

1/8 tsp. pepper
¼ C. evaporated skim milk
4 tsp. vegetable oil

Preheat oven to 500°. Cut fish into 4 serving pieces, if necessary. Roll cornflakes into fine crumbs. Add salt and pepper. Pour milk into shallow pan and dip fish in milk, then in crumbs. Arrange fish on baking sheet sprayed with vegetable pan spray. Sprinkle oil over fish and bake for 10 minutes.

Rosemary Stuchel

Ken's Meatless Meat Loaf

4 C. cooked rice
3 T. soy sauce
4 T. margarine
2 T. onions
1 C. cooked peas
4 scrambled eggs

6 C. Special K cereal
14 oz. carton cottage cheese
6 beaten eggs
1 pkg. dry onion mix
¼ C. oil

Add soy sauce to cooked rice, then set aside. Brown onion in 2 T. of margarine. Scramble eggs in 2 T. margarine and season to taste with salt and pepper. Mix cooked peas with half of the scrambled eggs. (Save remaining half of eggs for top.) Mix together cereal, cottage cheese, 6 beaten eggs, onion mix, and oil. Mix this with all other ingredients, except for eggs to be spread over top. Bake in 9x13-inch pan at 350° for 1 hour.

Sheila Algreen

Wanda's Macaroni & Cheese

½ lb. elbow macaroni
4 to 6 qts. water
3 tsp. salt
10 ozs. Longhorn style cheddar
cheese

Small amount of cooking oil
2½ C. milk
2 T. flour
½ C. milk

For ½ pound of elbow macaroni, bring 4 to 6 quarts of water to a rapid boil. If desired add 3 tsp. of salt. Slowly add ½ lb. of macaroni. Return to rapid boil, stirring frequently. Boil for 8 to 10 minutes. Use a little cooking oil in the boiling water when cooking macaroni to prevent sticking. Drain when cooked. Use a 2½ -quart casserole for macaroni and cheese. Slice 10 ozs. of Longhorn style cheddar cheese into small pieces. Pour 2½ C. of milk over macaroni and cheese. Add a white sauce of 2 large tablespoons of flour and ½ cup milk. Bake in oven at 350⁰ for 50 minutes.

"This recipe is my eight year old's favorite!"

Pam Palmer

Mostaccioli Supreme

2 (6½ oz.) cans chunk light
  tuna in water
4 eggs (lightly beaten)
2 C. small curd cottage
  cheese
2 C. shredded Monterey Jack
  cheese
⅓ C. sliced green onions,
  including tops
¾ C. dairy sour cream

¼ tsp. salt
¼ tsp. pepper
¼ tsp. ground nutmeg
1 (12 oz.) pkg. mostaccioli
  macaroni (cooked)
⅓ C. grated Parmesan cheese
Paprika & parsley flakes
  for garnish

Drain tuna. Combine eggs, cottage cheese, Jack cheese, onion, sour cream, salt, pepper, and nutmeg. Stir in macaroni and tuna. Pour into buttered 13x9-inch casserole dish. Sprinkle with Parmesan, paprika, and parsley. Cover dish with foil and bake at 350⁰ for 45 minutes. Let set for 10 minutes. Makes 6 to 8 servings.

Kathleen Kordick

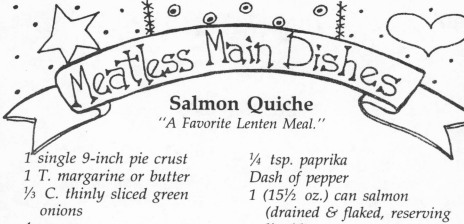

Meatless Main Dishes

Salmon Quiche
"A Favorite Lenten Meal."

1 single 9-inch pie crust
1 T. margarine or butter
⅓ C. thinly sliced green
   onions
4 eggs
½ C. milk
½ tsp. salt

¼ tsp. paprika
Dash of pepper
1 (15½ oz.) can salmon
   (drained & flaked, reserving
   liquid)
6 ozs. (1½ C.) shredded Swiss
   cheese
Parsley

Prepare pie crust and heat oven to 375⁰. In a small skillet, melt margarine or butter and saute' onions until crisp-tender. In a large bowl combine eggs and milk, beating until smooth. Add salt, paprika, pepper, and onions. Mix well. Stir in salmon and all reserved liquid. Sprinkle cheese in bottom of pastry-lined pan. Pour salmon mixture over cheese and bake at 375⁰ for 45 to 50 minutes or until knife inserted in center comes out clean. Let stand 10 minutes before serving. Garnish with parsley.

Hint: Cover edge of pie crust with strip of foil during the last 15 minutes to prevent excessive browning.

Joanne Gasiel

Wild Rice Bake

1 C. cubed cheddar cheese
1 C. Velveeta cheese (cubed)
½ C. minced onion
1 C. wild rice (rinsed)
1 C. black olives (sliced)

2 cans mushrooms (drained)
¼ C. oil
1 can tomatoes (undrained)
1 C. boiling water

In a greased 3-quart casserole layer the following: cheddar cheese, Velveeta, minced onion, wild rice, black olives, mushrooms, and oil. Quarter tomatoes and arrange on top. This can be prepared the night before and refrigerated. Dot with butter, season with salt and pepper. Add 1 C. boiling water before baking. Bake covered at 350° for 1½ hours. Uncover and bake for ½ hour longer. Let rest at least 15 minutes before serving.

Rosemary Stuchel

Pies

Apple Tree
By: Henry Miller

(Reprinted with Permission from the Madison County Historical Society)

Arthur Goshorn, Sr., publisher of the Winterset News, wrote an account of a chance meeting in his early years with Jesse Hiatt. It seems that Goshorn and his father were returning from a trip and met Jesse Hiatt in his wagon on a country road between Winterset and Peru. The account ran as follows:

"Cap't, you know a good apple," said the kindly old man picking an apple from the bottom of the wagon. "Don't you think that is a fine apple? Here is one for the boy too," and he tossed me one that I caught on the fly. While he told father about having discovered a new apple in his orchard and what a remarkable apple it was, I ate the first Delicious apple I ever saw. Mr. Hiatt talked as long as father would listen to him about that apple and we drove on.

"It's a good apple," I said. "Good enough," said father, "but not wonderful. Some tree peddler has sold him that apple tree and he has forgotten it." Hiatt told us that the tree was a sprout that had come up from a tree in his orchard and that he had named it the Hawkeye. "It is the equal of any apple on earth," he said enthusiastically. Several times after that, I saw Mr. Hiatt in Winterset and he always had an apple in his hand and he was talking apple. But he never could interest any local man in the Hawkeye apple. Nobody realized that he had really discovered the equal of any apple that grew.

Swedish Apple Pie

3¾ C. flour
¼ C. sugar
1/8 tsp. salt

1½ C. oleo
½ C. cold water

FILLING:
8 C. sliced apples
1½ C. sugar

1 T. cinnamon

1 egg (slightly beaten)

Combine flour, ¼ C. sugar, and 1/8 tsp. salt in bowl. Cut in oleo until like pie crust. Sprinkle with ½ C. water and make ball. Roll out half of dough to fit 12x18-inch pan. Spread apple-sugar mixture over bottom crust and top with crust; seal edges. Cut slits in top crust and brush with egg mixture. Bake at 425⁰ for 15 minutes. Lower temperature to 350⁰ and bake for 30 minutes more or until light brown. Cut into squares and serve.

Shirley A. Bittinger

Apple Cranberry Pie

3 C. sliced peeled apples
2 C. fresh cranberries
1 C. packed brown sugar
½ C. white sugar

⅓ C. flour
1 tsp. cinnamon
2 T. butter

Combine all ingredients and put in pie crust and bake for 1 hour at 350⁰. You can use pastry strip lattice on top of pie. Or make it a 2-crust pie.

Francis Radke

French Cran-apple Pie

4 C. sliced peeled apples
2 C. fresh or frozen
   cranberries
¾ C. white sugar
¼ tsp. nutmeg

¼ C. flour
¼ C. firmly packed brown
   sugar
½ tsp. cinnamon

TOPPING:
½ C. flour
⅓ C. firmly packed brown
   sugar
¼ tsp. cinnamon

Dash of nutmeg
¼ C. margarine or butter
⅓ C. chopped pecans

Prepare pie crust for 9-inch pie pan. Heat oven to 375⁰. In a large bowl combine apples and cranberries. In a small bowl combine remaining filling ingredients and mix well. Add dry ingredients to fruit and toss to coat. Pour filling into pastry lined pan. In a small bowl combine all topping ingredients, except margarine and pecans. Using pastry blender or fork, cut in margarine until crumbly. Stir in pecans and sprinkle evenly over top of pie. Bake at 375⁰ for 55 minutes or until apples are tender and crust and topping are golden brown. Cover edge of crust with strips of foil after 15 to 20 minutes of baking to prevent excessive browning.

Francis Radke

Basic Cream Pie or Pudding

¾ C. dry milk
⅔ C. white sugar
4 T. cornstarch
1/8 tsp. salt

3 egg yolks
2¼ C. hot water
2 T. oleo
1 tsp. vanilla

For Basic Cream Pie: Put dry ingredients in top of double boiler. Divide 3 eggs. Add 2¼ C. hot water to egg yolks and add to dry ingredients. Cook until thick. Remove from heat and stir in 2 T. oleo and 1 tsp. vanilla.

VARIATIONS:
For Banana Cream Pie: Line cooked pie crust with sliced bananas that have been dipped in lemon juice and water and drained well.

For Coconut Cream Pie: Stir ¾ C. coconut into cream mixture after oleo and vanilla. Sprinkle ¼ C. coconut on top of meringue before baking.

For Chocolate Cream Pie: Sift 3 to 4 T. cocoa into dry ingredients before adding egg yolks and water.

For Butterscotch Cream Pie: Use 1 C. packed brown sugar instead of white sugar and increase cornstarch by 1 T. Also stir in 1 tsp. Mapleine (maple flavoring) as well as vanilla flavoring.

For Raisin Cream Pie: Stir in 1 C. of raisins that have been boiled in 1½ C. water for 2 to 3 minutes. Drain raisins and use water for the water added to egg yolks. (Better raisin flavor.)

For Peanut Butter Pie: Mix ¾ C. powdered sugar with ½ C. peanut butter, using fork until it is all crumbs. Reserve 1 T. of crumbs for top of meringue before baking. Half of the crumbs go on the bottom of the baked shell and the other half of crumbs is added after oleo and vanilla to cooked cream mixture. Pour into baked shell and top with meringue and sprinkle with crumbs and bake.

Shirley and Bud Bittinger

# ☆ Pies ☆

Meringue for Cream Pies

3 egg whites
¼ tsp. salt
⅓ C. sugar

1 T. dry cornstarch
1 tsp. vanilla
½ tsp. cream of tartar

Beat egg whites until frothy and double in size. Sprinkle in ⅓ C. white sugar, mixed with 1 T. dry cornstarch and cream of tartar. Beat until egg whites are stiff and all sugar is dissolved, about 4 to 5 minutes. Add vanilla carefully. Place meringue on top of cream pie and bake at 400° for 12 to 15 minutes, until light brown.

"Bud and Shirley make the pies for the North Side Cafe!"

Shirley and Bud Bittinger

Weepless Meringue

1 T. cornstarch
2 tsp. cold water
½ C. boiling water

3 egg whites
Dash of salt
6 T. sugar

Mix together cornstarch and cold water. Add to ½ C. boiling water. Cook over low heat until it thickens. Set aside to cool. Beat until stiff the egg whites, dash of salt, and sugar. Add cooled cornstarch mixture to beaten egg white mixture. Bake at 350° for 20 minutes or until golden brown.

Anna King

344

Buttermilk Pie

2 C. sugar
1 tsp. cinnamon
1 tsp. nutmeg
1 tsp. vanilla
2 T. cornstarch

¼ lb. (1 stick) melted butter
   or margarine
3 large eggs
1 C. buttermilk

Mix the first 7 ingredients on slow speed until well blended and uniform. Add the buttermilk and mix well. Pour into unbaked 9-inch pie shell and bake at 350° for 40 minutes or until set and brown on top.

Norma Porter

Mom's Cherry Pie

PIE FILLING:
3 cans tart red pitted cherries
1¼ C. sugar

¼ C. flour
¼ tsp. almond extract

PIE CRUST:
2 C. flour
¼ C. cold water

½ C. Wesson Oil
1 tsp. salt

In a large bowl mix the sugar and flour. Add cherries and toss until fruit is coated. Mix in almond extract. To Make Crust: Mix ingredients with fork, divide in 2 and roll each half between waxed paper. Transfer crust into a 9-inch pie plate. Fill with cherry mixture and top with top crust. Seal and flute edge. Brush top with milk. Sprinkle with sugar and cut slits in top crust. Cover edges with foil and bake at 375° for 30 minutes. Remove foil and bake for 20 to 30 more minutes or until the top is golden brown.

Joan Hilton

Chocolate Crusted Pie

CHOCOLATE SHELL:

1¼ C. sifted flour   ½ tsp. salt
⅓ C. sugar   ½ C. shortening
¼ C. cocoa   ½ tsp. vanilla
2 to 3 T. water

VANILLA CHIFFON FILLING:

1 env. gelatin (unflavored)   ¼ C. milk
4 egg yolks (slightly beaten)   1¼ C. milk
⅓ C. sugar   ½ tsp. salt
1 tsp. vanilla   Another ¼ C. sugar
4 egg whites (stiffly beaten)

For Shell. Sift together flour, sugar, cocoa, and salt. Cut in shortening until particles are the size of small peas. Add vanilla. Sprinkle water over mixture, tossing lightly with fork until dough is moist enough to hold together. Roll out on floured board or pastry cloth to an 11 inch circle. Fit pastry loosely into 9-inch pie plate. Fold edge to form standing rim and flute. Prick crust with fork. Place dough "trimmings" in second pie pan and bake at 400° for 8 to 10 minutes. Do not overbake. Cool. Crumble baked, cooled trimming, and save for crumb topping.

For Filling: Soften 1 envelope unflavored gelatin in ¼ C. milk and set aside. Combine 4 egg yolks (slightly beaten), 1¼ C. milk, and ½ tsp. salt. Cook over boiling water until mixture thickens, stirring constantly. Remove from heat and add 1 tsp. vanilla and the softened gelatin. Beat well with rotary beater. Chill until mixture begins to thicken. Beat 4 egg whites until stiff. Beat in ¼ C. sugar gradually. Fold egg whites carefully into cooked egg and gelatin mixture. Pour into cooled, baked shell and let chill for 3 to 5 hours. Top with 1 C. heavy cream, whipped and sweetened (or use 8 ozs. Cool Whip). Sprinkle with the chocolate crumbs

Kathleen Kordick

Coconut Pie - Makes Its Own Crust

4 eggs
1¾ C. sugar
½ C. flour
¼ C. melted butter

2 C. milk
1½ C. coconut
1 tsp. vanilla

Combine in order given. Pour into greased 10-inch pie pan. Bake at 350⁰ for 45 minutes until golden brown. Cool.

Teresa Hoffelmeyer

Fudge Pie

1 C. soft butter
2 C. powdered sugar
4 eggs
1 baked pie shell

4 sqs. chocolate (melted)
1 tsp. vanilla
½ tsp. salt

Cream butter and sugar until very light and fluffy. Add eggs, 1 at a time, beating thoroughly after each addition. Add chocolate, slightly cooled and beat thoroughly. Add vanilla and salt. Pour into baked pie shell and refrigerate at least 4 hours. Serve with whipped cream or Cool Whip.

Margaret Tiernan

Pies

Lemon Pie

Pastry shell
5 eggs
1½ C. sugar
1 C. Half & Half
¼ C. margarine (melted)
3 T. lemon juice

2 tsp. finely shredded
  lemon peel
1 T. flour
1 T. cornmeal
1½ tsp. vanilla

Prepare pastry shell and line bottom with foil. Bake at 450⁰ for 5 minutes. Do not prick pastry. Only partially bake shell. Beat eggs lightly, just until mixed. Stir in sugar, Half & Half, melted margarine, lemon peel, lemon juice, flour, cornmeal, and vanilla. Mix well and pour into partially baked shell. Cover edges with foil and bake at 350⁰ for 25 minutes. Remove foil and bake for 20 minutes more, until knife inserted in center comes out clean. Cool and serve with whipped cream.

Ann Winjum

Millionaire Pie

1 (8 oz.) can crushed
  pineapple
1 (8 oz.) pkg. cream cheese
1½ C. powdered sugar

1 (8 oz.) carton Cool Whip
⅔ C. chopped pecans
1 (9-inch) baked pie shell

Drain pineapple. Cream together cream cheese and sugar. Fold in ½ carton Cool Whip and pineapple. Add nuts, reserving 2 T. for top. Put into baked crust and top with remaining half of Cool Whip. Top with chopped nuts and chill for 3 to 4 hours.

Irene Kelly

Lemon Meringue Pie

1 baked pie shell
1⅓ C. sugar
½ C. cornstarch
¼ tsp. salt
1¾ C. water

4 eggs (separated)
2 T. butter or margarine
1 T. lemon rind
½ C. lemon juice (4 lemons)

MERINGUE:
4 egg whites
¼ tsp. cream of tartar

½ C. sugar

Combine 1⅓ C. sugar, cornstarch, and salt in saucepan. Gradually stir in water. Cook over medium heat, stirring constantly until mixture comes to a boil. Boil for 1 minute, then remove from heat. Beat egg yolks slightly in a small bowl. Slowly mix in about ½ C. of the hot cornstarch mixture. Slowly stir back into remaining mixture. Cook, stirring constantly for 2 minutes over low heat. Remove from heat and stir in butter and lemon juice. Pour into pie shell. Beat egg whites with cream of tartar until soft peaks form, then add sugar a little bit at a time until firm peaks form. Put meringue on top of pie and bake in hot oven (400⁰) for 10 minutes. Best served cold.

"Our children always ask for a birthday pie instead of cake and this is the pie they always ask for."

Linda Hermanstorfer

Pies

Mincemeat for Pies

3 bowls ground meat
1 bowl suet
2 bowls raisins
2 bowls vinegar
2 bowls beef broth
5 bowls apples
1 bowl molasses

2 bowls white sugar
2 bowls brown sugar
4 T. cinnamon
1 T. salt
1 T. cloves
1 T. nutmeg

Cook meat and grind. Add other ingredients and cook for a few minutes. I put in plastic containers and put in freezer or you can can it in jars. (Note: 1 bowl equals 1½ C.)

"This was an old Pitzer church recipe that they made and sold for years."

Katherine Hartman

Peanut Butter Pie

2 (3 oz.) pkgs. cook & serve
  vanilla pudding
4 C. milk
½ C. creamy peanut butter

¾ C. confectioner's sugar
1 (9-inch) pie shell (baked)
Whipped cream

In a saucepan cook pudding and milk over medium heat until thickened and bubbly. Remove from heat and cool. In a bowl cut peanut butter and confectioner's sugar together with fork until crumbs form. Set aside about 3 T. crumbs and pour the remainder into pie shell. Pour pudding over crumbs and chill until set. Top with whipped cream sprinkled with remaining crumbs

Barb Schmitz

Mock Pecan Pie

¾ C. sugar
¾ C. corn syrup
¾ C. oatmeal
1 unbaked pie shell

2 eggs
⅓ C. soft margarine
1 tsp. vanilla

Mix all together and pour into unbaked pie shell. Bake at 350⁰ for 35 to 40 minutes.

Margaret Tiernan

Southern Pecan Pie

1 C. white Karo syrup
¾ C. sugar (white)
3 large eggs
2 T. melted butter
1 C. pecans (coarsely chopped)

4 T. orange juice
4 T. grated orange rind
8-inch unbaked pie crust
Whipped cream

Beat eggs slightly. Add sugar, syrup, juice, and rind. Stir in butter. Spread pecans over pie shell and pour filling over them. Bake at 350⁰ for 45 minutes. You might prefer just a little less orange juice.

Maxine Brunsmann

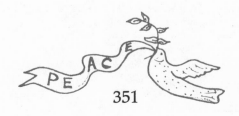

351

 ☆ Pies ☆

Amana Pumpkin Pie

1 (9-inch) pastry shell
1 C. honey
1 C. sour cream
2 T. pumpkin pie spice or
   1 tsp. cinnamon, ½ tsp.
   ginger & ¼ T. cloves

1½ C. cooked or canned
   pumpkin
½ tsp. salt
1 T. cornstarch
3 eggs (slightly beaten)
½ C. coarsely chopped walnuts

Preheat oven to 400°. In a large bowl blend until smooth the honey, sour cream, pumpkin, spice, salt, and cornstarch. Fold in slightly beaten eggs and turn into pastry shell. Sprinkle walnuts over top and bake for 45 to 55 minutes or until knife inserted near center comes out clean.

Joanne Gasiel

Pumpkin Pie Maletas

9-inch pie shell (unbaked)
2 eggs (beaten)
2 C. pumpkin
1 C. sugar
1½ C. milk

½ tsp. salt
¾ tsp. cinnamon
½ tsp. ginger
¼ tsp. allspice
¼ tsp. cloves

Combine all ingredients and pour into pie shell and bake in moderate oven until shell is light brown and pumpkin has set.

"This recipe has been my favorite given by a neighbor lady and is always good!"

Elma Tracy

Rhubarb Custard Pie

1 unbaked crust
2 eggs (lightly beaten)
2 T. milk (optional)
1½ C. sugar

3 T. flour
½ tsp. nutmeg
3 C. rhubarb
1 T. butter

Mix egg and milk together. Stir in the flour, sugar, nutmeg, and rhubarb. Pour into unbaked shell and dot with butter. Cover with lattice top crust and bake until brown at 400°.

Mrs. Albert Hill

Georgia Waller's Sour Cream Raisin Pie

1 egg
1 C. sugar
1 C. sour cream
1 T. vinegar

1 tsp. nutmeg
1 tsp. cinnamon
1½ to 2 C. dark raisins (soak in water & check for stems)

Add vinegar to sour cream. Stir in sugar and beaten egg. Add the spices and raisins. Put in a pie shell and bake at 350° for 45 minutes to 1 hour (until it sets up). (I lattice the top.) To brown top put under broiler a few minutes.

Variation: Of late I've been substituting Egg Beaters for the egg and using lite sour cream. Tastes about the same (not quite as rich) but better for you.

"This was my grandmother Wiedemeier's sour cream raisin pie and it has become a HOLIDAY MUST in our family!!"

Pies

Sour Cream Raisin Pie

½ C. water
1 C. sugar
1 C. sour cream
3 egg yolks
1 tsp. vanilla

1 C. raisins
1 C. sweet milk
Pinch of salt
2 large tsp. flour

Boil raisins in water for 15 minutes. Mix flour and sugar together. Add milk, cream, and beaten egg yolks. Cook slowly until thick. Add vanilla and cooked raisins. Put in a baked pie shell and cover with meringue.

Mary Lou Foley

Sour Cream Raisin Pie

1 whole egg or 2 yolks
1 C. sour cream
½ C. sugar
2 T. flour

¾ tsp. cinnamon
½ tsp. nutmeg
2 C. seedless raisins
   (uncooked)

Mix everything together and put in unbaked pie crust. Bake at 350° for about 40 minutes.

Mrs. Albert Hill

Strawberry Pie

2½ C. boiling water
1½ C. sugar
5 T. cornstarch

2 pkgs. strawberry Jello
½ C. boiling water
1 baked pie shell

Cook the first 3 ingredients until thick and boiling. Remove from heat and add 2 pkgs. Jello which have been dissolved in ½ C. boiling water. Let cool, then add 1½ pt. fresh strawberries. Pour into pie shell and let cool in refrigerator for 1 hour or more.

Patsy Bence

Strawberry Parfait Pie

1 (3 oz.) pkg. strawberry Jello
1¼ C. hot water

1 pt. vanilla ice cream
1 graham cracker crust

Dissolve Jello in hot water in a 2-quart saucepan. Add ice cream by spoonfuls, stirring until melted. Pour into pie crust and chill until firm. Dot with Cool Whip.

Bev Maxwell

355

Pies

Pecan Strawberry Pie

MERINGUE CRUST:

3 egg whites
¼ tsp. baking powder
1 C. sugar
1 tsp. vanilla

12 soda crackers
  (finely crushed)
½ C. broken pecans

FILLING:

1 pt. fresh or 16 ozs. frozen
  strawberries
½ lb. marshmallows

½ pt. heavy cream (whipped)
Few drops of red food coloring
  (optional)

For Crust: Beat egg whites and baking powder until frothy and soft peaks form. Add sugar gradually, beating until whites are stiff and glossy; add vanilla. Fold in cracker crumbs and coarsely chopped pecans. Spread in buttered 9 or 10-inch pie plate, building up sides to form shell. Bake at 325⁰ for 30 minutes. Cool.

For Filling: If using fresh strawberries, wash, hull, mash, and sweeten. Allow to stand while preparing crust, then drain reserving juice. Or, thaw and drain frozen berries, reserving juice. Heat ½ C. strawberry juice and add marshmallows. Cook, stirring until marshmallows are melted. Chill until partially set. Fold whipped cream and berries into marshmallows. Add a few drops food coloring, if desired. Pile into cooked crust and chill until serving time. Garnish with whole berries.

Kathleen Kordick

Toll House Pie

2 eggs
½ C. flour
½ C. white sugar
½ C. packed brown sugar
Whipped cream or ice cream

1 C. melted butter
(cooled to room temp.)
1 (6 oz.) pkg. chocolate chips
Unbaked pie shell

Preheat oven to 325⁰. In a large bowl beat eggs until foamy. Beat in flour, white sugar, and brown sugar until until well blended. Blend in melted butter. Stir in chocolate chips. Pour into pie shell. Bake at 325⁰ for approximately 1 hour. Very rich! Serve with ice cream or whipped cream. (Can use a top crust, if desired.)

Harriet Nevins

Frozen Pie Crusts

4 C. flour
¾ C. Crisco
1 T. sugar
1 T. salt

1 egg (slightly beaten)
½ C. water
1 T. vinegar

Mix flour, Crisco, sugar, and salt together. Mix egg, water, and vinegar together. Mix with flour mixture and stir until smooth and pliable. Can be divided into 5-6 portions and shaped into balls, placed in plastic bag, flattened, and frozen for future use. When needed, remove from freezer, thaw, and roll as for any pie dough. The beauty of this dough is that it never gets tough.

"My favorite time saver!"

Margaret Tiernan

Heavenly Pie Crust

2 to 2½ C. flour
⅔ to 1 C. lard

6 to 7 T. cold water
1 tsp. salt

Blend lard, flour, and salt in bowl until it becomes crumbly. Add water, a little at a time until you can form a ball. Flour your working area well. Place dough on this and flour again. Roll very gently until 1/8-inch thick. It's very important to not handle the crust very much. Add flour to the rolling pin if you have trouble. Place in pie plate and trim edges. Add your favorite filling. Wet the rim of crust with water. Top with next crust, seal edges together, and flute. Take a knife and put slits in top and sprinkle with sugar. Bake at 375⁰ for 1 hour. Fillings may vary.

I grew up on a farm, and as you know, all farm wives are GOOD cooks. My mom was one of the best! As a little girl, I remember being by her side in the kitchen, watching when she made all kinds of good things, especially pie.

My mom and I had only twenty years together. She was my best friend and I have many loving memories of her for which I feel very fortunate. I felt that my life was only beginning when she died and there was so much more I wanted to share with her, but that was not God's will.

One day, not long after Mom had died, I tried to make an apple pie to cheer up Dad. As it baked, the crust didn't bake down with the filling, so when I cut it - it crumbled! I ended up with lots of tough crust and very little apple filling. Needless to say, it wasn't Mom's.

I didn't attempt to bake another pie until after I married Gary. Being a new bride, I wanted a perfect pie just like Mom's. As I was adding the ingredients and remembering my mom's perfect crusts, I was becoming more and more frustrated and upset. I just couldn't seem to get it to the right consistency and I could feel tears beginning to sting my eyes. Then, suddenly, it was as though my mom was right beside me and my hands became hers. What a warm, loving, indescribable feeling.

That night as we were eating dessert, Gary just couldn't get over how someone as young as I could make such a flaky pie crust. I knew, however, that it really wasn't someone so young. Thanks Mom!

Nancy T. Emmert

Pastry for Two-Crust Pie

1 C. shortening (I use ½ lard
  & ½ Crisco, but you can
  use all Crisco)

3 C. flour
1 tsp. salt (scant)
12 T. cold water

Add shortening and flour to salt. Mix with fingers, then add water until flour is damp. Turn on lightly floured board and roll out. Bake at 350º.

"I could not make good pie crust, but this one never fails for me."

Martha Street

Pie Crust

1½ C. flour
1 tsp. baking powder
½ tsp. salt

5 T. lard or shortening
4 T. water

Mix flour, baking powder, and salt. Add lard, just until crumbly. Add water and roll out on floured surface. Should be enough for one 9-inch double pie crust or two single crust.

Mrs. Albert Hill

Pies

Crumb Crust

1 C. flour   1/4 C. sugar
1 stick oleo (cold)

Put flour and sugar in a small mixing bowl. Cut in cold oleo. Beat together with mixer until all is in fine crumbs. Press into pie pan and bake until light golden brown. This works well for cream/pudding pies.

Ruth Eivins

Crumble Pie Crust

1 C. flour   1/2 C. nuts or coconut or
1/4 C. brown sugar   a combination of both
1/2 C. butter

Mix and spread in a 9x13-inch pan. Bake at 350° for 15 minutes. Remove from oven and stir immediately. Press crumbs into a 9-inch pie plate. Reserve 3/4 C. of crumbs for topping on pie. This crust can be used with all cream pies.

Jill Kordick

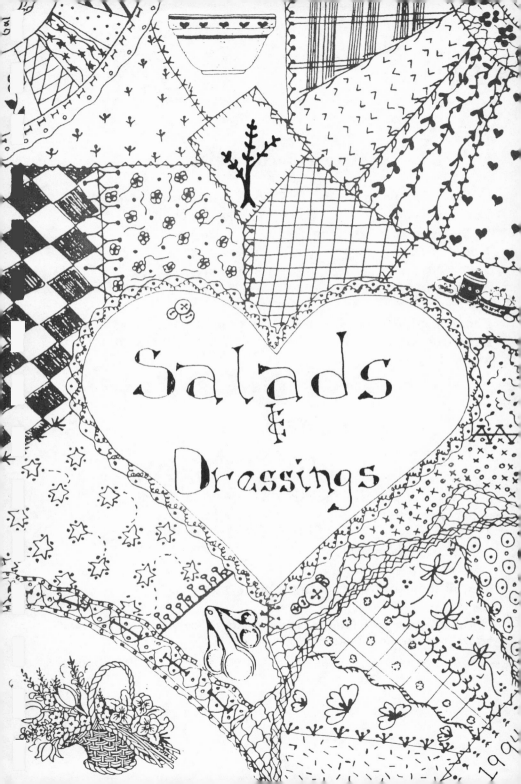

Salads
&
Drassings

Salads & Dressings

Apple Bacon Salad

¼ tsp. garlic powder
⅔ C. oil
½ lb. bacon (fried & crumbled)
1 head of lettuce (torn)
3 red apples (sliced)
2 tsp. lemon juice

½ C. grated Parmesan cheese
3 green onions (sliced)
1 C. croutons
½ tsp. pepper
¼ tsp. salt
1 egg (use egg substitute)

Combine oil, lemon juice, and garlic powder. Stir in apples. Add remaining ingredients and toss until all traces of egg disappear. Makes 8 servings.

Barbara Heck

Apple Salad

5 apples (not peeled) (cored & cut into small pieces)
15 large dates (pitted & chopped)

1 C. seedless grapes (cut in half)
1½ C. Cool Whip

Mix all the above together for a quick salad.

"I make this salad for holiday potlucks or family get-togethers - easy to fix and gets a great reception at meals."

Doris Dolton

Apple Salad

1 (20 oz.) can pineapple chunks
2 qts. chopped apples
2 C. halved seedless grapes

1¼ C. nuts (try cashews)
1 C. chopped celery

DRESSING:
¼ C. butter
¼ C. sugar
1 T. lemon juice

2 T. cornstarch
1 C. mayonnaise

Drain pineapple, reserve the juice, and set chunks aside. Prepare the dressing. In a small saucepan combine the pineapple juice, butter, sugar, and lemon juice. Bring to a boil over medium heat. In a small bowl, combine the cornstarch and enough water to make a smooth mixture. Remove juice mixture from heat and add cornstarch mixture to the bubbling juice. Return to burner, reduce heat, and cook until mixture is thick and smooth. Chill. Whisk in the mayonnaise. (This can be done a day in advance.) Place the pineapple chunks in a large bowl and add the rest of the salad ingredients. Toss well, then add the chilled dressing.

Maureen Roach

Cinnamon Apple Salad

2 (3 oz.) pkgs. lemon Jello
½ C. red cinnamon candies
2 C. unsweetened applesauce
1 T. lemon juice
Dash of salt

½ C. broken walnuts
2 (3 oz.) pkg. cream cheese
¼ C. milk
2 T. mayonnaise

Dissolve Jello and cinnamon candies in 3 C. of boiling water. Stir in applesauce, lemon juice, and salt. Chill until partially set. Blend softened cream cheese, milk, and mayonnaise together. Add to Jello mixture on low speed. Stir in walnuts and chill until firm.

Debby Corkrean

Candied Apples

1½ C. sugar
1½ C. water
Few drops of red food coloring

2 sticks cinnamon or more
4 or 5 apples or more
depending on size

Use pan where you can put apple slices in one row. Cook apples and prick with fork to see if they are done. Take out and add next batch.

"I like these for the holidays. They are old fashioned."

Martha Street

Blueberry Salad

2 (3 oz.) pkgs. grape or
   blackberry Jello
1 (16 oz.) can crushed
   pineapple (don't drain)

1 (16 oz.) can blueberry pie
   filling
2 C. boiling water

TOPPING:
1 (8 oz.) pkg. cream cheese
1 (8 oz.) carton sour cream
½ C. sugar

1 tsp. vanilla
1 C. chopped pecans

Mix the Jello, pineapple, pie filling, and water until dissolved. Pour
in a 9x13-inch dish to congeal overnight.

For Topping: Using a mixer combine the cream cheese, sour cream,
sugar, and vanilla. Spread this over the salad and sprinkle pecans
on the top.

Pam Palmer

Marie's Broccoli Salad

2 bunches broccoli
1 small red onion
8 ozs. shredded mozzarella
   cheese

1 small jar bacon bits
1 C. mayonnaise
½ C. sugar
2 T. red wine vinegar

Chop broccoli and onions. Mix all ingredients together and let set for 1 hour or preferably overnight.

"This recipe was given to me by Karey Miner McCauley's mother who lives in Maryland."

Mildred Waltz

Broccoli Salad

1 head of broccoli
½ C. raisins

6 slices crisp bacon
¼ C. salted peanuts

DRESSING:
½ C. mayonnaise
½ C. sour cream

2 T. sugar
3 T. prepared mustard

Cut broccoli into small pieces and add raisins, bacon, and peanuts. Mix together dressing and stir in broccoli mixture. Refrigerate.

Phyllis Patrick

Broccoli Cauliflower Salad

4-6 small green onions
1 bunch fresh broccoli
1 head of cauliflower
1 (10 oz.) pkg. frozen
    petite peas
1½ C. mayonnaise

1 C. plain yogurt
1 T. garlic powder or
    1 T. powdered dill weed
2 T. sugar
1 tsp. salt

Cut veggies into bite-sized pieces and place in bowl. Mix together mayonnaise, yogurt, garlic powder, sugar, and salt; add to vegetables. Cover and refrigerate overnight before serving. Makes approximately 8 servings.

Margaret Tiernan

Broccoli Slaw

¼ C. oil
⅓ C. cider vinegar
½ C. sugar
1 bag broccoli slaw
1 bunch green onions (chopped)

1 pkg. chicken flavored Roman
    noodles (uncooked)
1 C. cashews
1 C. sunflower seeds

To make dressing: Mix the oil, cider vinegar, and sugar together with the powder packet from the noodles.

Break-up noodles and toss with the broccoli and onion. Pour the dressing over this. Add the cashews and sunflower seeds about 1 hour before serving.

Bev Maxwell

Cauliflower-Pea Salad

1 medium head cauliflower
1 medium onion
1½ C. frozen peas
1 C. plain yogurt (or cream)

1 tsp. salt
½ tsp. pepper
2 tsp. dill weed

Break cauliflower into small pieces. Add diced onion and partially thawed peas. Combine all other ingredients and pour over veggies, stirring until all are well coated. Put in covered bowl and refrigerate for 24 hours before serving.

Margaret Tiernan

Cherry Salad

2 C. dark sweet cherries
  (drained)
1 C. pineapple tidbits
  (drained)
½ C. pecans
2 T. sugar

6 T. juice (3 lemon,
  3 pineapple)
4 T. butter
½ lb. marshmallows
1 C. cream (whipped)

Combine cherries, pecans, and pineapple. Make a dressing by combining sugar, eggs, lemon, pineapple juice, and butter. Cook until thick in top of a double boiler, stirring constantly. Remove from heat and stir in the marshmallows until partly melted. When cool, stir in fruit and nut mixture. Fold in whipped cream and chill for several hours before serving.

Harriet Nevins

Holiday Fair Cherry Salad

1 (3 oz.) box cherry Jello
1 C. boiling water
1 can cherry pie filling

1 to 1½ C. crushed pineapple
   (drained)
Coconut

Combine Jello and water, stirring until dissolved. Add cherry pie filling and pineapple. Chill in refrigerator until set, stirring once in awhile. Garnish the top with flaked coconut. Use a medium salad bowl. It makes about 1-quart. If you want a larger salad, just double the ingredients.

Dorothy Hochstetler

Chicken-Rice Salad

2 C. cooked chicken or turkey
1 C. cooked rice (cooked in
   chicken broth) (drain & chill)
1 (16 oz.) can bean sprouts
   (drained)
1 C. chopped celery
1 C. coarsely shredded carrots

2 T. chopped green pepper
2 T. soy sauce
¼ C. French dressing
¼ tsp. salt (optional)
¼ C. mayonnaise
1 C. frozen peas

Combine all ingredients, except mayonnaise and peas. Chill and just before serving, toss with mayonnaise and still frozen peas. Serves 8 to 10.

"Because of it's simple ingredients and capacity to serve several people with a small amount of meat, this salad, along with some dry crackers and a small bit of fruit, was presented at a women's meeting as a "meager meal" to call attention to the plight of the hungry people of the world. We all liked the salad so much we asked for the recipe."

Jean Gillespie

Chinese Chicken Salad

3 C. lettuce
1½ C. chopped chicken
1 (8 oz.) can water chestnuts
½ C. julienne carrots

¼ C. sliced green onions
¼ C. chopped red cabbage
¼ C. frozen pea pods
(optional)

DRESSING:
3½ T. soy sauce
2 T. rice vinegar
2 T. vegetable oil
1 T. sugar

½ tsp. garlic powder
½ tsp. pepper
1 can Chow Mein noodles

Mix all salad dressing ingredients together and toss at serving with the Chow Mein noodles. Serves 4.

Joanne Nichols

Chicken Salad for 25

2½ qts. small cubes, cooked
  chicken (3½-4 lbs. chicken)
5 C. fine celery (diced)
1 oz. lemon juice or
  more, to taste
2 C. mayonnaise or
  more to taste

Salt, to taste
1 (10 oz.) jar salad type green
  olives (drained & chopped)
1 (4 oz.) jar diced pimento
  (optional)
¼ lb. toasted blanched
  almonds

Mix in order given and refrigerate 2 to 3 hours before serving. Keep cold!!!

Ruth Cunningham

Special Chicken Salad

2 C. diced chicken or turkey
½ C. chopped celery
½ C. chopped cashews
¼ C. thinly sliced quartered
   radishes
2 T. chopped green onions

2 T. pimentos (chopped)
1 tsp. seasoned salt
⅔ C. Miracle Whip
1 T. lemon juice
   (fresh or frozen)
1 tsp. dill weed

Mix all ingredients together well and chill at least 4 hours before serving.

"This special salad was served at a Cursillo I helped with in Des Moines in 1980. Also used for daughter Sheryl's wedding at St. Joseph in Winterset, June 1978 and at Shirley and Bud's 25th wedding anniversary, September 28, 1993."

Shirley Bittinger

Chicken Salad

5 C. chopped cooked chicken
1 C. pineapple tidbits
1 C. water chestnuts (sliced)
1 C. sliced celery
½ C. slivered almonds

4 T. chutney
1 C. sour cream
1 C. mayonnaise
1 tsp. curry powder

Combine chicken, pineapple, water chestnuts, celery, and almonds. Chill. Combine chutney, sour cream, mayonnaise, and curry powder. Stir into chicken mixture.

Ann Winjum

Christmas Salad

1 (14 oz.) can sweetened
condensed milk
1 (21 oz.) can cherry pie
filling
8 ozs. marshmallows (miniature)

1 (No. 202) can crushed
pineapple (drained)
1 (No. 202) carton of
Cool Whip

Mix pie filling, pineapple, and condensed milk together. Add marshmallows and finally fold in Cool Whip. Chill and serve. Can be frozen and served this way. (Optional: Can add a few drops of red food coloring for darker red color.)

Kathy Thompson
Ruth Cunningham

Cold Fruit Compote

1 lb. dark pitted sweet cherries
1 lb. sliced peaches (drained)
1 (12 oz.) pkg. dried apricots
½ C. orange juice

¼ C. lemon juice
1 T. grated orange peel
1 T. lemon peel
¾ C. brown sugar

Place cherries with juice into 1½-quart casserole dish. Add peaches, apricots, orange juice, lemon juice, and grated peels. Sprinkle with brown sugar and bake, covered at 350⁰ for 1½ hours. Cool and refrigerate overnight. Serves 10.

Fonda Bass

Kentucky Fried Chicken Cole Slaw

⅓ C. sugar
½ tsp. salt
1/8 tsp. pepper
¼ C. milk
½ C. mayonnaise

¼ C. buttermilk
1½ T. white vinegar
2½ T. lemon juice
1 whole cabbage (chopped fine)
1 medium carrot (chopped)

Mix together the first 8 ingredients. Add to chopped cabbage and carrot. Chill for 2 hours.

Violet Brunner

Cranberry-Raspberry Salad

1 (6 oz.) pkg. raspberry Jello
2 C. boiling water
1 (16 oz.) can whole berry
   cranberry sauce
½ C. pecans

2 (10 oz.) pkg. frozen sliced
   strawberries (thawed)
Lettuce leaves
Whipped topping

Put Jello in a large mixing bowl. Pour in boiling water and stir until dissolved. Add cranberry sauce and break-up pieces with a spoon. Add strawberries and pecans. Stir well and pour into a 6-cup mold. Cover and refrigerate overnight. Unmold by dipping in warm water for a few seconds. Put on plate with lettuce leaves on it. Serve with whipped topping.

Harriet Nevins

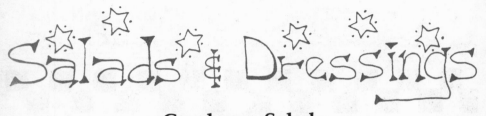

Salads & Dressings

Cranberry Salad

4 C. cranberries
1 (16 oz.) can crushed
  pineapple
2 C. sugar

¼ tsp. cinnamon
¼ tsp. allspice
¾ C. water

Cook all ingredients until thickened. Cool and serve at your next holiday meal!

Cindy Watson Pottebaum

Crunchy Salad

1 lb. cabbage (chopped) (can
  use packaged cole slaw mix)
5 T. chopped green onions

½ C. sunflower seeds
1 pkg. chicken Ramen noodles
½ C. slivered almonds

DRESSING:
2 T. wine vinegar
½ C. vegetable oil
2 T. sugar

Seasoning from Ramen
  noodle package

Crush noodles and brown in a little butter with the sunflower seeds and almonds. Just before serving toss cabbage, seeds, almonds, noodles, and onions with dressing.

Barbara Heck

Cucumber Salad

4 cucumbers (peeled & sliced)   1 medium onion (sliced)

MIX:
1½ C. Miracle Whip   ½ C. vinegar
½ C. sugar   Salt & pepper, to taste

Cover cucumbers and onions with Miracle Whip mixture. Let sit overnight in covered plastic bowl in refrigerator before eating.

Pam Palmer

Delicious Rice Salad

1 C. rice   2 C. Cool Whip
2 C. water   2 pkgs. frozen strawberries or
3 C. milk   raspberries
1 C. sugar   2 T. cornstarch

Cook the rice in the water until water is gone. Add the milk and sugar. Cook until it is absorbed by the rice. Cool completely. Add 2 C. Cool Whip. Mix the thawed strawberries or raspberries and the cornstarch. Boil until thick and clear. Cool well. Cover rice and refrigerate until ready to serve.

Shirley Privratsky

Frozen Banana Salad

2 (3 oz.) pkgs. cream cheese
½ tsp. salt
½ C. mayonnaise
1 C. sugar
2 T. lemon juice
½ C. crushed pineapple

2 sliced bananas
½ C. walnuts
½ C. maraschino cherries
  (cut in fourths)
2 C. Cool Whip

Mix cream cheese, salt, mayonnaise, sugar, and lemon juice. Beat well. Add bananas, pineapple, nuts, and cherries. Fold in Cool Whip, pour into 8-inch cake pan, and freeze. When ready to serve, softened slightly, slice, and serve on lettuce leaf.

Berta Kordick

Frozen Fruit Salad

1 can peaches
1 can pineapple
1 can mandarin oranges
Maraschino cherries

1 pkg. miniature marshmallows
1 medium carton Cool Whip
1 large box vanilla pudding
Nuts

Drain fruit and reserve 1½ C. juice. Cook pudding using fruit juice until thick. Add marshmallows. Cool and add fruit, nuts, and Cool Whip. Can freeze until ready to serve.

Katherine Hartman

Fruit Salad

1 can crushed pineapple
1 can mandarin oranges
1 box orange Jello
1 box tapioca pudding

1 box vanilla pudding
¾ C. miniature marshmallows
1 (8 oz.) carton Cool Whip

Drain juices from fruit and add water to make 3 cups of liquid. Add Jello and pudding; cook until it thickens. Cool. Add fruit, marshmallows, and Cool Whip. Refrigerate until set.

Ethel Lamb

6 Cup Fruit Salad

1 C. pineapple bits
1 C. coconut
1 C. seedless grapes (halved)

1 C. mandarin oranges
1 C. maraschino cherries
1 C. Cool Whip

Mix all ingredients together and refrigerate until ready to serve.

"This goes great with holiday meals and takes little time to prepare. Looks fancy and great for holiday get-to-gethers when you don't have a lot of time. At big family meals you may want to double the recipe."

Doris Dolton

Salads & Dressings

Green Goddess Salad

DRESSING:

1 C. mayonnaise
⅓ C. chopped parsley
3 T. anchovy paste
1 T. lemon juice

⅓ C. sour cream
3 T. finely chopped chives
3 T. tarragon vinegar
Dash of freshly ground pepper

SALAD:

1 head of romaine lettuce
1 head of curly endive

1 C. croutons
½ C. sliced black olives

Combine all dressing ingredients and chill at least 2 hours. Combine lettuce, endive, olives, and croutons with dressing just before serving. Makes 12 servings.

Barbara Heck

Green Pea Salad

1 can peas (drained)
½ C. diced sweet Gherkins
   pickles
1 or 2 sliced hard-boiled eggs

Salad dressing (Miracle Whip)
¾ C. diced cheese
   (Velveeta or cheddar)

Mix altogether with salad dressing (to your taste). Chill and serve.

Josephine Sitkiewicz

Gum Drop Salad

DRESSING:
1 C. sugar
1 T. vinegar
1/8 tsp. salt

¾ C. pineapple juice
4 T. flour
1 C. whipped cream

SALAD:
½ lb. miniature marshmallows
½ lb. small gum drops
  (cut in two or sliced)
½ C. nutmeats

1 lb. red & white seedless
  grapes (halved)
1 small bottle maraschino
  cherries (halved)

For Dressing: Blend sugar, flour, and salt. Add liquids and cook in double boiler until thick. Cool. Fold in whipped cream.

For Salad: Add salad ingredients to cooled dressing and refrigerate. This salad can be made one day ahead of serving time.

Margaret Tiernan

Holiday Fruit Compote

1 lb. mixed dried fruit
¾ C. small pearl tapioca
6 C. water (divided)
5 apples (peeled & cubed)

1 C. sugar
Ground cinnamon
Ground cloves

Place fruit, tapioca, and 4 C. water in large saucepan. Cover and let stand overnight. The next day, add apples, sugar, and 2 C. water. Bring to a boil. Add a dash of cinnamon and cloves to your taste. Reduce heat and simmer for 45 to 60 minutes until tapioca is transparent. Can be served warm or cold.

Fonda Bass

Macaroni-Broccoli Salad

1 C. Miracle Whip salad
   dressing
1/8 C. chopped parsley
1 tsp. dry basil
1 garlic clove (crushed)

1 (8 oz.) pkg. mild cheddar
   cheese
2 C. cooked broccoli
1 C. colored macaroni
2 medium raw tomatoes

Cook the macaroni and cool. Add cooked broccoli, parsley, basil, garlic, and salad dressing and mix. Put tomatoes and cheese on top. Chill and stir before serving.

Mrs. Albert Hill

Macaroni Salad

1 C. mayonnaise
½ C. Carnation milk
¾ C. sugar
½ C. vinegar

8 ozs. curly macaroni
Chopped green peppers
3 carrots (shredded)
1 can ripe black olives (sliced)

Cook and drain the macaroni. Add the desired amount of green pepper, the carrots, and olives. Mix the mayonnaise, Carnation milk, sugar, and vinegar. Mix well with the macaroni mixture and let set overnight. Will keep up to 2 weeks in the refrigerator.

Sue Finnell

Mandarin Orange Sherbet Salad

1 large pkg. orange Jello
1 pt. orange sherbet
1 can mandarin oranges

2 bananas (sliced)
1 C. whipping cream
  (whipped)

Dissolve Jello in 2 C. boiling water. Add sherbet (that has been removed from freezer for 5 to 10 minutes) and stir until dissolved. Chill until partly set. Add the whipped cream and fruit. Mix thoroughly and pour into 9x13-inch pan and let set up in refrigerator.

Luella Fairholm

Salads & Dressings

Mandarin Salad

½ C. slivered almonds
2 whole green onions (chopped)
½ head of Romaine lettuce
1 (11 oz.) can mandarin
   oranges (drained)

3 T. sugar
½ head of Iceberg lettuce
½ C. chopped celery
1 crisp apple (chopped)

DRESSING:
½ tsp. salt
Dash of pepper
2 T. sugar
Dash of Tabasco sauce

¼ C. vegetable oil
1 T. chopped parsley
2 T. vinegar

In a small pan over medium heat, heat almonds and sugar, stirring constantly until almonds are coated and sugar is dissolved. Watch carefully as they burn easily. Cool and store in airtight container. Mix all dressing ingredients and chill. Mix celery, lettuce, and onions. Just before serving add almonds, oranges, and apple. Toss with dressing. May be prepared early in the day and assembled just before serving.

Kathleen Kordick

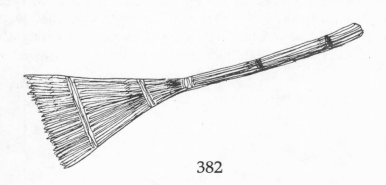

Marinated Carrots

5 C. carrots (sliced)
1 medium onion (diced)
1 green pepper (diced)
1 can tomato soup
½ C. salad oil

1 C. sugar
¾ C. cider vinegar
1 tsp. salt & pepper
1 tsp. prepared mustard

Cook carrots until tender. Drain and cool. Combine all remaining ingredients and marinate carrots in mixture at least 12 hours. Drain and serve.

Kathleen Kordick

Marinated Vegetables

⅓ C. salad oil
1 T. red wine vinegar
1 T. lemon juice
1 tsp. salt
½ tsp. black pepper
1/8 tsp. garlic powder

1 T. ground dill weed
4 C. raw vegetable pieces, such
as: mushrooms, radishes,
broccoli, cauliflower, carrots,
celery, cucumbers, tomatoes,
olives & onions

Mix oil, vinegar, juice, and spices. Pour over prepared vegetables in bowl with tight-fitting lid and let stand for 2 to 3 hours. Tip bowl several times before serving to coat all vegetables well.

Margaret Tiernan

Molded Spinach Salad

1 pkg. lemon gelatin
¾ C. boiling water
1½ T. vinegar
½ C. mayonnaise
¼ tsp. salt
½ C. chopped celery

2 T. minced onion
1 pkg. frozen, chopped spinach
  (thawed & drained)
1 C. cottage cheese
  (small curd)

Dissolve gelatin in boiling water. Add 1 C. cold water. Add vinegar, mayonnaise, and salt. Put in freezer tray and chill until firm 1-inch around sides. Turn into bowl and beat until fluffy, using mixer. Add celery, onion, spinach, and cottage cheese. Pour into 1-quart mold and chill.

Elizabeth M. Edwards

Mostaccioli

1 lb. mostaccioli pasta
6 drops yellow food coloring
1½ C. vinegar
1½ C. sugar
2 T. yellow mustard

1 tsp. garlic salt
1 tsp. pepper
1 onion (chopped fine)
1 cucumber (chopped fine)

Cook the pasta according to package directions. (Add the food coloring to the pasta water.) Mix the vinegar, sugar, and spices; heat to boiling. Add the onion and cucumber. Mix with the pasta.

Becky Conrad

Overnight Salad

IN 9x13-INCH PAN LAYER:

1 head of lettuce
(torn in bite-size pieces)
Spread with 2 C. Hellman's
mayonnaise
2 T. sugar over mayonnaise

8 slices bacon (crumbled)
1 small onion (chopped)
1 pkg. frozen peas
(do not thaw)
4 ozs. shredded cheddar cheese

Cover tightly and refrigerate overnight.

Variation: 2 hard-boiled eggs (chilled and sliced) may be added, also other optional layers like ½ C. diced green pepper and 1 C. diced celery or carrots.

"This is a great salad which I use when I entertain. I served it in January of 1980 when we had vice-president Mondale for lunch."

Carita Kelleher

Pasta-Cabbage Salad

8 ozs. vermicelli
1 medium head of cabbage
(shredded)
2 grated carrots
½ C. chopped celery
½ C. chopped green pepper

½ C. grated onion
½ C. sour cream
3 T. sugar
½ pt. mayonnaise
2 T. vinegar
Salt, to taste

Cut vegetables. Cook vermicelli according to directions. Combine sour cream, sugar, mayonnaise, vinegar, and salt. Mix all together and chill.

Fonda Bass

Pineapple Salad

2 pkgs. Knox gelatin
½ C. cold water
1 C. nuts
2 C. sugar
2 C. grated cheese

3 C. Cool Whip
2 (16 oz.) cans crushed
    pineapple
1 jar maraschino cherries

Dissolve the Knox gelatin in the water. Boil sugar and pineapple for 5 minutes. Add to gelatin mix and let cool. Add nuts, cheese, and cut-up maraschino cherries. Fold in Cool Whip and refrigerate. Serves 16 people.

Harriet Nevins

Pink Champagne Frozen Salad

1 (8 oz.) pkg. cream cheese
    (softened)
¾ C. sugar
1 (No. 2) can crushed
    pineapple (drained)

1 (10 oz.) pkg. frozen sliced
    strawberries (with juice)
2 bananas (quartered & sliced)
1 (8 oz.) carton Cool Whip

Stir all ingredients together and put in 9x13-inch dish (or larger). Freeze. Serve frozen or slightly thawed.

"A very special neighbor, Margie Clark, made this salad for Lacey's baptism. Margie and Eddie have been our daughter's Winterset grandparents."

Jean Pletchette

Pistachio Salad

9 ozs. Cool Whip
1 small pkg. instant pistachio
  pudding

1 large can crushed pineapple
  (do not drain)
1-2 C. marshmallows (small)

Combine dry pudding mix and pineapple, stirring well. Add marshmallows and fold in Cool Whip. Chill for at least ½ hour.

Cindy Watson Pottebaum

Potato Salad

2 lbs. potatoes (about 6
  medium sized, cooked)
¼ C. finely chopped onion
1 tsp. salt
1/8 tsp. pepper

¼ C. Italian salad dressing
½ C. mayonnaise
½ C. chopped celery
2 hard-cooked eggs (chopped)

Mix all together and chill. Serve when ready.

Margaret Tiernan

Pretzel Salad

2⅔ C. broken pretzel twists
¾ C. margarine
¼ C. sugar
8 ozs. cream cheese
  (softened)
1 C. sugar

8 ozs. whipped cream
10 ozs. frozen strawberries
1 (8 oz.) can crushed
  pineapple
1 large pkg. strawberry Jello

Melt margarine and stir into pretzels and sugar. Press into 9x13-inch pan and bake at 350⁰ for 10 minutes. Cool completely. Cream sugar and cream cheese together. Fold in whipped cream and spread over cooled pretzel mixture. Refrgerate. Drain juice from strawberries and pineapple. Measure enough juice and water to make 2 cups. Boil water and juice; add Jello to dissolve. Cool until set, then add strawberries and pineapple. Pour over cream cheese layer and refrigerate.

Kim Algreen

Raspberry Salad

2 small boxes red
   raspberry Jello
2 boxes frozen raspberries
1 large carton Cool Whip

1 (3 oz.) pkg. cream cheese
   (softened)
½ C. chopped pecans
3¼ C. hot water

Combine 2 C. of hot water with 1 box of Jello, the raspberry juice may also be used, but don't go over 2 C. of liquid total. Add the raspberries and let set. To second box of Jello add the remaining 1¼ C. hot water. When partially set, mix and add the softened cream cheese. Stir in the Cool Whip and pecans. Spread over the first layer of Jello and chill.

Sue Finnell

Red Raspberry Salad

2 pkgs. raspberry Jello
2 C. boiling water
1 lb. can applesauce

1 frozen pkg. red raspberries
   (undrained)

TOPPING:
1 lb. pkg. miniature
   marshmallows

1 (8 oz.) carton sour cream
1 carton whipped cream

Dissolve Jello in water and add applesauce and raspberries. Pour into 9x13-inch glass baking dish and place in refrigerator. Let it cool and set up. Mix marshmallows and sour cream together and chill. Whip 1 carton whipping cream and add to marshmallow mixture. Spread on top of set-up Jello mixture.

Marilyn McNamara

Salads & Dressings

Raw Fresh Vegetable Salad

1 bunch fresh broccoli
1 head of cauliflower
  (flowerettes)
1 can pitted black olives
  (drained & sliced)

1 red onion (chopped fine)
1 basket (sliced) mushrooms
1 basket cherry tomatoes
1 (6 oz.) jar stuffed green
  olives (drained)

DRESSING:
2 env. Good Season's Italian
  dressing
⅔ C. oil

¼ C. vinegar
2 T. water

Pour dressing over veggies and add cherry tomatoes before serving. Note: Can be made the day before and refrigerated.

Patricia Morris

Sauerkraut Salad

1 qt. kraut (drained & cut
  fine with scissors)
½ C. green pepper (cut in
  fine pieces)
½ C. green onions (cut in
  fine pieces)

½ C. celery (cut in fine
  pieces)
½ C. cider vinegar
1½ C. sugar

(Note: Do not use green tops or dry onions.) Combine the kraut, onions, celery, and green pepper in a large mixing bowl. Bring sugar and vinegar to boiling. Let cool and pour over kraut mixture and mix well. Place in a tight container and refrigerate for 48 hours. Do not freeze. Mix well before serving. This will keep indefinitely in refrigerator. Serves 10.

Ruth Cunningham

Ribbon Salad

2 (3 oz.) pkgs. strawberry Jello
2 (3 oz.) pkgs. lime Jello
1 (3 oz.) pkg. lemon Jello
8 ozs. cream cheese
1 C. water

1 C. marshmallows
1 (15 oz.) can crushed
  pineapple (drained)
1 small carton Cool Whip

Dissolve lime Jello in ¾ C. hot water, then add ¾ C. cold water. Pour into 13x9-inch pan and let set up. Combine lemon Jello, cream cheese, 1 C. water, and marshmallows. Cook over low heat until Jello and marshmallows dissolve. Let cool, then add pineapple. When almost set, add Cool Whip. Spread on top of lime Jello and let set up. Dissolve strawberry Jello in ¾ C. hot water, then add ¾ C. cold water. Let cool until almost set, then pour on top of lemon Jello mixture. Let set up and serve.

"This is my favorite salad that my Grandma Dermody makes. It's a holiday tradition at Grandma's house."

Jessica Hermanstorfer

Salads & Dressings

Spinach Rice Salad

1 C. uncooked rice
½ C. Italian salad dressing
1 tsp. soy sauce
¼ C. sugar

2 C. fresh spinach (torn into
  bite-size pieces)
½ C. chopped green onions
½ C. cooked bacon (chopped)

Cook rice, according to package directions and drain. Combine Italian salad dressing, soy sauce, and sugar. Pour over rice, cover, and chill. Add spinach, onions, and bacon before serving. Good!

Nancy M. Corkrean
Fonda Bass

Super Salad

1 head of cauliflower
  (cut in chunks)
1 head of broccoli

4 stalks of celery
  (cut in chunks)
1 pkg. thawed frozen peas
  (not cooked)

DRESSING:
1 lb. bacon (fried & crumbled)
¼ C. minced onion
1½ C. mayonnaise
¼ C. sugar (more or less)
¼ C. Parmesan cheese (pieces)

2 tsp. vinegar
¼ tsp. salt (optional)
A little pepper
Chunks of Colby & cheddar
  cheese (optional)

Toss together in a very large bowl and serve.

Sue Stuchel

Tomato & Onion Salad

1 mild white onion (sliced)
12 C. water
1 tsp. salt
2 large bunches spinach (about
   2 lbs. total) (stems removed)
Salt & pepper

2 large tomatoes (sliced)
½ C. palm vinegar or ¼ C.
   distilled white vinegar &
   ¼ C. water
1 tsp. sugar

In a bowl combine onion, 4 C. of water, and salt; let stand for 30 minutes. Drain, rinse, and drain again. Rinse spinach well. Pour remaining 8 C. of water into a 4 to 5-quart kettle. Bring to boil over high heat. Add spinach and cook just until wilted (about 1 minute). Drain, rinse, and squeeze dry. Arrange spinach on rimmed serving plate. Top with onions and tomatoes. In a small bowl, stir together vinegar and sugar. Season to taste with salt and pepper; drizzle over salad. Makes 6 servings.

Marvin & Mira Imes

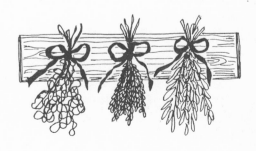

Vegetable Salad with Sweet-Sour Dressing

1 C. chopped green pepper
1 C. sliced celery
½ C. sliced green onions
2 T. diced pimento
1 (16 oz.) can Green Giant
   sliced green beans (drained)
½ C. cider vinegar

1 (12 oz.) can Green Giant
   Niblets Golden whole kernel
   corn (drained)
½ C. sugar
½ tsp. salt
½ tsp. pepper
¼ C. canola oil

In a large bowl combine green pepper, celery, onions, pimento, green beans, and corn. In a small bowl, blend remaining ingredients and pour over the vegetables. Cover and refrigerate for several hours or overnight. Makes 10 (½ C.) servings.

Joanne Gasiel

Taco Salad

1 lb. ground beef
   (fried & cooled)
½ lb. longhorn cheese (grated)
4 diced tomatoes
1 chopped onion
4 diced stalks of celery
1 can red kidney beans
   (drained)

1 head of lettuce
   (torn into pieces)
1 C. taco sauce
¾ C. Miracle Whip
¼ C. catsup
¼ tsp. chili powder
1 bag nacho cheese Doritos

Combine ground beef, cheese, tomatoes, onion, celery, and kidney beans with a head of lettuce. Combine taco sauce, Miracle Whip, catsup, and chili powder in a small bowl. Whisk together and use as a salad dressing. Top with nacho cheese Doritos.

Sue Stuchel

Top Ramen Salad

1 lb. pkg. shredded cabbage
3-4 chopped green onions
2-3 oz. pkg. slivered almonds

¼ C. sunflower seeds
¼ C. sesame seeds
1 pkg. Ramen noodles (chicken)

DRESSING:
½ tsp. pepper
1 tsp. Accent
½ tsp. seasoning from Ramen
   noodle package

1 T. sugar
3 T. vinegar
1 tsp. salt
½ C. oil

Mix dressing ingredients together ahead of time and refrigerate. Also toss together cabbage and onions ahead of time. Toss and bake almonds, sunflower seeds, and sesame seeds together at 350° for about 15 minutes. At the last minute before serving, break up 1 pkg. of dry chicken flavored Ramen noodles into cabbage. Add nuts and dressing; toss well.

Kim Algreen

Sweet Salad Dressing

Juice from a 20 oz. can of
   pineapple
1 T. flour

½ C. sugar
Pinch of salt

Mix, heat, and stir. Cook until it starts to thicken a little.

Mrs. Albert Hill

Celery Seed Dressing

⅔ C. sugar
2 tsp. lemon juice
1 tsp. powdered mustard
1 tsp. salt
¼ tsp. white pepper

1 small onion (minced)
⅓ C. cider vinegar
1 C. vegetable oil
1 tsp. celery seed

Place the first 6 ingredients together and half the vinegar in a blender jar. Blend well. With blender still running, add the oil and remaining vinegar. Blend thoroughly. This method prevents dressing from separating. Stir in the celery seeds.

Nancy M. Corkrean

Soups & Sandwiches

Love One Another

1994

Soups & Sandwiches

Lenten Soup Suppers:

During Lent, on Wednesday evenings, we have Mass at 6:00, followed by a soup supper and then religious ed. class. For our soup suppers we ask all students to bring a can of soup, any kind. We divide these soups into two pots; one with the tomato based soups and the other with chicken noodle types of soup. Fruits, raw vegetables, crackers, and breads are contributed by parishioners. Sometimes, parishioners will bring homemade soups, a special treat! In this section, you will find some of our favorite soups often enjoyed during Lent.

Bean Soup Served in The Capital, Washington D.C.

2 lbs. #1 white Michigan beans

Smoked ham hock
Salt & pepper, to taste

Cover beans with cold water and soak overnight. Drain and recover with water in pan. Add smoked ham hock and simmer slowly for about 4 hours until beans are tender. Add salt and pepper. Just before serving, bruise beans with large spoon enough to cloud. Serves 6.

Ruth Cunningham

Soups

Beef Barley Wild Rice Soup

Olive oil
1 lb. cubed (½-inch) beef, floured
1 onion (chopped)
3 cloves garlic (minced)
¼ tsp. Tabasco sauce
Black pepper
½ tsp. dried crushed basil

½ tsp. dried crushed oregano
1 C. canned stewed tomatoes
4 (14½ oz.) cans beef broth
½ C. barley
⅓ C. wild rice
2 stalks celery (chopped)
1 carrot (finely chopped)

Saute' onion in olive oil until it is translucent. Add beef cubes and brown. Add beef broth, tomatoes, garlic, Tabasco, and pepper. Cover and simmer for 2 hours or until meat is tender. Add spices, barley, and rice. Cook for 1 hour. Add vegetables and cook for another ½ hour.

Clif Neel

Soups & Sandwiches

GOVERNOR'S RESIDENCE
DES MOINES, IOWA 50312

Broccoli and Cheese Soup

2 T. finely chopped onion
2 T. margarine
3 T. flour
½ tsp. salt
1/8 tsp. pepper
2 C. milk

1 C. American cheese
2 chicken bouillon cubes
1½ C. water
1 (10 oz.) pkg. frozen chopped
 broccoli

In a large pan cook onions in butter until tender. Stir in flour, salt, and pepper until well blended. Add milk and cook until thickened, stirring constantly. Add cheese and stir until melted. Remove from heat. In a separate pan dissolve bouillon in water and bring to a boil. Add broccoli and cook until done. Do not drain. Add broccoli to mixture.

Chris Branstad

Soups

Bread Crumb Dumplings and
Your Favorite Soup or Stew

1 C. flour
3 tsp. baking powder
½ tsp. salt
1 C. dry bread crumbs
2 T. shortening
1 egg (well-beaten)

¾ C. milk
1 T. grated onion
Dash of pepper
1 can soup (tomato soup
   is great)

Prepare soup and have simmering on stove. Measure flour, baking powder, and salt in bowl. Add bread crumbs. Cut in shortening. Add well-beaten egg, milk, onion, and pepper. Mix gently, just until all is moistened. Drop by tablespoons into gently boiling soup or stew. Cover and boil for 12 to 15 minutes without removing lid. Makes 10 to 12 medium-sized dumplings that are light and delicious.

Joanne Gasiel

Chili

3 lbs. ground beef
   (browned & drained)
½ onion (chopped)
1 large can tomato juice
4 T. uncooked rice

2 cans chili beans
½ tsp. salt
¼ C. sugar
1 tsp. chili powder or
   more, to taste

Mix all ingredients. Add water if this is too thick for you. Cook in a crock pot on low for 6 to 8 hours or cook in 250° oven for 2 to 3 hours. Freezes well.

Joan Hilton

Soups & Sandwiches

Classic Chili Recipe

1 lb. ground beef
½ C. chopped onion
¼ C. chopped green pepper
1 (16 oz.) can tomatoes
   (cut-up)
1 (8 oz.) can tomato sauce

1 bay leaf
1 tsp. dried oregano leaves
   (crushed)
Shredded cheddar cheese
1 (15 oz.) can chili style beans
   in chili sauce

In a large skillet brown ground beef, onion, and green pepper until meat is browned and vegetables are tender. Drain off fat. Stir in tomatoes, beans with sauce, tomato sauce, bay leaf, and oregano. Bring to boil, then reduce heat. Cover and simmer for 30 minutes. Makes 5½ C., about 4 servings. Top with shredded cheddar cheese.

John M. Watts Sr.

Chili (Hot)

2 lbs. coarsely ground beef
1⅓ C. chopped onion
½ C. chopped green pepper
⅓ C. chopped celery
2 cloves of minced garlic
1 (16 oz.) can diced tomatoes
1 (15 oz.) can tomato sauce
1 T. tomato paste
3 T. sugar

3 T. canned chopped green
   chili peppers
3 T. chili powder
½ tsp. ground cumin
1 tsp. bottled hot pepper sauce
1 bay leaf
1 (15 oz.) can beans
½ C. beer

Brown meat with onions, green pepper, celery, and garlic. Add rest of the ingredients, except beans and beer. Simmer, uncovered for 60 minutes, stirring occasionally. Add beans and beer; simmer for ½ hour.

Ann Winjum

Soups

Crock Pot Chili

1 lb. ground beef
3 cans chili beans
1 large can stewed tomatoes
  (chopped)
1 medium onion (chopped)
1 small stalk of celery (chopped)

4 C. tomato juice
½ tsp. garlic salt
½ tsp. chili powder
¼ tsp. pepper
¼ tsp. Tabasco sauce

Brown ground beef. Combine ground beef and all ingredients in crock pot. Mix well, cover, and cook on high for an hour. Reduce to simmer and cook for at least 4 hours. May cook all day, if desired.

Mary Anne Snyder

Ground Beef (Curly Soup)

2 small potatoes
1 lb. ground beef
1 large onion
2 bay leaves
2 or 3 whole allspice

1 (8 oz.) carton sour cream
1 or more cups of milk
2 T. vinegar
Flour, to thicken
2 C. water

Cut up potatoes and cook in 2 C. of water. Fry ground beef, drain fat from meat and add to potatoes and water. Add onion, bay leaves, and spice. Add sour cream and milk, then vinegar. Mix small amount of water and flour to thicken. Remove bay leaves and spices before serving.

"This recipe comes from my husband Norberts mother. It is called curly soup because of the vinegar curdling the milk. This recipe came from the depression era."

Josephine Sitkiewicz

Soups & Sandwiches

Irish Stew

2 lbs. lamb
1 lb. onion
4 stalks celery
1 leek

½ lbs. carrots
2 ozs. barley
1½ lbs. potatoes
¾ pt. cold water

Cut meat into 1-inch cubes. Season well with salt and pepper. Slice onions thinly and other vegetables thickly. Pack alternate layers of vegetables, barley, and meat into oven-proof casserole dish. Start with onions and end with potatoes. Pour water over, cover, and cook for 1½ to 2 hours at 325⁰. Baste from time to time. Raise oven temperature to 425⁰, uncover, and brown potatoes.

Nancy Corkrean

St. Patrick's Day

There are many legends about St. Patrick. St. Patrick is said to have explained the mystery of the Trinity using a green shamrock and pointing out that it has three leaves but is still one plant. It is also said that he charmed all the snakes in Ireland into the sea where they drowned.

Our parish celebrates St. Patrick's Day with a family get-together where Irish Soda Bread, Irish Stew, Scones, and other Irish foods are served.

Last year we were even visited by a wee leprechaun who gave all the children little gifts!

Soups

Minestrone Soup

¼ C. oil
1 clove minced garlic
1 C. chopped onion
1 C. chopped celery
2 (6 oz.) cans tomato paste
1 (10½ oz.) can beef broth
2½ qts. water
1 C. chopped cabbage

1 (10 oz.) pkg. frozen peas &
   carrots
2½ tsp. salt
¼ tsp. pepper
½ tsp. rosemary
1 can kidney beans
   (not drained)
1 C. dry elbow macaroni
Parmesan cheese

Heat oil in a large kettle and saute' garlic, onion, and celery for 5 minutes. Stir in tomato paste and the next 7 ingredients. Bring to boil, cover, and simmer for 1 hour. Add remaining ingredients, except cheese, and cook for 15 minutes longer. Garnish with Parmesan cheese. Freezes well. Makes 8 to 10 servings.

"This has been one of my favorite recipes, because when our children were small, ALL FOUR of them loved it!!!"

Mary Anne Roby

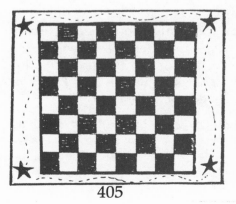

Soups & Sandwiches

Quick and Easy Minestrone

5 large stalks of celery
   (cut-up)
1 large onion (cut-up)
2 T. salad oil
¼ lb. spaghetti
2 (No. 2) cans kidney beans
1 C. cubed squash

1 C. tomato juice
1 tsp. salt
½ tsp. pepper
1/8 tsp. thyme
1/8 tsp. oregano
1/8 tsp. paprika
¼ lb. American cheese

Saute' celery and onion in salad oil in covered pan. Cook spaghetti in salted water, do not drain. Add celery, onion, beans, squash, tomato juice, salt, pepper, and spices. Simmer until squash is tender. Grate cheese and add last. Simmer until cheese melts. Makes 6 large servings.

Irenee S. Tracy

Great Grandma Burch's Potato Soup

1 lb. bacon (diced & browned)
5 lbs. potatoes (peeled & diced)
2-3 onions (diced)
Seasoned salt, to taste

A little lemon pepper
1 T. flour
Shredded cheddar cheese

Brown and drain the bacon. Add half of the diced potatoes and brown. Drain and add diced onions and brown. Add remaining potatoes and cover with water. Season with seasoned salt and a little lemon pepper. Cook for 2 to 3 hours until liquid is cooked down and then add milk. Cook until hot. Add 1 T. flour to thicken. Serve with shredded cheddar cheese on top.

"This has become the Christmas Eve meal tradition in our home since Mark's grandmother taught me how to make it after we were married."

Karen Gronemeyer

Soups

Famous-Barr's French Onion Soup

1¼ lbs. peeled onions
3 ozs. butter or margarine
1 tsp. freshly ground pepper
1 T. paprika
1 bay leaf

1½ tsp. salt
1½ qts. canned beef bouillon
½ C. all-purpose flour
1 C. white wine (optional)
1 T. Kitchen Bouquet

Slice onions 1/8-inch thick (use food processor if available). Melt butter and place onions in it. Saute' slowly for 30 minutes in a large soup pot. Add all other ingredients, except bouillon. Saute' over low heat for 10 minutes more. Add bouillon and simmer for 1 hour (may simmer longer). Adjust color to a rich brown with caramel coloring or Kitchen Bouquet. Season with salt, to taste. May refrigerate at this point, if desired.

For Proper Serving: Heat soup and fill individual heat-proof bowls with 8 ozs. of soup. Top with French bread cubes and 2 ozs. grated Swiss cheese. Place under broiler until brown, approximately 5 minutes.

"Famous-Barr is the name of a nice department store chain in St. Louis similar to Younkers. This soup is served in their restaurant. This soup was dearly loved by my mother-in-law who often requested that I make it for our Christmas Eve meal."

Joy Drury

Soups & Sandwiches

Taco Soup

1 lb. ground beef
½ C. chopped onion
1 (29 oz.) can stewed tomatoes
  (cut-up)
2 (16 oz.) cans kidney beans
1 (16 oz.) can tomato sauce

1 env. taco seasoning mix
1 avocado (peeled & chopped)
Shredded cheddar cheese
Corn chips
Sour cream

Cook ground beef and onion until meat is browned. Drain off excess fat. Add taco seasoning, undrained tomatoes, tomato sauce, and undrained kidney beans. Simmer, covered for 15 minutes. Add avocado and serve. Pass cheese, chips, and sour cream to top each serving. This makes 6 servings.

Marianne Eivins

Hot Tomato Soup

2 T. vegetable oil
1 med. onion (sliced or diced)
2 stalks celery (sliced)
  (if desired)
1 qt. tomato juice

2 C. chicken broth
Salt & pepper, to taste
Tabasco sauce (if desired)
2-3 dashes cayenne pepper
Crushed red pepper (if desired)

(Note: We like this medium hot and add just a pinch of the crushed red pepper, but no Tabasco sauce.) Heat oil in soup pot and saute' the onion and celery. Add the tomato juice and chicken broth. Add salt, pepper, and simmer gently for 30 to 40 minutes.

"This is a great warm up soup for those cold days when nothing else warms you up."

Linda Hermanstorfer

Soups

Vegetable Cheese Soup

1 C. shredded potatoes
½ C. chopped celery
½ C. chopped onion
½ C. chopped carrots
4 T. butter
3 C. chicken broth

2 C. milk
½ C. flour
12 ozs. shredded Velveeta
  cheese
1 tsp. parsley
½ tsp. pepper

In a Dutch oven, saute' vegetables in butter until tender. Add chicken broth and simmer for 30 minutes. Thoroughly blend flour and milk. Add to soup base. Add the shredded cheese, parsley, and pepper. Cook soup on low heat until cheese is melted.

Sue Stuchel

R.K.'s Favorite Vegetable Soup

1 C. chopped potatoes
1 C. chopped carrots
1 C. chopped celery
½ C. green pepper (chopped)
1 C. chopped onion
1 tsp. salt
Pepper, to taste

4 T. butter
3 C. chicken broth
2 C. milk
2 cans cheddar cheese soup
1 can cream of celery soup
½ C. flour

Cook vegetables in butter until tender - do not brown. Add chicken broth and simmer for 30 minutes. Blend milk into flour and add, along with soups to vegetables and broth mixture. Cook and stir until thickened. May be served in crock pot. Serves 8 to 10.

Fran Cesca

Soups & Sandwiches

Barbecue Beef Burgers

1½ to 2 lbs. ground chuck
1 onion (diced)
1 C. diced celery
1 T. flour
1 T. sugar
1 tsp. salt

¼ tsp. pepper
1 bottle catsup
1 T. mustard
1 T. Worcestershire sauce
1 (15 oz.) can chili beans

Brown ground chuck, onion, and celery. Mix flour, sugar, salt, pepper, catsup, mustard, and Worcestershire sauce. Add to meat, then add beans and simmer.

Marilyn McNamara

Pillows

3 lbs. ground beef
1 small head cabbage (shredded)
½ C. soy sauce
1 T. Accent
2 T. cornstarch

3 loaves frozen bread dough
  (thawed)
1 beaten egg
Poppy seed
Parmesan cheese

Cook meat and cabbage. Add soy sauce and Accent. Simmer for 20 minutes, uncovered. Sprinkle cornstarch over meat and mix well. Remove excess grease and let cool. Cut bread dough into 10 even pieces. Flatten to about the size of your hand and place 2 T. meat into center. Shape into ball and brush with egg. Sprinkle poppy seeds and Parmesan cheese over top. Bake at 375° for 15 minutes.

Kim Algreen

410

Pepperoni Bread

1 loaf frozen bread (thawed)
Pepperoni slices

½ lb. grated sharp cheddar cheese

FILLING:
2 eggs
Dash of garlic powder

1 tsp. oregano

Thaw out loaf of frozen bread dough for 2 hours, just until soft, but not starting to rise. Roll out to size of jelly roll pan. Spread with ½ of the filling mixture. Sprinkle on the cheese and pepperoni slices. Roll as you would a jelly roll. Seal edges and cut in half to make 2 loaves. Brush with remaining filling mixture. Slit top with knife and bake on greased cookie sheet at 350⁰ for 35 to 40 minutes or until golden brown. Makes 2 loaves. (For fillings, use anything you like as pizza toppings.)

Kathleen Kordick

Sloppy Joes

2 lbs. hamburger
2 T. onion (chopped)
2 tsp. mustard
1 C. ketchup
4 T. vinegar

2 tsp. water
2 T. flour
1½ tsp. chili powder
2 T. brown sugar
2 T. Worcestershire sauce

Brown hamburger and onion. Add remaining ingredients and simmer for approximately 1 hour.

Kim Algreen

Soups & Sandwiches

Sausage Bread

¾ lb. Italian sausage
½ lb. lean ground beef
1 loaf frozen bread dough
1½ C. mozzarella cheese

¼ tsp. anise seed
Garlic salt, onion salt, dried
    red pepper & oregano,
    to taste

Set out bread dough to thaw. Brown sausage and ground beef with anise seed and other spices. When bread dough has thawed and risen, spread out on greased cookie sheet (as if you were going to make a pizza). Sprinkle sausage mixture evenly over dough. Sprinkle cheese evenly over sausage mixture. Starting at the edge roll-up like a jelly roll, place seam side down, and tuck under the ends. Let rise another 30 minutes and then bake at 350° for 35 to 40 minutes or until golden brown. *"This is really good served with potato soup."*

Mary Anne Snyder

Sausage Loaf

1 loaf French bread (16 ozs.)
8 ozs. bulk pork sausage
⅓ C. onion (chopped)
1 clove of garlic (minced)
1 egg

1 T. mustard, (divided)
2 T. chopped parsley
¾ C. sharp Cheddar cheese
½ C. grated Parmesan cheese
¼ C. olive oil
1 tsp. pepper

Slice bread in ½ lengthwise. Slightly hollow out each ½, leaving a ½-inch thick layer of bread. With fork, mash bread into small crumbs. Cook sausage, onion, and garlic in skillet over medium heat until meat is brown; drain. In a large bowl, combine crumbs, meat mixture, egg, 1 tsp. mustard, and parsley; set aside. Using blender, process the cheeses, oil, 2 tsp. mustard, and pepper until mixture forms paste. Spread cheese mixture evenly over inside of bread. Fill with meat mixture and place halves together. Wrap in foil and bake at 350° for 30 to 35 minutes. Cut into 1-inch thick slices. Makes 16 servings.

Teresa Hoffelmeyer

tea

TEA
TIME

Friends are forever

1994

In this section you will find recipes especially selected for more elegant entertaining, such as wedding showers, women's luncheons, etc. You will also find some typically English recipes for other special occasions.

Jam is a tea time tradition, served with scones, breads, and incorporated into desserts and cake recipes. We have included several recipes for jams or jellies in this section for that reason. However, these are more typically American recipes, especially the corn cob jelly which is an Iowa favorite.

Take Time for Tea

When visitors arrive in my native country of England, a cup of tea is usually offered. Brewed in a tea pot and served piping hot, it is Britain's most popular drink. Iced tea is altogether an American drink.

In northern England where I was from, "tea" was usually the evening meal, much as supper is here. On special occasions, afternoon tea would be served formally to friends at about 4:00 p.m. with finger sandwiches and cake. If dinner followed later in the evening, we children were "off to bed." An aunt once told me that, "Little pigs have big ears," so I suppose our curiosity was stimulated by being excluded from grown-up activities.

From our history books we learned that tea arrived in England in the late 1600's. Some felt it had medicinal properties, while others viewed it with suspicion. Rumors even circulated that drinking tea would yellow one's skin. This, because it was known that the Chinese had long been avid tea

(Continued on Next Page)

(Take Time for Tea - Continued)

drinkers. Newly arrived, tea was very expensive and drunk only by the rich, but as the tea trade grew it became more affordable and eventually the entire nation took to tea drinking.

For many of us, afternoon tea still evokes memories of Victorian England: beautiful linens, fine porcelain china, an array of tiny sandwiches, scones and cakes, and ladies with needlework in their fingers and time on their hands.

Reality, of course, is different. Another aunt of mine fell off her bicycle while riding on a narrow cobbled street. Feeling slightly dazed she was surprised when a kind lady rushed out of her house and said, " 'Ere luv 'av a cup of tea.'' My aunt looked at the cup of tea and told the woman she couldn't drink anything because she felt sick. Later, she told us the cup was so stained that she would have rather died than taste that tea!

Still in England, going out for tea is a timeless tradition. Both tourists and natives look for their favorite nostalgic setting: a friend's house, a tea shop in a country village or seaside resort, or in one of London's most elegant hotels. Take your choice, but do take time for tea!

Sheila Algreen

Tea Time

Strawberry Ice

7 C. fresh strawberries
2 C. sugar

1¼ C. orange juice
1 C. fresh lemon juice

Puree' strawberries in blender. In a large bowl combine puree', sugar, orange juice, and lemon juice. Let stand at room temperature for 2 hours. Pour into 9-inch square pan and freeze. When frozen about 1-inch on all sides of pan place in mixing bowl and beat until mushy. Return to pan and freeze until slightly frozen. Beat again and then freeze until firm. Serve with mint leaves and a drizzle of raspberry liqueur over top. May be served at the end of your meal, between courses or by itself.

Teresa Hoffelmeyer

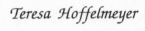

Cold Strawberry Soup

3¼ lbs. frozen pureed'
   strawberries
½ tsp. cinnamon
½ tsp. salt
1 C. frozen orange juice
   concentrate

1 C. water
¼ C. burgandy wine
5 cloves
3 T. cornstarch
½ gal. vanilla ice cream
1 qt. light cream

Mix first 7 ingredients and bring into a boil. Blend in cornstarch and cook until thickened. Cool and remove cloves. Add ice cream and light cream. Stir until blended. Refrigerate for 1 hour. Garnish with fresh strawberries and mint leaves. Serves 10 to 12.

Teresa Hoffelmeyer

Strawberry Soup

2 pts. strawberries
¼ C. brown sugar
¼ C. heavy cream

1 C. white wine
¾ C. sour cream

Puree' strawberries. Blend everything together. Chill and serve with fresh sliced strawberries on top. Serves 6.

Sheila Algreen

Tea Room Chicken

6 ozs. wild rice mix (cooked)
1 (16 oz.) pkg. frozen chopped broccoli
3 C. cooked diced chicken
1 C. shredded Velveeta cheese
1 C. fresh mushrooms (sliced)
½ C. mayonnaise

1 can cream of mushroom soup
¼ tsp. dry mustard
¼ tsp. curry powder
Parmesan cheese
½ C. cracker crumbs
1 T. butter

In a 9x13-inch pan, layer rice, broccoli, chicken, cheese, and mushrooms. In a separate bowl combine mayonnaise, soup, mustard, and curry powder. Pour over chicken mixture. Sprinkle with Parmesan cheese. Saute' crackers with butter and sprinkle over cheese. Bake at 350⁰ for 30 to 45 minutes or until bubbly.

Ann Winjum

Tea Time

Pinwheel Sandwiches

1 loaf of brown bread
1 loaf of white bread

Butter (softened)

FILLINGS SUCH AS:
Cooked asparagus tips
Very finely chopped egg
   with mayonnaise

Crab or lobster paste
Ham & cream cheese
   with herbs

Bread must be thinly sliced. Trim off crusts. Spread with butter and spread on soft filling. Roll up each slice. Chill, covered with plastic wrap. Cut into thin pinwheels and serve immediately.

Sheila Algreen

Tea Sandwiches

8 ozs. cream cheese
1 pkg. Hidden Valley Ranch
   dressing

1 T. lemon juice
Party rye bread
Cucumber

Mix first 3 ingredients until creamy and spread on rye bread. Top with slices of cucumber.

Maureen Roach

Watercress Tea Sandwiches

6 ozs. cream cheese
¼ C. sour cream
2 C. chopped watercress

Sliced firm white bread
Salt & pepper, to taste

Mix Cream cheese with sour cream. When light and fluffy mix in watercress evenly. Add salt and pepper. Spread on bread with crusts removed. Cut into triangles.

Sheila Algreen

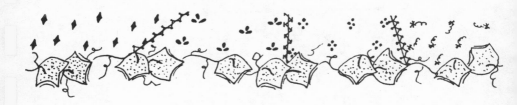

Apricot Brandy Cake

CAKE
1 C. butter (softened)
3 C. sugar
6 eggs
1 tsp. orange extract
1 tsp. almond extract
½ tsp. lemon extract

3 C. flour
½ tsp. salt
¼ tsp. baking soda
1 C. sour cream
½ C. apricot brandy

GLAZE:
1 C. sugar
½ C. water

2 T. apricot brandy

TOPPING:
32 ozs. apricots (drained &
    cut into small pieces)

1 T. cornstarch
2 T. apricot brandy

For Cake: Cream butter and sugar. Add eggs, 1 at a time and blend well. Stir in extracts. In a small bowl combine dry ingredients and add to creamed mixture alternating with sour cream and brandy. Pour into greased 9½-inch Bundt pan. Bake at 325⁰ for 1 hour and 10 minutes or until tests done. Cool for 10 minutes and then remove from pan. Pour warm glaze over top and cool completely.

For Glaze: Bring sugar and water to a boil in saucepan until slightly thickened. Remove from heat and add brandy.

For Topping: Heat apricots in saucepan. Combine cornstarch with apricot brandy. Stir into apricots and cook until thickened. Spoon over cake.

Sheila Algreen

Almond Tea Cakes

2 C. butter or oleo
¾ C. sugar
¾ C. packed brown sugar
2 egg

4 tsp. almond extract
4 C. flour
1 tsp. baking powder

FILLING:
1 egg white
½ C. sugar
½ C. ground almonds

½ tsp. lemon juice
Milk
Sliced almonds

For Dough: In mixing bowl cream together butter and sugars. Add egg and extract, mixing well. Add flour and baking powder (dough will be soft). Chill.

For Filling: Stir egg white, sugar, ground almonds, and lemon juice in a small bowl.

Remove small portions of dough at a time from refrigerator. Place 1-inch balls of dough into minature muffin cups, pressing slightly onto sides and bottom. Place ½ tsp. filling into each and cover with quarter size circles of dough. Brush with a little milk and top with sliced almonds. Bake at 350⁰ for 20 minutes or until golden brown. Makes 5 dozen.

Fonda Bass

420

The Royal Battenberg Cake

CAKE:

1½ C. flour
1 tsp. baking powder
Pinch of salt
¾ C. sugar
¾ C. butter
8 oz. can almond paste

3 eggs
1 tsp. vanilla
1 to 2 T. milk
A few drops of red food
  coloring

APRICOT GLAZE:

12 ozs. apricot jam
Juice of ½ lemon

2 T. water

Grease loaf pans and line with waxed paper. Grease again and sprinkle with flour. (Discard excess flour.) Preheat oven to 350° and bake for 15 to 20 minutes.

For Cake: Measure dry ingredients into bowl and add the rest of the ingredients except food coloring and almond paste. Beat until smooth. Pour half of the batter into 1 pan and color the other half pale pink. Pour into second pan and bake. Cool on rack. Remove waxed paper. When cold, trim crusts and cut into 2 equal slices lengthwise. Warm the glaze and brush on strips of cake. Put 1 pink strip on top of a plain strip and vice versa to make a checkered rectangle. Soften almond paste by kneading. Roll out on lightly sugared board. Shape it into rectangle the length of reshaped cake and wide enough to wrap around sides, top and bottom of cake. Leave ends uncovered. Brush more glaze on cake and then wrap and press the almond paste around cake. Make seam on bottom. Turn cake right side up and scallop edges of almond paste with fingers. Lightly scorce the top in a lattice pattern with knife.

"This is named for the British Royal Family."

Sheila Algreen

421

Cindy's Birthday Cake

CHEESECAKE:
2 (8 oz.) pkgs. cream cheese
¾ C. sugar
2 large eggs
2 tsp. vanilla extract

3 (1 oz.) sqs. semi-sweet
    chocolate (melted & cooled)
1 C. sour cream

CAKE:
2 C. unsifted cake flour
1 T. baking powder
½ tsp. salt
1 C. sugar
⅓ C. vegetable oil

3 large eggs (separated)
⅔ C. cold water
1 T. vanilla
¼ tsp. cream of tartar

For Cheesecake: In a large bowl with electric mixer, beat cream cheese until fluffy. Gradually add sugar, beating. Add eggs (1 at a time) beating after each addition. Fold in vanilla, chocolate, and sour cream until well blended. Pour into greased 9-inch springform pan and bake at 325⁰ for 35 to 40 minutes. Cool on wire rack at room temperature for 1 hour. Loosen from side of pan with spatula. Remove side of pan and refrigerate until cold.

For Cake: In a large bowl, stir flour, baking powder, salt, and ¾ C. sugar. Make a well in center of flour mixture. Add oil, egg yolks, water, and vanilla. Beat with wire wisk until smooth. In a small bowl combine egg whites and cream of tartar. Beat until frothy with electric mixer. Beat in remaining ¼ C. sugar until stiff peaks form. Fold this into flour mixture. Divide batter into two 9-inch round greased baking pans and bake at 325⁰ for 35 to 40 minutes. Cool on wire racks 10 minutes in pan, then turn cakes out onto racks and cool completely.

(Continued on Next Page)

(Cindy's Birthday Cake - Continued)

FROSTING:

2 C. whipping cream
¼ C. confectioner's sugar

2 T. cocoa
1 tsp. vanilla extract

In a bowl combine cream, sugar, cocoa, and vanilla. Beat with electric mixer until stiff. On a serving plate place one cake, right-side up. Spread with ⅓ C. frosting. Invert cheesecake over frosted cake layer and then remove bottom of pan. Spread with ⅓ C. frosting and top with remaining cake, right-side up. Frost top and sides of cake.

Teresa Hoffelmeyer

Jean's Cheshire Meringue

16 Ritz crackers (crushed)
1 oz. flaked almonds
2 ozs. finely chopped walnuts
3 egg whites

1 tsp. vanilla
1 tsp. baking powder
1 C. sugar

TOPPING:

½ pt. sweet whipped cream
   (fresh preferable)

Grated sweet chocolate

Beat egg whites until stiff. Sieve sugar and baking powder; add to egg whites gradually. Beat again. Stir in crumbs, nuts, and vanilla. Put mixture in 2 pie pans and bake at 300° for 35 to 45 minutes, making sure it's dry all through. Cool meringue and put 1 piece of meringue on plate. Cover with whipped cream and sprinkle with chocolate. Place second meringue on top and cover all over with whipped cream. Sprinkle chocolate over all.

"This was served to us on a 1991 visit to the County of Cheshire, England."

Sheila Algreen

English Trifle
(A special Tea-Time Favorite)

3 or 4 sponge cupcakes
    (can use Hostess)
6 macaroons
¾ C. sweet sherry

1 C. raspberry jam
1¼ C. pastry cream
2 C. whipped cream

PASTRY CREAM:

2 C. milk
4 egg yolks
6 T. sugar
6 T. flour

1 tsp. cornstarch
1 tsp. butter
1 tsp. vanilla

For Pastry Cream: Scald milk. In pan combine yolks, sugar, flour, and cornstrach. Add hot milk and cook for 3 minutes until smooth and thick. Dot with butter, cool, and add vanilla.

For Trifle: In a deep bowl put sponge cupcakes cut in half crosswise. They are better if a little dry. Crumble 6 macaroons over them. Pour sherry over them and let stand for 15 minutes. Spread thickly with raspberry jam. Pour cool pastry cream over trifle. Add whipped cream and decorate with a pinch of macaroon crumbs. Can be made into two layers.

"Over the years, this dessert has become a favorite on Christmas eve. Before children tear into presents, adults have a delicious "decadent" taste of trifle."

Sheila Algreen

Pecan Torte with Chocolate Glaze

TORTE:

4 large eggs (room temp.)
(separated)
1 C. granulated sugar
2 T. sifted cake flour

½ tsp. salt
½ tsp. baking powder
1 T. orange juice or white rum
2 C. very finely ground pecans

FILLING:

½ C. heavy cream
1½ tsp. grated orange zest
½ tsp. vanilla extract

¼ C. confectioner's sugar
1 tsp. light corn syrup

FROSTING:

6 ozs. semi-sweet
chocolate chips

½ C. sour cream
Speck of salt

For Torte: Preheat the oven to 350⁰. In a mixer bowl, beat the egg yolks until thick and light, about 2 minutes. Gradually add the granulated sugar and then beat for another 2 minutes so the mixture is well combined. By hand, stir in the cake flour, salt, baking powder, and juice or rum. In another mixer bowl, beat the egg whites until very stiff. Fold half of the nuts into the yolk mixture, then add half of the egg whites to the egg-nut mixture and repeat, ending with the egg whites. Pour into 2 well-greased 8-inch cake pans and bake for 25 to 30 minutes or until the tops are golden brown and spring back when lightly touched with your finger. Cool on a rack for 20 minutes, then remove from the pans.

For Filling: Pour the cream into a chilled mixer bowl and add the orange zest, vanilla, confectioner's sugar, and corn syrup. Beat until stiff. Place one cake layer on a round plate and spread with all the filling. Top with the remaining layer and refrigerate.

For Frosting: Mix the chocolate morsels in a double boiler over hot, not boiling water. Stir in the sour cream and salt; mix gently. Remove from the heat and spread on the sides and top of the torte. Garnish with chocolate leaves or sprinkle with chopped pistachio.

Nancy M. Corkrean

Tea Time

Holiday Tarts

BOTTOM LAYER:
½ C. butter   1 C. flour
1 (3 oz.) pkg. cream cheese

RASPBERRY FILLING:
¼ C. red raspberry preserves

ALMOND PASTE TOPPING:
1 egg   Coarsely chopped almonds
½ C. sugar   to sprinkle on top
½ C. almond paste

For Bottom Layer: Beat together the butter and cream cheese. Stir in flour and chill for 1 hour. Shape into 1-inch balls and press into ungreased mini-muffin cups.

For Filling: Spoon ½ tsp. red raspberry preserves into each tart.

For Topping: Spoon 1 rounded teaspoon of almond paste mixture over preserves and sprinkle with coarsely chopped almonds. Bake at 325⁰ for 25 to 30 minutes. Cool in pan and remove. Makes 24 tarts.

Joann Ritter

426

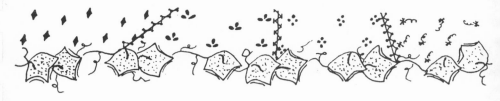

Orange Juice Bread

½ C. butter
1¼ C. sugar
2 eggs
1½ C. flour

1 tsp. baking powder
¼ tsp. salt
¼ C. orange juice
¼ C. milk

ICING:
1 T. lemon juice
1 T. orange juice

⅓ C. sugar

Cream butter and sugar. Beat eggs and add. Sift flour, baking powder, and salt. Mix orange juice and milk. Add liquids alternately with dry ingredients and creamed mixture. Butter 11x4x3-inch loaf pan or 2 small loaf pans. Line bottom of pan with waxed paper and butter the paper. Bake at 325° for 45 minutes. Combine lemon, orange juice, and sugar in saucepan. Cook over medium heat and brush bread with icing as soon as they are taken from the oven.

Joann Ritter

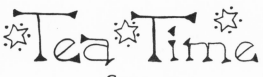

Scones

1½ C. flour
2 ozs. Crisco or margarine
1 oz. sugar
Pinch of salt
1 tsp. baking powder

Raisins, to taste
1 egg
½ C. milk
Grated orange peel

Grease a cookie sheet. Cut Crisco into flour. Add sugar, salt, and baking powder. Add raisins and orange peel. Beat egg and milk together. Add until it is biscuit consistancy. Roll out on floured board and cut into approximately 12 rounds. Bake at 375⁰ for 10 to 15 minutes.

Scones
(Old English Recipe)

1 C. flour
½ tsp. salt
2 ozs. margarine
1 oz. sugar

½ C. milk
Milk for glazing
Raisins, to taste

Sift flour and salt. Add raisins and cut in margarine to fine bread crumb stage. Add sugar. Mix to soft dough stage with milk. Roll on floured board and cut into rounds. Brush with milk. Bake at 375⁰ for 10 to 15 minutes.

3 T. strawberry jam   ¼ lb. butter

Blend until smooth and spread on warm scones.

"As a child in England, my mother made the above scones in an oven heated by a coal fire. She cooked one side and then flipped them over to finish cooking. These scones need to be eaten immediately and do not store well." (W.W. I Era)

Phyllis Patrick

Aunty Nancy's Old English
Christmas Plum Pudding

1 C. sifted flour (8 ozs.)
1 tsp. soda
1 tsp. salt
1 tsp. nutmeg
1 tsp. cinnamon
¼ tsp. mace
1½ C. raisins (cut fine) (½ lb.)
1½ C. currants (cut fine)
   (½ lb.)
¾ C. finely chopped citron
   (¼ lb.)

¾ C. finely chopped lemon &
   orange peel
½ C. chopped walnuts (4 ozs.)
2 C. bread crumbs
   (loosely packed)
2 C. ground suet (16 ozs.)
1 C. brown sugar (8 ozs.)
3 large eggs (beaten)
5 T. currant jam (2 ozs.)
¼ C. sherry or brandy or
   fruit juice

Sift together dry ingredients. Mix in raisins, currants, citron, lemon, and orange peel, walnuts, and bread crumbs. Mix together and blend in remaining ingredients. Pour into well-greased 2-quart mold. Cover tightly and steam on stove in boiling water for 6 hours. Add boiling water as needed. Serve hot with sauce. Serves 14 to 18.

SAUCE:
¼ C. sugar
2 T. cornstarch
¼ tsp. salt
1 egg

2 C. milk
1 T. butter
2 tsp. vanilla extract

(Continued on Next Page)

(Plum Pudding - Continued)

Mix together in double boiler the sugar, cornstarch, salt, and egg. Stir in milk and cook over low heat to boiling. Boil for 1 minute. Cool and blend in butter and vanilla extract.

"Traditionally the plum pudding was full of surprises. Before baking, tiny silver thimbles, small silver horseshoes, and silver threepenny bits (coins) were added. It had to be eaten with great care. A silver thimble found by a young lady meant being forever an old-maid. The horseshoe of course, meant a lucky year ahead. A silver threepence could be kept or spent. My cousin Rita and I loved this ritual at Christmas and our grandad always found a coin. In later years, we realized the coin was popped in his mouth at an appropriate moment! As little girls though, we just thought him very lucky."

Sheila Algreen

Date Pudding

1 egg	¾ C. sugar
1 C. dates (chopped)	1 T. shortening
1 C. boiling water	Pinch of salt
1 C. nuts (chopped)	1¾ C. flour
1 tsp. soda	1 tsp. vanilla
½ tsp. baking powder	

Combine egg, dates, nuts, and boiling water. Mix together the remaining ingredients, then mix all together and bake at 325° for about 30 minutes. Serve with whipped cream.

"I think this was probably my mother's favorite recipe. We never had a Thanksgiving or Christmas dinner together that she didn't bake it."

Wanda Martin

Suet Pudding

2 C. grated suet
5 C. flour
1 lb. raisins

2 C. water
1 lb. butter (not margarine)
1 lb. brown sugar

Blend grated suet into flour with your hands. Work it quite awhile. Blend in raisins with hands. Add water and it will be very stiff. Should not be sticky, about like pie crust, but not as soft. Work it about half an hour and add more flour if needed so it is not sticky. Divide in half and roll about ½-inch thick on floured surface. Mix butter and brown sugar together and place in center of dough. Fold dough up around it and roll out other half. Fold it around the other direction and seal well by pinching dough together. Put on piece of old sheet or some kind of strong material and tie in a ball. Tie top securely and I let set overnight where cold. Put in deep kettle on a trivet or jar rings in boiling water (about 2 inches). Steam for 4 to 6 hours adding boiling water when needed.

"This was a Steven's holiday tradition. Considering the calorie—cholesterol count, it is probably akin to eating poison. Leftovers can be frozen and it reheats well in the microwave."

Frances Stevens

Earlham, Originally a Quaker Settlement in Madison County

The Society of Friends (Quakers) began in England in 1648. Because of their belief in extreme simplicity in dress, speech, worship, and lifestyle, they were first ridiculed and then persecuted. Refusing to join the Church of England or to give up their ideals, they began traveling to America to settle. Here they continued their strong belief in non-violence by opposing all slave ownership and worked to improve relations with native American Indians. They were among the first groups to promote equal rights for women and were very active in the underground railroad to free slaves. Their numbers have continued to grow both in England and America.

Alberta Kisling Shares some Quaker History . . .

The town of Earlham, in northern Madison County was incorporated in 1870. The Rock Island Railroad came west from Des Moines in 1869. Quantities of corn were shipped out of Earlham. A group of Quakers settled there and built a four year high school known as the Earlham Academy. In the 1890's the community purchased the building and changed the name to the Earlham High School. In 1920 a larger school was built and the old school was sold to the Masonic Temple.

One Quaker family, George and Deborah Standing and their five sons came from England on the ship the "Idaho." The trip took two weeks. They came by train from New York to Muscatine, Iowa. In 1870 they heard a farm might be available in the Earlham Quaker community. George walked most of the 200 miles to Earlham where he bought an 80 acre

(Continued on Next Page)

(Quaker History - Continued)

farm for $5.00 an acre. It took as long to move his family, 3 horses, 2 cows, and a wagon from Muscatine to Earlham as it took to come from England to America, two weeks.

To plant their first crop of corn and soybeans they chopped a series of holes in the plowed sod and dropped the seed in by hand. They raised sorghum, turnips, and potatoes. Wheat was an important Iowa crop and there were many mills on the river for grinding the wheat into flour.

At first there were no fences so the children had to round up the livestock each night. One of the cows wore a bell so she could be located by the tinkle.

They planted 100 apple trees. An old stagecoach road passed near that grove of apple trees and bands of Mesquakie Indians occasionally camped east of the Standing farm.

Deborah adjusted to pioneer life - a great change from city life in England. She preserved the wild fruits: plums, strawberries, gooseberries, and crab apples. I have included her recipe for suet pudding as well as other family favorites that have been handed down to me.

'Tis a gift to be Simple

Great Grandmother Standing's Suet Pudding

1 C. chopped suet
1 C. sweet milk
2 C. raisins
1 C. molasses
2 C. flour

1 tsp. soda
1 tsp. cinnamon
1 tsp. ground cloves
1 tsp. nutmeg

Mix ingredients well. Fill greased mold or tin can ¾ full. Cover with waxed paper and tie with string. Steam for 2 hours in a pan of boiling water on stove. Add more water as needed. Serve warm with sauce below.

SAUCE:
1 C. sugar
1½ T. flour
1 C. boiling water

1 tsp. vanilla
1 T. brown sugar

Add boiling water to sugar and flour. Bring to full boil, then add vanilla and brown sugar.

Alberta Kisling

Grandaughter Alberta's Christmas Wassil

3 qts. apple cider
2 sticks cinnamon
1½ tsp. nutmeg
½ C. honey
⅓ C. lemon juice

2 tsp. lemon rind
2 (No. 2) cans pineapple juice
3 whole oranges
Whole cloves

Heat cider and cinnamon sticks in large pan. Bring to a boil, then let simmer, covered for 5 minutes. Add remaining ingredients. Simmer for 5 minutes longer. Press cloves, ½-inch apart into the 3 oranges. Place in baking pan with water and bake at 325⁰ for 30 minutes. Add to wasil and serve hot.

Alberta Kisling

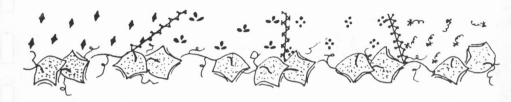

Grandma Lorene Standing's Apple Rings

SYRUP:

1½ C. sugar
2 C. water

DOUGH:

2 C. flour
2 T. sugar
3 tsp. baking powder
1 tsp. salt
6 T. shortening
⅔ to ¾ C. milk

FILLING:

3 C. tart juicy apples (diced)
1 T. butter
½ tsp. cinnamon

Cook for 5 minutes in 9x13-inch pan the 1½ C. sugar and 2 C. of water. Sift flour, 2 T. sugar, baking powder, and salt; cut in shortening. Add milk and stir to make soft dough. Roll dough ⅓-inch thick into oblong 6x12-inches. Spread with diced apples and dot with butter. Sprinkle with cinnamon and roll in a long roll. Slice 1½-inch thick and place in pan of boiling syrup. Bake immediately in 450° oven for 20 to 25 minutes.

Alberta Kisling

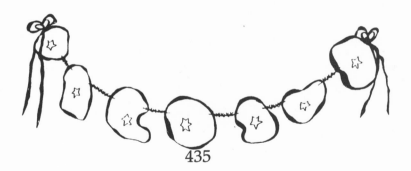

Tea Time

Lemon Curd or Lemon Cheese

½ C. butter
4 large lemons
   (need juice & grated rind)

4 beaten eggs
2 C. sugar

Melt the butter on low and add the rind and lemon juice. Stir in eggs and sugar, mixing well. Continue heating until it thickens. Tastes great on a bagel with cream cheese.

Phyllis Patrick

Rhubarb Butter

4 C. rhubarb (cut-up)
1 T. cinnamon
½ tsp. allspice

1 tsp. cloves
1 pkg. Sure-Jell
5½ C. sugar

Mix the first 5 ingredients. Bring to a hard boil. Add sugar and boil for 2 minutes, stirring constantly so mixture won't stick. Put in jars and seal. (For color, red food coloring can be added.)

Jeanette Neel

Corncob Jelly

12 *bright red cobs*   3 *C. sugar*
3 *pts. water*   6 *red hots*
1 *(1¾ oz.) pkg. Sure-Jell*

Boil broken cobs in water for 30 minutes. Remove from heat and strain liquid. If liquid doesn't measure 3 cups, add enough water to make 3 cups. Add Sure-Jell and bring to a rolling boil. Add sugar and boil for 2 or 3 minutes or until jelly consistency. (Put the red hots in with the liquid.) Pour into 8 small baby food jars that have been sterilized. Seal with paraffin. To make corncob jelly, you must use field corn not sweet corn. Field corn has red cobs and is grown to feed cattle and pigs.

Early pioneers could make jelly from corncobs when fruit was not available. I am sure they didn't have Sure-Jell, but knew of other ways to make their jelly set.

The Cosmopolitan Federated Club of Earlham chose to have a booth and sell corncob jelly at the first Covered Bridge Festival in 1970. The Festival Committee wanted to have all things raised or made in Madison County.

When the Cosomopolitan Club was dissolved, the Ingenue Federated Club of Earlham took over the corncob jelly project. We picked corn by hand and shelled the corn to get our cobs. We put our jelly in recycled baby food jars and decorated the tops with calico dust hats; some were painted and sometimes decorated with corncob slices.

Two years ago the Federal Food Administration required that all kitchens making jellies, jams or candies for sale be inspected. Due to the inconvenience and expense, we dropped the project. Now I only make it for our own use. It is my grandchildren's favorite jelly.

Each year people still stop at our Covered Bridge Booth and ask for corncob jelly. Some would use it for gifts or favors or send it to out-of-state relatives or friends.

Gretchen Brittain

Rhubarb Preserves

7 C. rhubarb (diced) 1 can blueberry pie filling
1 large (6 oz.) box red raspberry Jello

Cook ingredients together for 15 minutes on low heat. Put in containers that are handy and freeze. Very good!

Florence Stalheim

Vegetables

Peas Onions

Peppers Corn Green beans

Asparagus Pie

25 fresh asparagus spears or
   1 (10 oz.) pkg. frozen
⅓ C. butter
5 T. all-purpose flour
2 C. milk
2 tsp. lemon juice
¾ tsp. curry powder
   (optional)

½ tsp. celery salt
1/8 tsp. black pepper
1 baked 9-inch pie shell
4 hard-cooked eggs
   (peeled & sliced)
½ C. grated cheddar cheese
Paprika

Preheat oven to 350⁰. Trim the fresh asparagus spears and cut into 1½-inch lengths. Place in a skillet with enough water to barely cover. Cook, covered for 2 to 3 minutes or until just done; drain and set aside. If using frozen asparagus, thaw spears on paper toweling, then cut into 1½-inch lengths. You need 1⅔ to 2 C. of chopped asparagus. In a medium saucepan melt the butter and add the flour. Cook over medium-low heat until the mixture bubbles up in the pan, but do not allow the roux to brown. Add the milk all at once and whisk and cook until the mixture thickens. Add the lemon juice, curry powder, celery salt, and pepper. Cook mixture over low heat for 2 to 3 minutes, then remove from heat. In the baked pie shell, alternate layers of asparagus and sliced eggs. Pour the sauce over the asparagus (it will be very thick) and spread out evenly. Top the sauce with the grated cheese and sprinkle paprika over all. Bake for 40 to 45 minutes or until sauce bubbles up in the middle and the cheese is a deep golden brown. Remove from oven and allow pie to stand for 10 minutes before cutting into wedges.

"This recipe was given to me by Maureen Roach (Larry Lantz's wife). Larry prepared it for a potluck which I attended. I "begged" her for the recipe and have been enjoying ever since. I have since had many requests for this recipe every time I take it to a potluck! Thanks Larry and Maureen!"

Larry Lantz
Joy Drury

St. Joseph's Smorgasbord
By: Mildred Waltz

St. Joseph's Smorgasbord started the first or second spring Monsignor Higgins was here. (1956)

Each of the four Altar and Rosary Society divisions was to come up with a project. The division chaired by Dorothy Bass discussed the idea of a smorgasbord and since nothing like this had been done locally, we decided to give it a try.

By the third year, the Smorgasbord had grown so much that it was no longer a project that just one division could handle so the whole Altar and Rosary became involved. About this time, it was also moved from the VFW Hall to the Community Building because more space was needed. The first year it was in the Community Building, I was the chairperson and during the planning stage I broke my arm. Luckily Marguerite Gallery came to the rescue and together we carried it off. We had people cooking some of the food in their homes. The VFW let us use their big roaster and ovens. We fried chicken at Tim Osborn's cafe with Anna King in charge there. I remember the late John Cunningham standing for hours carving the roasts.

The Smorgasbord grew from about 200 people to well over 1,000. Many of Monsignor Higgin's friends came from Des Moines. He really enjoyed the event and stayed the day visiting with all the people. It was an event the community looked forward to and was held the first Sunday after Easter. It was a big job, but very rewarding as we all worked together, men, women, and children.

Sometime in the late '70s it was dropped, as people became busier. Although it was a great community builder, every time Fr. Palmer mentions resurrecting the event we quickly change the subject, as those of us who at one time or another were in charge remember the work involved.

441

Vegetables

Baked Beans for Smorgasbord

8 (No. 2½) cans beans or
   3 gallon can
4 C. catsup
6 tsp. prepared mustard

Salt & pepper, if needed
4 C. brown sugar
2 C. diced bacon
1½ C. chopped onions

Mix and bake for 4 hours at 325°. Uncover the last 45 minutes. Makes approximately 50 servings. Need to use four 9x13-inch pans.

"This recipe was sent to me on a post card (3 cent) post marked March 16, 1961. I was still a new bride, married November, 1960. The smorgasbord committee got the recipe from Bill and Dorothy Good who operated a popular bakery and lunch spot on the square. It became a popular staple at all Kelleher Family gatherings."

Carita Kelleher

Calico Beans

¼ lb. bacon (cut-up)
1 lb. ground beef
¼ C. onion (chopped)
½ C. brown sugar
½ C. catsup
1 (15 oz.) can kidney beans

1 (16 oz.) can pork & beans
1 (15 oz.) can butter beans
1 (15 oz.) can green beans
2 T. vinegar
1 tsp. dry mustard

Brown bacon, meat, and onion; drain. Add remaining ingredients and bake at 300° for 1½ hours. This may be cooked in a crockpot and let cook on low for 6 to 8 hours. You may use lima beans instead of butter beans.

Debby Corkrean

Nevada Beans

6 slices bacon (cut into pieces)
1 large onion (chopped)
1 (16 oz.) can baked beans
1 (15 oz.) can red kidney
  beans (undrained)
1 (15 oz.) can butter beans
  (drained)

½ C. catsup
¼ C. yellow mustard
¼ C. Worcestershire sauce
2 T. brown sugar
1 T. dark molasses

Cook bacon and onion until tender, about 10 minutes. Combine with beans, catsup, mustard, Worcestershire sauce, brown sugar, and molasses. Pour into 2-quart greased casserole and bake, uncovered at 350⁰ for 1 hour. (Can be mixed up a day ahead and baked when needed. I have put them in a large crock or oblong dish.) Makes 10 to 12 servings.

Rosemary Stuchel

Broccoli Cheese Casserole

1 pkg. frozen cauliflower
1 pkg. frozen brussel sprouts
1 pkg. frozen broccoli (chopped)

1 (8 oz.) jar Cheez Whiz
1 can mushroom soup

Cook vegetables as directed on package. Drain well. Put in casserole dish and add cheese and mushroom soup. Mix and bake for ½ hour in moderate oven.

Luella Fairholm

Vegetables

Broccoli Casserole

2 pkgs. frozen broccoli
¾ C. Minute Rice (uncooked)
¼ C. margarine (melted)
½ C. onion
1 can cream of mushroom soup

1 can cream of celery soup
1 small jar Cheez Whiz
Slivered almonds
Paprika

Cook broccoli as directed and drain. Melt margarine and mix in onion, soups, cheese, and rice. Layer in a buttered casserole dish the broccoli and soup mixture. Sprinkle with paprika and slivered almonds. Bake, uncovered at 350⁰ for 30 to 40 minutes.

Joan Hilton

Broccoli and Cauliflower Casserole

2 pkgs. frozen broccoli/
   cauliflower
1 can cream of chicken soup
1 can cream of celery soup

1 (8 oz.) jar Cheez Whiz
2 small cans French fried
   onions

Thaw frozen vegetables and put in casserole dish. Blend cheese and soups. Heat until well mixed and pourable. Pour over vegetables and add 1 can of onions, stirring gently. Bake at 350⁰ for 45 minutes. Add 2nd can of onions to top and bake for 15 more minutes.

Norma Porter

444

Broccoli and Rice Casserole

1 C. Minute Rice
1 C. boiling water
1 stick margarine
½ C. celery
½ C. onion (chopped)

1 can cream of mushroom
   soup
1 (4 oz.) jar Cheez Whiz
1 pkg. (box) frozen chopped
   broccoli

Put 1 C. Minute Rice in 2-quart casserole dish and add 1 C. of boiling water, cover, and let set. Saute' margarine, celery, and chopped onion. Add cream of mushroom soup and Cheez Whiz. After cheese melts add to rice. Cook and drain frozen chopped broccoli. Add to rice mixture and mix well. Bake at 350⁰ for 30 minutes. (Can also be microwaved for 5 minutes on medium and then for 5 to 8 minutes on High.)

Dorothy J. Kellogg
Patricia Morris

Buffet Supper Rice

"You either love this recipe or hate it! Be brave!"

1 C. chopped onion	½ tsp. salt
¼ C. margarine	1/8 tsp. pepper
4 C. hot cooked rice	3 (4 oz.) cans mild green
2 C. sour cream	chilies
1 C. cottage cheese	2 C. sharp cheddar cheese
1 bay leaf (crumbled)	(grated) or Monterey Jack
Parsley	

Cook onion in margarine until soft, but not brown. Mix with rice, sour cream, cottage cheese, bay leaf, salt, and pepper. Drain and chop chilies. In a large buttered casserole spread ⅓ rice mixture, ⅓ chopped chilies, and ⅓ cheddar cheese. Repeat twice and bake, uncovered at 325⁰ for 25 minutes. Garnish with parsley. Serves 10 to 12.

"The surprise flavor in this casserole goes well with chicken, ham or roast beef."

Sharon Johnson

Carrots and Cheese

4 C. carrots (sliced & cooked)	½ stick of oleo
1 large onion (sliced)	Buttered bread crumbs
¾ to 1 lb. Velveeta cheese	

Cook carrots and onions until done. Drain and pour into 8x8x2-inch pan. Melt cheese and oleo together and pour over carrots and onions. Top with buttered bread crumbs, if desired and bake at 350⁰ for 30 minutes or until bubbly.

Kathleen Kordick

Cabbage Rolls

2 lbs. ground beef
¼ lb. ground pork
½ C. rice (uncooked)
Salt & pepper

1 medium onion
1 (8 oz.) can tomato sauce
1 medium head cabbage

Mix the ground beef and pork in a large bowl. Add the seasoning, rice, and finely chopped onion; mix well. Steam the head of cabbage for easy removal of leaves. Add 1 tsp. of vinegar to the water along with the cabbage. Place a heaping tablespoon of meat mixture into a cabbage leaf and roll tight. Place in roaster and pour the tomato sauce over all and add 1 tsp. of shortening. Add 1 tomato sauce can of water. (I add about ¼ C. water to start with and add more as needed.) Bake at 325° for 1½ hours. Makes about 16 to 20 cabbage rolls.

Shirley Privratsky

Escalloped Carrots

4 C. cooked carrots
1 medium onion (diced)
3 T. butter
1 can cream of celery soup
½ tsp. salt

Dash of pepper
½ C. grated cheddar cheese
1½ C. seasoned stuffing mix
   (dry) or croutons
¼ C. melted butter

Place carrots in the bottom of a casserole dish. Saute' the onion in 3 T. butter. Combine the onion with the soup, salt, pepper, and grated cheese. Spoon over the carrots. Toss the stuffing mix (croutons) with the ¼ C. butter. Sprinkle over the soup mixture and bake at 350° for 30 to 40 minutes.

Jana Corkrean

Golbaki - Cabbage Rolls

1 large head of cabbage
½ C. regular rice
1½ lbs. ground beef
Salt & pepper, to taste

1 small onion (minced)
½ tsp. garlic powder
1 egg

TOMATO SAUCE:
4 slices bacon (diced)
1 small onion (chopped)

1 (8 oz.) can tomato sauce
1 bay leaf

Remove core from cabbage and scald in boiling water. Remove leaves, 1 at a time and set aside. Cook rice in boiling water for about 10 minutes; drain. Brown ground beef and onion together until lightly brown. Mix beef mixture, rice, egg, and seasonings. Place a large spoonful of meat mixture on each cabbage leaf. Fold and roll. Chop leftover cabbage and place in bottom of casserole baking dish. Arrange cabbage rolls on top. Pour tomato sauce over rolls, cover, and bake at 350⁰ for about 1 hour.

For Tomato Sauce: Brown bacon and add onion, sauteing' for several minutes. Add tomato sauce, bay leaf, salt, and pepper (to taste). Simmer for about 2 minutes.

Corn and Broccoli Casserole

1 pkg. frozen broccoli (thawed)
¼ C. fine bread crumbs
1 can creamed corn
1 T. butter

¼ tsp. salt
1 egg (beaten)
1 T. minced onions

Butter casserole. Mix half of the bread crumbs with other ingredients. Pour into casserole and sprinkle on balance of bread crumbs. Bake at 350° for 45 minutes.

Margaret Tiernan

Corn Noodle Casserole

1 pkg. frozen noodles
¼ lb. chopped American
   cheese
1 tsp. sugar

¼ lb. oleo
2 (15 oz.) cans creamed corn
½ tsp. pepper
½ tsp. salt

Cook and drain noodles. Add cheese, butter, and sugar until melted. Add corn, salt, and pepper. Pour into greased casserole dish and bake at 350° for 40 minutes. Serves 8.

Joanne Nichols

Vegetables

Scalloped Corn

2 C. whole kernel corn
1 C. milk
2 eggs (beaten)
1 tsp. salt

2 T. butter
2 T. flour
2 T. sugar

Combine all ingredients in oven-proof dish, mixing well. Bake at 350° for 30 minutes, stirring occasionally.

Irene Kelly
Joan Hilton

French Fried Onions

6 medium mild white onions
   (sliced ¼ -inch thick)
2 C. milk

3 eggs
All-purpose flour

Pour beaten eggs and milk into shallow pan. Drop separated onion rings into egg mixture, swishing until all are well coated, then dip into flour until coated, a few at a time. Fry in deep, hot fat until crisp and golden. Salt just before serving.

Margaret Tiernan

Onion Puff

2 *large onions*   2 *tsp. butter*

BATTER:
2 *large eggs*   ¾ *C. flour*
2 *T. melted butter*   ¾ *tsp. salt*
¾ *C. milk*

Heat oven to 375°. Slice onions ¼-inch thick and saute' in butter in 9-inch cast iron skillet over high heat until lightly browned and tender. Pour batter over sauted onions in skillet. Bake for 45 minutes. Best when served immediately.

Teresa Hoffelmeyer

Cheesey Potatoes

1 *pkg. Southern style hash*   1 *T. dried onion*
  browns or green pepper style   1 *can cream of chicken soup*
1 *tsp. salt*   ½ *C. milk*
¼ *tsp. pepper*   8 *ozs. sour cream*
½ *C. oleo*   2 *C. Cheez Whiz*

Mix all together and put into a 9-inch square pan, sprayed with Pam. Bake at 350° for 1 hour. (1½ recipe makes a full 9x13-inch pan.)

Joanne Nichols

Vegetables

Buffet Potato Casserole

1 (2 lb.) pkg. frozen hash brown potatoes
½ C. butter or margarine (melted)
1 pt. sour cream
1 can condensed cream of chicken soup

2 C. shredded cheddar cheese
1 tsp. salt
¼ to ½ tsp. pepper
2 C. cornflake crumbs
½ C. butter or margarine (melted)
½ C. chopped onion

Combine potatoes and ½ C. butter in large bowl. Stir in sour cream, soup, onion, cheese, salt, and pepper. Place in greased 13x9x2-inch baking dish. Combine cornflake crumbs and ½ C. melted butter. Sprinkle over top and cover with foil. Bake at 350⁰ for 20 minutes. Uncover and continue baking for 20 minutes. Note: This casserole can be made in advance and refrigerated. If so add 10 minutes to baking time.

Variations: May use 1½ C. longhorn cheese in place of cheddar. You may also cook uncovered.

Kim Algreen
Cheryl Emanuel
Pam Palmer
Patricia Morris

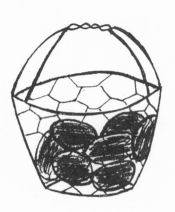

Hash Brown Casserole

8 C. frozen hash browns
½ C. chopped onion
2 cans cream of celery soup

⅔ C. milk
1 (6 oz.) pkg. cream cheese
8 ozs. cheddar cheese (grated)

Mix soup, milk, and cheese and heat. Pour over potatoes and dot with butter. Bake at 350⁰ for 1 hour and 15 minutes. Cover with foil the first half hour, uncover for last half hour, then sprinkle with cheddar cheese the last 15 minutes.

Rosemary Gronstal

Potato Dish

6 potatoes (unpeeled & diced)
1 C. water

½ C. oleo (melted)
1 pkg. dry onion soup mix

Mix water, oleo, and soup mix together. Layer potatoes in greased 9x13-inch pan and pour mixture over potatoes. Bake at 350⁰ for 45 to 60 minutes or until tender.

Marilyn McNamara

Minnesota Wild Rice

1½ C. wild rice
4 C. water
1 tsp. salt
1 small onion

4 strips of bacon (diced)
4 green onions (sliced)
6 fresh mushrooms (sliced)

Rinse rice thoroughly. Add water, salt, and onion. Cover and simmer until tender for 45 minutes. Remove onion and drain rice. Dice the bacon and fry until crisp; add the green onions and mushrooms which have been sliced thinly and cook until tender. Add the rice and season with salt and pepper.

Helen Sawyer

Vegetable Medley

1 bag broccoli, cauliflower, carrot, fanfare (thawed & drained)
1 can cream of mushroom soup

⅓ C. sour cream or yogurt
¼ tsp. pepper
1 (4 oz.) jar pimiento
1 can French fried onions
1 C. shredded cheddar cheese

Combine vegetables, soup, ½ C. of the cheese, sour cream, pepper, pimiento, and ½ the can of French fried onions. Pour into a 1-quart casserole and bake, covered at 350º for 30 minutes. Top with remaining cheese and onions, then bake, uncovered for 6 minutes longer.

For Microwave: Prepare as above. Cook, covered, on High for 8 minutes, turning when halfway through. Top with remaining cheese and onions. Cook, uncovered on High for 1 minute or until cheese melts.

Margaret Tiernan

Zucchini

3 C. thinly sliced zucchini
1 C. Bisquick
½ C. minced onion
½ C. grated Parmesan cheese
2 T. snipped parsley
½ tsp. salt

½ tsp. seasoned salt
½ tsp. dried marjoram or
  oregano leaves
1 clove of garlic (minced)
½ C. vegetable oil
4 eggs (slightly beaten)

Grease oblong pan. Mix all ingredients and spread in pan. Bake at 350⁰ for 25 minutes or until golden brown. (I even add 1 pound of ground beef which is browned and drained.)

Marine Brunsmann

Vegetables

A patchwork of Recollections & Stories

CELEBRATE THE LORD'S NEW DAY

1994

"Boomerang"
By: Cheryl Weltha

(Reprinted with Permission from The Madisonian)

For many Winterset High School graduates, the high school yearbook - The "Boomerang" - may be gathering dust somewhere on a forgotten shelf. But for Pete Tran, a 1968 foreign exchange student from Vietnam, the Winterset yearbook represented a ticket to freedom as Tran escaped with only it and the clothes on his back from the war-torn country.

Yearbook his ID . . .

"This (1968 Boomerang) was my ID . . . it was my proof that I had been to America," Tran said upon his return to Winterset after 25 years away.

Unlike a real boomerang, Tran's return to America involved several years of planning an escape for himself and other family members. After his return in 1968 to Bien Hoa, South Vietnam, Tran found life there going from bad to worse.

He went on to receive a law degree, married, and had two children. After the Communist take-over in 1975, he secretly began escape plans. He gained inspiration knowing that his own father had successfully planned his family's escape from North Vietnam to the south.

"The Communists controlled everything...even our thought," said Tran. "They'd rather kill ten people to get just one possible CIA informer."

Tran said the odds were against him from the outset. He was highly educated, Catholic, had worked for the U.S. Embassy and he had been a student in America, all strikes against him, in the view of the local Communist government. The threat of being sent to a so-called 're-education camp', as his

458

parents had been, was ever present. After being accused of having had CIA connections, Tran went underground, moving from town to town to elude the Communists.

"I couldn't tell anyone about the planned escape, not even my family," he explained, "If they knew, we could be caught."

Pretends to be a Fisherman . . .

About a year before his escape, Tran moved his family to the sea coast after obtaining permission to work in a fishing cooperative. This was the first major step in his escape plan. It took a year of pretending to be a fisherman before he and his family were prepared to escape.

"We had to get permission for everything...we had to buy fish on the black market out on the sea to show the Communists when we got back at night," he said.

The night of the country's annual celebration of the Communist revolution, Tran and 46 family members quietly stepped into a ten-foot long river boat (with a crawl space below) and, without any equipment or experience, set sail on the open sea. Their hopes were to see an American ship or for the boat to land in nearby Malaysia.

"All we knew was to go south and turn right," said Tran, whose only guide was Polaris - the north star.

The crowded family traveled three days and nights, and then met with Thai pirates who stole everything they had, including Tran's wedding and school rings. Thanks to the aid of a Thai fisherman, the group made it to the shore of Thailand.

Tran had to quickly assess the situation there, which turned out to be unfriendly. He stalled for time with the authorities in order to learn what was safe. An appointment with a UN representative fell through.

"We had to follow orders, but I would try to find a way out of it," he said, explaining that the Thai government was towing the boat people back out into the sea, supposedly en route to refugee camps, but cutting the ropes and leaving them stranded.

Recollections

Send letters to U.S. . . .

At this time while staying in an 'isolation' area, Tran sent letters soliciting help to the few contacts he had here in the U.S., which included Cliff Scholten, WHS prinicpal, and Bill and Jeneta Weltha, a family he had gone to St. Joseph Catholic Church with during his senior year. Scholten and several school groups raised about $500 and mailed it to a missionary in Thailand who passed the money on to Tran.

Meanwhile, Tran's letter to the Welthas family reached their new address in Palmyra, Missouri, after being sent to Winterset. Jeneta brought Tran's dilemma to the attention of a congressman and other people. In an odd turn of circumstances, the Tran family was allowed to come to the states because their two-year-old daughter needed heart surgery. In 1980, the Trans arrived in California for that surgery and have been in America ever since.

"I so appreciate the U.S. people who helped us," said Tran, who later became a U.S. citizen.

Tran shared his story with his 1968 WHS classmates at their 25-year reunion. He received a standing ovation plus an assurance of a new class ring from Scholten.

Today, Tran leads a busy life in San Jose, California, with his wife and four children. He works as a correctional officer for the Santa Clara County Jail as well as being a realtor. He is currently taking a correspondence course with Taft University to become a lawyer, a position he had formerly earned in Vietnam. He also volunteers his assistance to ethnic groups in the San Jose area.

In reminiscing of his year here in 1968, Tran said he learned a lot and recalled that chorus with teacher Dean Leslie was his favorite subject. He proudly shows the water-stained pages of his own yearbook, entitled "Boomerang."

"This is very meaningful to me," he said. "I am like this Boomerang...I went out and then I came back."

A Surprise Ending

By: Emery Bubany
(Edited by Teresa Hoffelmeyer)

(Reprinted with Permission from the Madisonian)

In 1994, Winterset will celebrate its 25th Covered Bridge Festival! Most people who attend Covered Bridge expect to have a good time, but once in awhile someone also gets the surprise of a lifetime. The following is the story of a former Madison County resident and her surprise during the Covered Bridge Festival of 1989.

Louise Shehan Porter of West Des Moines decided to tour the historical complex during her visit that year. Marguerite Gallery, a former Winterset teacher and one-time postmaster, was telling those on the tour about the origin of the old log cabin at the complex and explaining how it was once part of a house.

Louise commented to Marguerite that her mother had told her she'd been born in a log cabin in Madison County. Marguerite began questioning this visitor and after showing her a picture of the house to which the log cabin had been attached, Louise realized that it was indeed the house where she was born, "My mother always told us girls we were born in a log cabin, but we thought she was exaggerating!"

Another surprise came when the two women discovered that Louise had been a student of Marguerite's in the third grade. Louise had fond memories of this special teacher's classes, but for Louise, her fondest memory was in 1945 when Marguerite gave her family gifts for Christmas. It was a time when they were struggling to make ends meet.

It should be noted that the log cabin where Louise and the rest of the Shehan family lived had at one time served as a post office. The postmasters would build rooms onto the log cabin and bring their families to live there. Because Marguerite had once been a postmaster, she paid to have this log cabin moved to the historical complex.

(Marguerite Gallery died in 1993, but her memory will live on in those who knew her and whose lives she touched.)

Saga of The One Room School
By: Lucille Russell

A poet once wrote: "Still sits the schoolhouse by the road a ragged beggar sunning." Very few one room schools survived. However, they were a most important part of our history. Those of us who attended these schools and later returned to teach in them were indeed privileged people.

The teacher taught all grades K through 8th, sometimes to thirty pupils. The subjects taught were the three R's, reading, writing, arithmetic, and also, geography, history, physiology, English, government, spelling, music, and science. While one class was reciting, the other children were preparing their lessons. The younger children learned a lot from listening to the older children reciting their lessons. On the playground the older boys and girls helped the little ones and looked after them. Everyone brought their lunch. The lunch hour was like a big family eating and visiting together.

Sometimes a teacher taught at the same school for several years and had a very positive influence on many young people's lives. Edith Bowles, who taught Walnut No. 5 for thirty-two years, was one of the best.

Besides teaching all grades, the teacher built the fires, swept the floors, nursed the sick and wounded, policed the playground and the two little outhouses, put on programs, and helped with coats and overshoes. She or he also raised and lowered the flag and carried the water from an outside well for drinking and washing of faces and hands. Sometimes the older children helped with the chores. They liked to dust, clean erasers, and wash blackboards.

The old schoolhouses were often the nerve centers of the neighborhood for young and old alike. There were "literary" meetings, where the folks gave readings, sang songs, had spell downs, and ciphering matches. The best speller was the one still standing after everyone else had incorrectly spelled a word, and the best in math could add, subtract, multiply, and divide faster than anyone else.

There were programs put on by the teacher and the pupils. These consisted of small plays, poems recited from memory, and songs. Often a box or pie supper was part of the entertainment. The ladies, young and old, brought fancy decorated boxes filled with good country cooking. These were auctioned off to the highest bidder, who then ate with the lady who brought the box. The money was used for needed school equipment.

Elections were held in some of the schools. In the 30's and 40's many schools held monthly Parent-Teacher Association meetings. This was a community get together, a social time for the families and the teacher to communicate and get to know each other better.

Many great men and women of America got their early education in the one room rural schools.

The Bear in The Woods of Winterset
By: Jim Pottebaum, Veterinarian

(In our community, we have a family, the Rogers, who own a menagerie of exotic animals. The following event occurred the day the Rogers moved from one farm to another.)

One Tuesday afternoon, I was called out to help capture a 325 pound black bear on the loose. The owners were transporting the bear from one cage to another when the bear broke through the back door of the horse trailer and jumped out onto the road. The male bear whose name was Custer ambled up into some brush and trees nearby. The owners immediately stopped the truck and trailer. Scott Rogers got out to follow the bear and his wife Theresa quickly drove to town to get help to catch Custer.

Recollections

When Theresa excitedly related the problem to me, I called Iowa State University to get instructions on which and how much tranquilizer to use to subdue the large bear.

Armed with syringe and drugs, we quickly returned to the site. Now the problem was getting the untamed bear to hold still while I crept up to it to poke it with a needle. Luckily, the bear had a sweet tooth, and Scott had a Milky Way bar to share. As the bear nibbled, I jabbed him with the syringe. He roared, jumped, and reeled around. I promptly dropped the syringe and ran. Luckily, enough tranquilizer was injected to make the bear a little groggy and move with slow reflexes, so that I could administer the rest of the drug dose. Soon the cranky, loose bear was completely asleep and would remain so for about an hour.

Now another problem presented itself: How to move the bear from the brush up on the hill back down to the trailer parked on the road. When I went down to my truck to get a rope, I became aware of nearly a dozen cars parked on the pavement with people watching the whole event. A pick-up load of construction workers volunteered to help me. They enjoyed the chance to hold and carry a live bear out of the woods. Soon the bear was back inside the horse trailer and the rear door fortified to stay shut. As the crowd dispersed, my secretary nervously called to me on my 2-way radio. Apparently a passerby had seen the commotion earlier and had raced to town. The sheriff's office had been notified that someone had been mauled on the hillside by a five hundred pound bear; our office had been called for reinforcements, and the sheriff was on the way. The story was corrected quickly, and the unusual event was over.

Both the *Madisonian* and *Des Moines Register* featured the event.

She Finds Her Winter Coat Served Well in WWII
By: Alan Koonse

(Reprinted with Permission from the Madisonian)

In 1945, a young Winterset girl made her own personal contribution to refugees in war-torn Europe. She gave what she could, an old winter coat.

In 1976, that simple donation brought a letter of heartfelt thanks from the daughter of a Czech woman who had received the coat 31 years ago.

Celine McLaughlin was a 12-year-old student at South Ward Elementary School in Winterset when she heard of the national appeal for clothing and money to aid the homeless, hungry, innocent victims of World War II's terror.

Her small donation had a special meaning for her. "During the war, everybody was very enthusiastic about doing anything they could to help the war effort," Celine recalls today.

Asked for Letter . . .

Because of her special interest in the project, she put a note in the pocket of the old coat before donating it. The message was simple and direct: She asked the person who received the coat to write to her.

Thirty years passed. Celine married John Waring, moved to Omaha, Nebraska, became the mother of seven children, and forgot about the note.

She forgot about it until recently, that is, when she received a letter from the daughter of the woman who had received - and used - the coat.

The letter said: "When you were 12 years old in 1945 after the Second World War, you gave a coat to be sent to the refugees in Europe. This coat was given to my mother in Czechoslovakia and she found your note in its pocket.

In Hard Times . . .

"The coat served my mother in hard times and she kept your note, gratefully, all these years.

465

Recollections

"Since 1947, my parents lived in Israel in the kibbutz. I found your note and decided to try and thank you, with my mother."

The letter was signed simply: "Sincerely, the daughter, Efrat Weil" The letter - addressed to Celine McLaughlin - was received in Winterset, and postmaster Marguerite Gallery forwarded it to Mrs. John Corkrean of Cumming, whom she knew to be Celine's sister.

Gallery, who had been one of Celine's teachers at the Winterset school when the clothing drive had taken place, said she remembered Celine McLaughlin's name when she saw it on the letter that came into the post office.

Didn't Remember Note . . .

Celine Waring said Efrat Weil's handwriting was "excellent" and she believes the girl is a teenager.

"To be real truthful, I don't remember putting the note in the pocket. And it probably didn't occur to me at the time that the recipient may not have been able to read English," she said.

"It amazes me that the child of this woman would be so appreciative. When I got the letter I was very excited," she said. Waring said her children and their friends have taken a keen interest in the letter that bridged a gap of more than 30 years. The family is planning to write Miss Weil soon, she said.

Celine Waring's family did write back to the Weil family. Through correspondence with the father, Shrage Weil, they learned that he had painted the Israeli Room in the JFK Performing Arts Center in Washington D.C. He also sent Celine a print of one of the paintings. Celine and her husband took the print into a shop in Omaha to be framed and were waited upon by a woman who became estatic when she saw the print. She was Jewish and had been in a Concentration camp and confirmed that Sharaga Weil was indeed a very famous Jewish artist.

466

Threshing Days
By: Martha Street

The following is my recollection of threshing days in our neighborhood when I was a child.

The threshers had a run of places they would go, all of which would be decided at a threshers meeting prior to threshing days. Our threshing crew consisted of my uncles and a few neighbors. The weather and how often the threshing machine and steam engine broke down determined when they got to our place. There were times when we only had an afternoon's warning before they arrived.

These days were fun for my sister, two brothers, and myself. We had to help, but our mother was the really busy one!

Feeding threshers was a big event. It not only included feeding the men, but their wives and children who came to help in the kitchen. Generally, both dinner and supper were served; however, some of the men went home to do their chores and did not stay for supper.

We kept the old world custom of serving lunch in mid-morning and mid-afternoon. The lunch consisted of a cold drink such as lemonade, coffee, sandwiches on homemade buns or bread and cookies. The kids and a mature helper served the lunch since the rest of the women were busy in the kitchen. In many cases there was a water boy with cold water in a stone jug, stopped with a corn cob cork, who brought the jug to each man for a cool drink.

A farm wife's reputation as a good cook depended upon this meal so it was no ordinary meal! There was competition among the wives in the threshing ring, and any wife who had not been able to help with a meal was given a detailed report from her husband of what others served.

The mainstay for many meals was fried chicken. Since there was no refrigeration, the wife would wring the necks, pluck feathers, and clean them ready for the frying pan that morning. From the garden came potatoes for mashing, cabbage for slaw, ripe tomatoes and cucumbers for slicing, green beans cooked with home-cured bacon, corn, and pickles. Homemade noodles were made if chicken soup was served and there were homemade bread or rolls, jellies, jams, and freshly churned butter. For dessert there would be fruit pies and cakes. If anyone had an ice cream freezer, ice was purchased in town and they made ice cream for pie a la mode!

The women prepared all the food in the kitchen on the big black cookstove that was fueled by wood. The temperature on a hot summer day rose to 90 or so in the kitchen while the bread and pies were baking. There was hot water in the reservoir on the back of the stove for washing dishes.

Before the men came for dinner a mirror was hung on a tree in the yard near the house. A basin was put on a bench with a pail of water and dipper. Soap, comb, and towel were beneath for the crew to use to clean up. There was much joking and laughter as they ate at the long table. Sometimes the table had to be reset for the next bunch if they could not all be served at one time.

After the men had overindulged and gone back to work, the dishes were washed and the women would begin preparing for the afternoon lunch and drinks, after which most of the women and their children would go home. A few might stay to help with supper, if needed.

Everyone was tired, but full, at the end of a long threshing day. The wife had usually been up since 5:00 a.m. on those days and it was nice to be able to sit down and breathe a sigh of relief that feeding the threshers was over for the year.

A Look Back
By: Teresa Hoffelmeyer

As I was looking over my recipes, I came upon my well-worn sweet pickle recipe. It is written in my great aunt Irene's hand on a sheet of stationery with the heading, "JENSEN HARDWARE - PLUMBING, HEATING, & SHEET METAL WORK - DEXTER, IOWA." This was my great uncle Carl's store which closed in the late 1950's. It was a special store to me, as this was where I got my first tricycle, swing set, and doll house. My uncle Carl was my favorite great uncle and I believe I was a favorite of his.

Actually, I had quite an assortment of great uncles, some of whom I saw frequently and others seldom. There was my great uncle Pete, a bachelor, quite stout, and completely bald. He would visit us on Sunday afternoons and bring Drew's chocolates. Then there was my great uncle Fat. I was always amazed that family and friends alike called him Fat, and it never seemed to bother him. My grandfather and some of these great uncles had a love of horses and mules and frequently participated in 4th of July parades, riding horse drawn carts and accompanied by grandchildren. (Perhaps they had ridden one too many horses because many of them, including my dad, have a bit of a bandy-legged walk, as if they just got off a horse, a trait more noticeable as they age. Fortunately, the women of the family have not inherited this walk.)

As a little girl, I remember going to Uncle Carl's and Aunt Irene's for Christmas dinner. The dining room table seemed endless as we passed plate after plate of food, including Irene's pickles. My parents, grandparents, and assorted relatives would all gather for those occasions. Aunt Irene was a perfectionist and never actually sat at the table to eat with us, but bustled about making sure everyone was well fed. Later, she would eat a small plateful in the kitchen.

Dexter at this time was a lively town with two grocery stores, a pharmacy, dry cleaners, and clothing store. We would gather in town at Christmas with all our country neighbors and Santa would visit, usually riding in a pickup, and give all

469

Recollections

the children candy. There were drawings too and occasionally we would win a turkey to roast for the holidays. Sadly, this small town is no longer the flurry of activity it once was and my great aunt and uncle's home no longer has the beautiful flower gardens and perfectly kept lawn.

After my great aunt and uncle died, their belongings were auctioned. I asked my dad if he would bid on their bedroom set for me, which he agreed to do as long as it didn't sell for more than $100. I did get the three piece bedroom suite and today I appreciate it as a beautiful antique, but at the time I only knew that the dresser had a special drawer where the toys were kept for us kids. That and the fact that it was theirs made it special to me.

First Communion
By: Fr. Frank Palmer

First Eucharist/Communion is for most a memorable experience. I can truly say that is true for me for several reasons!

To begin, I should mention that First Eucharist in St. Anthony's held a niche of honor all its own. Young people made their First Communion in 2nd grade. It was the highlight of the year. White was the traditional color for both boys and girls. Families were good about loaning attire, pants, dresses, or veils for those who could not afford to purchase them. Also it was always held on Mother's Day.

The ceremony as it was conducted by the Sisters of Humility had its own distinctive flavor emphasizing the honor or specialness of the occasion. Chosen boys from the first grade, "leaders" as they were called, would escort each first communicant from his place in the pew up to the sanctuary for reception of communion and then back again to the pew. Both leader and first communicant with hands folded demurely, paced themselves up the altar and back. All of this was synchronized in several practices under the watchful eye of Sr. Cyril, our second grade teacher who was in charge. As a first grader I was honored to be a leader/escort; I remembered how thrilled I was. I looked forward to making my First Communion the next year.

The following year I was a second grader. All through the year catechism lessons relevant to the Eucharist & Reconcilication (Confession/Penance as it was called back then) had to be memorized and learned along with prayers such as the Our Father, Hail Mary, and Act of Contrition. During the month of April we had practice sessions in the church. I had my first communion suit complete with black tie. We all looked forward to May.

Then the unexpected occurred. Two weeks before Mother's Day, my mother received a letter from my brother who was in the Navy (war time) indicating that he would be on a brief leave in Chicago and would be available for visit over Mother's Day weekend. Could she take the train up and stay with relatives?

I was asked to make a choice: go with my mother to see my brother or stay at home and make my first communion. I was torn, but I eventually decided to go with my mother. I remember how difficult it was for me to tell Sr. Cyril that I was not going to make my First Communion with the class. I remember how disappointed she was. The anguish was further compounded when I went to Mass on Mother's Day in Chicago. Coincidentally, it was the First Communion Mass for that parish as well. I tried to hide my tears as I watched the kids come down the aisle.

So I had to wait a whole year. As a third grader, I practiced with the second grade to receive my First Communion. May arrived; again my first communion suit was readied. Saturday morning we had our final practice for Mass the following Sunday morning. Relatives were invited to the Mass and

Recollections

brunch following. I woke up Sunday morning excited. I dressed, wandered into the kitchen, and there on the table were cookies that my mom had made for brunch. Without thinking, I ate two of them. I suddenly realized that I had broken the Eucharist fast (midnight fast from solid foods was a requirement in those days). My mother was "fit to be tied." Once more, I had to tell Sr. Cyril that I would not be making my first communion. Judging from her reaction, I think she also was "fit to be tied."

Later on that afternoon, when things quieted down, Sr. Cyril stopped by and suggested that I make my First Communion the next day (Monday) at the morning school Mass. So the next morning, I dressed in my white suit and made my First Communion in the presence of the student body. As I did, I think Sr. Cyril and my mother gave a great sigh of relief!

White Communion Shoes
By: Karen Pommier

Back in 1957, I was an anxious second grader awaiting my First Holy Communion Day. Boy, was I surprised to wake up the day before and discover Mom had gone to the hospital to have a baby! She and Dad were awfully quiet about such things. My oldest sister, Margene, was delegated to take me downtown and buy a new pair of white shoes for my Communion Day. Not a pair of children's white shoes were to be found anywhere in town. A determined salesman offered me the only pair of white shoes he had in the store - a woman's pair, size 8½! He kindly included three pairs of foam insoles to help fill out the shoes.

Mom was so shocked when I showed up at her hospital doorway wearing shoes that were hopelessly huge on me.

At this Catholic hospital, I remember doctors and nuns giving me statues, holy cards, and money because it was a special day, and perhaps they felt sorry for this poor little girl with huge feet!

Some 20 years later, I found the shoes in my parents' basement. I laughed so hard when I put them on; they were still too big!

Corpus Christi
By: Fr. Frank Palmer

One of the warm memories that I have growing up as a youngster in my home parish was our annual celebration of the Feast of Corpus Christi (Latin for the "Body of Christ"). Its origin dates back into the 1300's. I don't know when it started in our parish or which of the pastors initiated it. All I remember is looking forward to it each year. It was a time honored tradition. We would have a big procession in the afternoon honoring the Sacrament of the Eucharist or the Blessed Sacrament as we called it. All of the Catholic parishes in the city were invited to participate together with their parish organizations. The Knights of Columbus with their color guard participated, as did the band of Dowling High School. Naturally the clergy were all present also.

The feast day occurs on the Sunday following Trinity, usually the first or second week of June, on the tail end of spring. Spring flowers are blooming, especially peonies. I remember how Msgr. Lalley, our pastor, on the Sunday of the celebration would spend the sermon time detailing the leaders of the various sections of the procession. It would be quite large.

The procession began at the parish church and proceeded through the neighborhood following a rectangular route. The Dowling band usually led the way, followed by the organizations. Msgr. Lalley, carrying the Blessed Sacrament flanked by six men carrying a canopy over him, was at the end. Many of those walking in the procession would drop petals of flowers. All along the route parishioners on both sides decorated their homes in festive colors emphasizing some theme honoring Jesus. I remember decorating our house with crepe paper, colors of red, white, blue. One year on our lawn adjacent to the street, I had formed the letters "Welcome Jesus." The decorating usually took a major part of the morning.

Traditionally, the procession stopped at three homes along the way. The parishioners at these homes had constructed beautiful outdoor altar shrines decorated with fresh flowers for the occasion. It would be at these homes that the procession would pause and celebrate Benediction; the people gathered there in prayer would be blessed. As the Blessed Sacrament passed by each of our homes, there would be a hushed reverence. Parishioners would join in one final prayer service of benediction on the parish grounds at the grotto of Mary. Then a huge parish Italian dinner followed, along with rides and games for children.

The procession with all of its solemnity and festivity is something that I still remember.

Advent and Christmas

The Jesse Tree
- An Advent Family Tradition

(You will need some type of tree, a small evergreen or artifical tree or a construction paper tree, etc. Children can draw, color, and cut out the suggested symbols for your tree.)

The Jesse tree is like a family tree for Jesus. Jesse lived about 1,000 years before Jesus, and it was his youngest son, David, whom God's prophet Samuel blessed. Samuel told David that through him a royal family would be established.

By making a Jesse tree and reading about David and the other important family stories of Jesus' heritage, children learn how each person on the Jesse tree helped prepare for the coming of Jesus. Some were born thousands of years before Jesus; others just shortly before his birth. Below you will find the names of the persons you will want to include on your Jesse tree and a short scripture passage that tells about each person. You are encouraged to read more than just the suggested scripture.

WEEK 1

Noah	*Gen. 7:1*	*ark*
Sarah & Abraham	*Gen. 17:19, Gen. 18:1*	*tent*
Joseph	*Gen. 37:3*	*coat of many colors*
Moses	*Ex. 20:1*	*tablet of Commandments*
Isaiah	*Mt. 4:13-16*	*scroll*

WEEK 2

Jesse	*Is. 11:1-2*	*tree stump with new growth coming out the top*
David	*1 Sm. 16:13, Lk. 2:4*	*royal crown*

Deborah	Jg. 4:4-5	scales of justice
Ruth	Ru. 1:16 & 2:7	bundle of grain
Jonah	Jon. 2:1, Lk. 11:29-30	whale

WEEK 3

Jeremiah	Jer. 18:1-6	clay pot
Elizabeth & Zechariah	Lk. 1:57, 29-64	writing tablet
John the Baptist	Mt. 3:4-6	river
Mary	Lk 1:30-31	heart
Joseph	Mt. 1:20	carpenter's tools

WEEK 4

Jesus	Lk. 2:7	crib
shepherds	Lk. 2:8-12	sheep
magi	Mt. 2:1-2	star
Simeon & Anna	Lk. 2:24-27 & Lk. 2:36-38	2 turtle doves
YOU	Mt. 12:50	What symbol of yourself will you hang on Jesus' family tree?

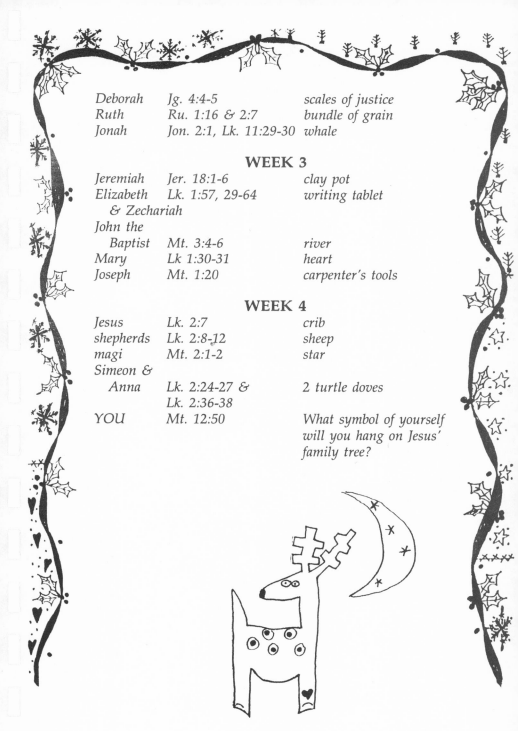

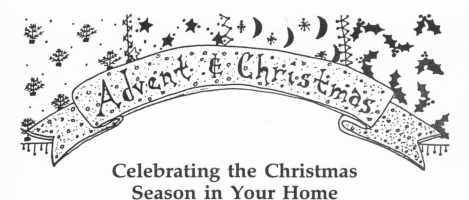

Celebrating the Christmas
Season in Your Home

By: Kathryn H. Schneider & Robert M. Hamma

(Copyright, December 1993 - Catholic Update, "Celebrating Christmas Season in Your Home.")
(Reprinted with Permission)

CHRISTMAS EVE . . .

Christmas Season begins on the evening of December 24th. Many of us celebrate by going to the evening Mass, sharing a special meal, and exchanging family gifts. For others, Midnight Mass is a special tradition. Some share a meal afterward. The variety of celebrations reflects the many family and ethnic traditions that make Christmas so wonderful.

Activity: Blessing Our Christmas Gifts

Before you open your gifts with your family or special friends, you might first gather together and offer this prayer:

Loving God, giver of all gifts, we thank you for these gifts before us. We have carefully chosen each one and wrapped it with love. As we now offer them to one another we thank you for the love we share and the joy you have given us by your coming among us on this night.

CHRISTMAS DAY . . .

During the four weeks of Advent we lit the candles on our Advent wreaths as we awaited the coming of Christ. Now on Christmas Day we proclaim the coming of Jesus, the Light of the World. The Gospel of John, read during the Mass of Christmas Day, proclaims: "The light shines in the darkness and the darkness has not overcome it." *(John 1:5)*

Activity: Christmas Candle

Place a large candle at the center of the Advent wreath or perhaps on your table to express the light of Christ among us throughout this season. Find a beautiful candle at a craft store or make one of your own. Choose a thick candle that is proportionately short, perhaps white, red, or green. You may wish to paint or carve a suitable symbol, such as a star, on the candle.

Here is a prayer for lighting the candle:

Leader: *Christ our light has come!*

All: *Christ our light has come!*

Leader: *Lord Jesus, you have come into the world to show us the infinite love of God. Dispel the darkness of our hearts with your light. Let your love shine upon us.*

All: *Christ our light has come!*

DECEMBER 26: Feast of St. Stephen . . .

Because St. Stephen was the first martyr, he is given the honor of being remembered on the day after Christmas. His martyrdom *(see Acts 6 and 7)* also reminds us that Jesus was to be rejected and put to death.

Stephen was one of the original seven deacons, appointed by the apostles to take care of the needs of the poor in the Church. Thus this day has been associated with caring for the poor and hungry, as the carol "Good King Wenceslaus" reminds us. In England and Canada this day is called Boxing Day because it was the day when the poor boxes were opened and their contents distributed to the needy.

Activity: Serving the Poor

This is a day to reflect on what we can do for the needy, not only during the season, but also throughout the year. Discuss with your family or friends or explore in your heart some specific ways you can get involved in ongoing service to the poor whether it be through prayers or direct service. Don't overlook simple activities like visiting a sick relative or friend, cheering up a lonely person, or making a contribution to a special charity.

DECEMBER 27: Feast of St. John, Apostle and Evangelist . . .

St. John is the second of the "companions of Christ" whose feast follows close upon Christmas. John is known as the beloved Disciple because of the special friendship he shared with Jesus. His feast day is a good occasion to recall the importance of Christian love and fellowship. Part of the traditional celebration of this day was the blessing and drinking of wine because, according to legend, St. John once drank a cup of poisoned wine without ill effect.

Activity: Remembering Our Friends

This is a day to remember those who share a special friendship with us, like John did with Jesus. It is fitting to drink a glass of wine or grape juice in their honor, especially if they are apart from us during the Christmas season. Invite each family member to name one special friend for whom he or she is most grateful. Then all take a drink together. This might be a good occasion to pray spontaneously for your own list of special friends.

A recipe for St. John's Wine is found in the beverages section of this cookbook.

DECEMBER 28: Feast of the Holy Innocents . . .

Matthew's Gospel reports how King Herod, out of fear and jealousy of this newborn king, "...ordered the massacre of all the boys in Bethlehem and its vicinity two years old and under..." *(Mt. 2:16)* Having been warned in a dream, Joseph took Mary and the baby and fled to Egypt. Jesus escaped, but these innocent little ones became the victims of Herod's insane fear.

Activity: Children in Need

Are there children in your neighborhood, school, or community who could use your help? Perhaps you could discuss with children in your life ways for them to reach out to children who need friends. Or, you could get involved in your local Christ Child Society. (Local chapters supply clothing to children in need.)

Make some vanilla pudding. Place a spoonful of raspberry or strawberry jam in the center. It symbolizes the blood of these tiny martyrs. This may sound gory, but may lead to some interesting discussions.

FEAST OF THE HOLY FAMILY . . .

This celebration takes place on the Sunday between Christmas and New Year's Day. The events surrounding the slaughter of the innocents and the flight into Egypt lead us naturally to consider the life of the Holy Family. Their life together is hidden from us until Jesus is 12 years old. Then we learn how he was separated from his parent on a pilgrimage to Jerusalem. What we do know of the life of the Holy Family reveals qualities such as courage, resourcefulness and patience that continue to speak to us as families today.

Activity: Celebrate Your Family

Celebrate your family or friends. Sit together in a circle. By turn, let each one name one or two good qualities of each person and thank God for him or her. Then mention one hope you have for each person in the coming year. End with a sign of peace and the Our Father. Another option could be for the family to hold hands at the meal prayer and for a father or mother to ask for God's blessing on the family.

Teach your children a new game, the Like-About Game. Next time they argue, make them stop and look each other in the eye and tell each other something they like about the other.

482

NEW YEAR'S EVE . . .

As the year comes to a close we look back and remember. We are grateful for the many ways God has blessed us and sorrowful at the pain the year may have brought us. All around us this day we hear the nostalgic words of the Scottish song "Auld Lang Syne:" "Should old acquaintance be forgot and never brought to mind...for auld lang syne" (literally, "for old long since"). The song evokes the memory of people and places from our recent and distant past. In faith we know that Christ, the beginning and the end, is present in every moment of our lives, uniting the people and events of the past, present, and future by his love.

Activity: Thanksgiving for the Year

Once again, sit together in a circle. Let each one name a good thing that happened during the past year and thank God for it. Then mention a hope for the coming year.

NEW YEAR'S DAY . . .

On this day we celebrate the Solemnity of Mary, the Mother of God. Following the ancient tradition of celebrating the octave (eighth day) of an event, we celebrate again the mystery of Jesus' birth, but this time with our eyes on Mary. This is actually the oldest feast of Mary in our calendar. When we celebrate her as the Mother of God, we are at the same time celebrating the divinity of Jesus who was truly human and truly God. In recent times January 1st has been designated as a day of prayer for peace. This recommendation calls us, as the new year begins, to pray and work for peace in our homes, in our nation, and in our world.

483

Activity: Blessing the New Year

Offer this prayer to ask God's blessing on the year ahead:

God our Creator, in your goodness you have given us the gift of life and this new year which lies before us. Help us to live each day with gratitude. Strengthen us to make peace in our families, in our neighborhoods, and throughout the world.   Amen.

In Conventry, England, it was a custom to visit one's godchild on New Year's Day and bring him or her a "God-cake." It might be fun to begin a tradition of somehow remembering your godchild or children on this day with a card or some small gift to let them know they are special to you and your family.

SOLEMNITY OF THE EPIPHANY . . .

The word *epiphany* is derived from the Greek word meaning "manifestation" or "appearance". On this day we celebrate the revelation of the birth of Jesus the Christ to all the nations. The Three Kings represent all the peoples of the earth. The traditional date for the celebration of Epiphany is January 6th. We now celebrate this feast on the Sunday after January 1st so that we may all participate in the liturgy.

In eastern regions of the early church, such as Egypt and Syria, Epiphany was the only celebration of Christ's birth. It included the remembrance of both his birth and his manifestation to the whole world. Like Christmas, Epiphany was celebrated on the day of winter solstice. But because the Eastern

484

calendar was 12 days behind the one used in Rome, Epiphany fell on January 6th. This is how the tradition of the Twelve Days of Christmas came about.

Today, Russia, Greece, Spain, Latin America, and other places follow this tradition and celebrate Christ's birth on January 6th. For us, the focus of Epiphany Sunday is on the manifestation of Christ to the world and the coming of the Three Kings. As today's first reading puts it: "Nations shall walk by your light and kings by your shining radiance." *(Is. 60:3).*

Activity: Blessing Your Home

Because this was the day the Three Kings visited the house of Jesus, the custom of blessing homes on Epiphany Day developed. After the blessing, the initials of their traditional names -- Caspar, Melchior, and Balthaser -- were written in chalk on the back of the door. They were enclosed by the year and connected by a cross in this way: $19 + C + M + B + 94$. You may wish to adapt this practice using crayon and paper.

Use this prayer to bless your home as you place the sheet on your door:

Lord Jesus, the Three Kings followed the star that led them to your home. Help us to find you in this house through the love we share. Bless our home and all of us during this year ahead.   Amen.

Have someone light and hold your Christmas candle during your blessing ceremony. This is a reminder that we are still in Christmas season.

As part of our parish tradition, we celebrate Epiphany with a party. We begin with family skating at our local skating rink, followed by a potluck at our parish hall. The closing celebration takes place in the church where we are visited by LaBefana, the ageless wanderer. She shares the story of her search for the infant, Jesus, and then gives small gifts to the children. One year each child got a small bag of frankincense and myrrh.

FEAST ON THE BAPTISM OF THE LORD . . .

Following our celebration of Christ's manifestation to the world on Epiphany we celebrate his baptism, the beginning of his public ministry to both Jews and gentiles. This celebration takes place on the Sunday after Epiphany Sunday.

Activity: Remembering Our Baptisms

As a family, share recollections of the baptism of each child. Bring out the baptismal candles, the christening gowns, or other remembrances of that day. Light the candles and reread the account of Jesus' baptism in Mt. 3:13-17. Then join hands and pray Our Father.

A tradition that we've adopted from the Lutheran church in Winterset is to give each child a rose the Sunday before his or her baptismal anniversary. The rose is to remind children of this special event, and it is hoped that parents will plan something special, perhaps the child's favorite meal by candlelight, a favorite dessert, etc. One family celebrates by having a brunch on the Sunday the child receives his or her rose with all the relatives invited.

A Christmas Memory
By: Elma Tracy

When I was eight or nine years old at Christmas, we had about 10 inches of snow. In those days there were no snow plows. Men cleared their own roads with scoop shovels just wide enough for a team and sled to pass through the drifts. The sled was a 26" high wagon box on two sets of runners pulled by a team of horses.

This Christmas we were having midnight Mass at our country church three miles from our home. While Mother, Dad, and we children were getting ready to go to church, my sister, who was older than I, harnessed the horses and hitched them to the sled. Dad had put straw in the bottom for a sort of cushion for us kids to sit on. He and Mom sat on a spring seat and he drove. They had a lap robe and Mom had a fur-lined coat. Dad had a sheepskin-lined storm coat. They made us kids keep covered with a horsehide robe as it was very cold.

Some folks had sleigh bells on their horse's harness and that really sounded nice to us. We didn't have any bells, but the runners on the sled made a sort of whining sound as they slid over the snow.

The church was lit by kerosene lamps held in brackets about six feet high on each side of the church. I think there were about five on each side of this small wooden church. The church had a very nice sounding bell which could be heard a couple of miles on a clear night.

The candles seemed nicer at night, and I didn't think the Mass was very long that night either. I really enjoyed it all, and we knew we would get our gifts when we got home. My older sister would keep

the wood stoves going while we were gone as she was also babysitting my younger brother.

After Mass we went back to the sled; Dad untied the team from the hitching post, and we crawled back under our horsehide robe. It seemed a long time going home. We were warm all huddled together and when we did near home, the sky in the east was turning light. We knew it wasn't long before it would turn red and it would be morning. Then Christmas Day would be here at last. We would have coffee cake for breakfast and would soon smell the stuffed chicken roasting in the oven for dinner. Our house would seem so warm and cozy, like no other day in the year.

Fond Memories
By: Victoria L. Williams

As I look back on my childhood, I have many fond memories from Sunday dinners and drives through the countryside to sledding parties at a friend's farm. But no memory is more precious than Christmas time.

Every year was rich with tradition. Christmas Eve Day was spent preparing for a trip to Grandma's house where we would spend the evening with my aunts, uncles, and cousins. Dinner was a feast with turkey and dressing, pumpkin pie, and of course, Grandma would make a special plate of spaghetti because she knew it was my favorite. After dinner, all the children would play upstairs, never very far from the

Christmas tree, somehow always knowing where our gift was and bragging if it was the largest. Names had been exchanged earlier in the season, and the game of guessing who had our name was complete when we arrived at Grandma's house. The excitement would build and finally when we thought we could stand it no more, our parents would announce that it was time to open the gifts. The cheers and laughter of us children put a smile on their faces as they passed out the gifts.

After the paper was picked up and the new toys were sprawled across the floor, talk would turn to Santa Claus. Would Santa reach our house before we got home or would we have to wait until morning to open our gifts? We all hoped he would put our town at the top of his list! As our parents watched us play, Dad and my uncles would quietly disappear. A short time later they would return, yawn and stretch, and say it was time to go home. We would run to get our coats and boots and pile in the car for the short trip home.

Before we left, Dad would call Cy. Cy was an old gentleman whom Dad worked with. He had no family to be with during the holidays, so several years before, Dad had invited him for Christmas dinner. He enjoyed it so much that we made sure that he was part of the family from then on. Cy would meet us in front of the house, and as we pulled up my sisters and I would jump out of the car and run up to the window hoping we would see the beautifully wrapped packages. And sure enough, Santa had miraculously arrived, the presents placed neatly under the tree with loving care. We sat around the living room and opened our gifts one by one. We were already half asleep by the time we went to bed that evening.

Christmas morning was spent getting ready for Christmas Mass. The church looked beautiful, decorated in red flowers, bows, and a large nativity scene on the altar. The choir sang perfect harmony throughout the Mass and the closing song was always "Joy to the World" which was accompanied by a trumpet. After Mass we joined my mother's family.

Grandma Mary and Grandpa Buck lived in a small town 30 minutes away from our town. The trip was short, but Grandpa was always impatient. By the time we arrived at his house and walked in the door, he was seated at the head of the table ready to eat. The adults would eat at the table and the kids would eat on trays in the living room. After dinner and the dishes were done, we would watch Dicken's "A Christmas Carol" while the adults played cards. The day was always relaxing with family talk and lots of love.

Many years have passed since then and my cousins and I are spread throughout the country with children and lives of our own. I only hope that I can give my children as many warm and happy memories as my parents gave me.

Nativity Scene

By: Mary Bricker
(Greenfield, Iowa)

When our children were young, my husband John started a yearly event, building a rustic outdoor nativity scene. It was always completed several days before Christmas and remained up until Epiphany.

The project was a family endeavor. The boys and their dad would tour the countryside for small evergreen trees that would become the sides of the stable or sawed off to make a wooden roof. Several weeks before Christmas, the girls would begin coloring Christmas scenes. These scenes were taped together and covered our picture window giving a backdrop of stained glass to our scene.

After the exterior was completed, the boys and their dad would bring in bales of hay for inside the stable and for the manger. The younger girls relinquished one of their prettier dolls for baby Jesus and wrapped the doll in white flannel. The Blessed Mary was a beautiful painting that Dad had painted. The painting was placed beside the manger and was draped with blue satin from a gown never worn. The day before it was to be worn, our first grade daughter came down with the measles. It was only fitting that it should adorn the Blessed Mary.

John was a vet and when everything was almost ready, he and our oldest son would take the vet truck and trailer and pick up two or three lambs and donkeys. They were placed in the stable. Then, the whole family gave John instructions on placing the blue lighting and the floodlights.

As people drove by and stopped, the girls opened their bedroom windows and sang Christmas carols.

Each year song birds would come to be a part of the scene, and we would inherit a stray dog and sometimes a cat. They would stay in the hay until the scene was taken down.

One year our scene was just completed, when what should appear but a big shaggy dog with a torn bleeding ear and a matted coat of dirty fur. The children dragged him into the house, and he allowed John to treat his ear. Then, we all worked cleaning him up until he was just beautiful. The children named him Sparky, and he immediately responded to that name.

Sparky was quite smart, could climb trees, and would herd our 4-H calf into the barn. With his big tongue, he lavished kisses on us all. During the day, he played with the children and helped them care for the donkey and lambs. At night, he would jump over the wooden fence and lay down by the lambs.

Although we kept his tummy full and poured our love upon him, he left the day after Epiphany.

Now the children have gone their own ways. It's been a long time since we had the nativity scene, but I still remember the peaceful, happy, simple times we shared.

WE BELIEVE IN ST. NICHOLAS

Our Ostentatious Christmas Tree

By: Mary Bricker
(Greenfield, Iowa)

My mother had just moved to California and as she was not able to take her Christmas decorations, we inherited them. Usually our tree was very simple, covered with popcorn balls and decorations the children made. This year, however, our tree was stupendous with fancy golden ornaments and huge red bulbs. We were so proud of our fancy tree.

We had been waiting for a phone call from our oldest daughter to let us know when she could be picked up in Des Moines. We got her call, but she said that she would need a ride all the way from Iowa City because the conductor would not allow her on the train. (Years ago there was a train from Iowa City to Des Moines.) It seemed she had a big Christmas surprise package that was too large to go on the train. It was decided that one of her sisters would drive to Iowa City to bring her home.

Upon their return, we knew why she wasn't allowed on the train. She had a gilded cage with the cutest little monkey in it. He was dressed in a colorful shirt, pants, and cap.

That evening after church, a group of the kids' friends came to see our monkey. Of course he had to be let out of his cage! Unfortunately, the crowd scared him and he scampered up our Christmas tree right to the very top, close to the ceiling. Before we could rescue him, the beautiful tree weaved back and forth, then came crashing to the floor. Our monkey survived, but the beautiful ornaments were pieces of splintered glass.

Maybe we were too proud of our tree. We all eventually realized the glamorous tree wasn't as important as our simple one. Christmas was, after all, being together as a family.

The Christmas Pageant
By: Joanne Nichols

I have many beautiful Christmas memories, however, the ones I can still close my eyes and nearly see are those when I was a child at Sacred Heart in Chariton. We always had a beautiful Christmas pageant at the Midnight Mass.

Mothers worked for weeks making the costumes for all the children in kindergarten through sixth grade.

We always had to lie down in bed around eight p.m. and sleep for a couple of hours. Then Mom would get us up to be at church by eleven for the procession that began shortly before midnight. The smallest angels led the way, all in long white robes with their wings outlined in gold tinsel. Each angel carried a candle into the darkened church and a colored ribbon indicating the nine orders of angels. I can still remember how thrilled I was the year I was chosen to be the angel who got to ring the bells at midnight and how heartbroken I was the year I was chosen to be the Blessed Mother in the beautiful light blue silk gown, but I got the chicken pox and couldn't go.

We also had the Three Kings and shepherds as part of the pageant leading up to midnight. The church was always packed with non-Catholics of the area too. I remember being tired and happy as we returned home about two in the morning from the pageant.

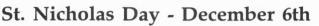

St. Nicholas Day - December 6th
By: Shirley Bittinger

My mother died in 1939 when I was 6 years old. When I was 9 years old, my father had to board my three younger brothers and myself in St. James Catholic Orphanage in Duluth, Minnesota. We only stayed a couple of years till Dad could make home arrangements for us all.

On December 5th, the nuns had us hang our long brown stockings at the end of our beds in anticipation of a vist from St. Nicholas. If we had been good children we would get candy and fruit from St. Nick, but if we had been naughty we would get a lump of coal.

I guess St. Nicolas decided we all had some good in us, as I never saw anyone get a lump of coal.

Recollections of Christmas
As told to Mary Anne Roby by her
99 year-old mother, Laura Pilmaier.

About one week before Christmas, the stores would decorate windows and families would put up crib scenes and other decorations, but the tree would always go up on the day before Christmas. During that week, almost every evening was spent baking cookies and candies to offer to guests who would visit between Christmas and New Year's Day. Most of the children believed in Santa until about 10 years of age. Santa always came on Christmas Eve and the custom was that he brought each child one special gift. There were no electric lights in those days so the trees were decorated with

495

real candles, popcorn, cranberries, and beautiful ornate ornaments. Buckets of water had to be kept around the tree for emergency use; still there were quite a few tree fires in those days and eventually the use of lit candles was discontinued.

The churches always had wonderful crib scenes, and the children always loved seeing this and waiting for the infant to be placed in the manger on Christmas Day.

We went to church in our horse driven carriage. Ours was very nice, and we were excited when our parents bought our beautiful new horse. The owner told us the horse wouldn't eat until we said, "Good morning" and shook his front hoof. That was always fun and we loved him very much. It was very nice being driven to church through the snow in our beautiful horse driven carriage.

My father was a wonderful chef so after church the relatives met at our house for a very festive dinner. Before the guests left, we sent each one away with a little stocking made of netting and filled with the cookies and candies made just before Christmas.

The Christmas festivities never ended until January 6th when St. Nicholas came and left us all a little bowl of oranges, candy, and nuts. That day was called "The Feast of Little Christmas" and after that people took down their trees, put away their decorations, and the holidays were over -- all except the memories which really do last a lifetime.

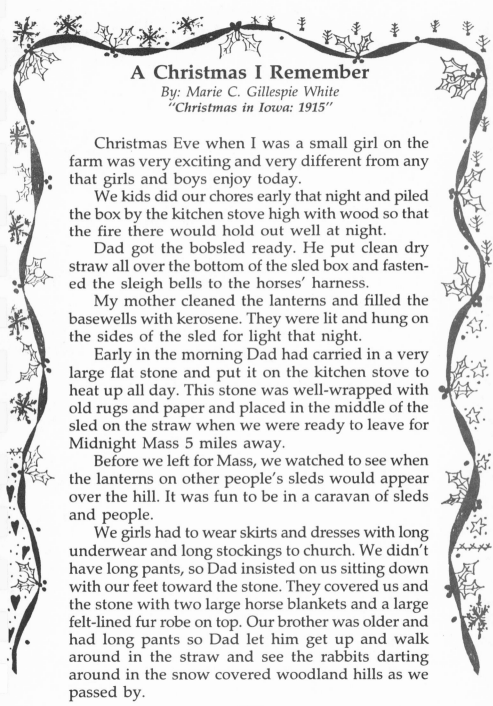

A Christmas I Remember

By: Marie C. Gillespie White
"Christmas in Iowa: 1915"

Christmas Eve when I was a small girl on the farm was very exciting and very different from any that girls and boys enjoy today.

We kids did our chores early that night and piled the box by the kitchen stove high with wood so that the fire there would hold out well at night.

Dad got the bobsled ready. He put clean dry straw all over the bottom of the sled box and fastened the sleigh bells to the horses' harness.

My mother cleaned the lanterns and filled the basewells with kerosene. They were lit and hung on the sides of the sled for light that night.

Early in the morning Dad had carried in a very large flat stone and put it on the kitchen stove to heat up all day. This stone was well-wrapped with old rugs and paper and placed in the middle of the sled on the straw when we were ready to leave for Midnight Mass 5 miles away.

Before we left for Mass, we watched to see when the lanterns on other people's sleds would appear over the hill. It was fun to be in a caravan of sleds and people.

We girls had to wear skirts and dresses with long underwear and long stockings to church. We didn't have long pants, so Dad insisted on us sitting down with our feet toward the stone. They covered us and the stone with two large horse blankets and a large felt-lined fur robe on top. Our brother was older and had long pants so Dad let him get up and walk around in the straw and see the rabbits darting around in the snow covered woodland hills as we passed by.

497

We loved our horses, especially that they pulled us through the snow and over the hills. Listening to the bells, the horses' feet treading through the snow, their little snorts while we were cozy and warm under the covers was adventuresome.

I was a wiggler and wanted to get up and run around in the straw but Dad said, "No." So I lay back in the straw and looked up at the stars, watched for some falling stars, and dreamed about an angel flying high in the sky, flying on its way to sing "Christ is Born."

When we arrived at the church, Dad tied the horses to the rack along side of the other horses and covered each of them with one of the blankets that had covered us. Mother made sure the stone was well covered with the fur robe so it would retain some of its warmth.

I loved going into church and seeing so many flickering candles in the beautiful shiny gold holders. I couldn't take my eyes away so I stumbled into the seat. The organ music was lovely too. You see we had no radio or T.V. in those days.

When we arrived home Dad took care of the horses and Mother prepared a big breakfast. We all were so hungry. It was good.

Now that we had been to church with Christ and prayed, we could open our presents. One present for each of us was the usual. Also, there was an orange and candy. Oranges were a rare fruit in our home and in most homes then.

We dressed in our warm night clothes in the living room by the light and the warmth of the hard coal burner stove.

Before we went upstairs to our cold rooms, Mother handed

us from the oven a warm brick wrapped in much paper. These we placed in our icy cold beds so we would cuddle down for the rest of the night.

We knew that on Christmas, tomorrow, we would make good use of our little sleds on our big hill.

Christmas at St. Anthony's
By: Fr. Frank Palmer

Imagine the whole left side of a church sanctuary filled with Dicken's Collectibles: cottages, houses, churches, storefronts, all radiantly lit and tucked amid folds of star studded paper against a backdrop of a decorated Christmas tree!

When I was growing up as a youngster in St. Anthony's parish in Des Moines, I had an uncle who made Christmas a memorable tradition for our family and really for the entire parish. His name was Ignatius or 'Uncle Noche' (his Italian derivative), as we called him. For as long as I can remember, he would construct the Christmas creche in our parish church. However, this was no ordinary creche; it was a picture book portrait from a European countryside. He would have a dozen or so full grown Christmas tress along the wall on the left side of the sanctuary; in the center of the trees, he would place the creche. He would surround the creche with miniature cottages and storefronts complete with figurines. He would have trails, slopes, receding snow areas, lights on the trees. It was a beautiful sight!

Ritually, he would begin his preparations right after Thanksgiving, coming to the church after work. Placing of the trees would be first; then the meticulous laying of starched paper over the desired area. He would fold and weave, placing the appropriate figurine or cottage where he wished. I remember going over to the church after school measuring each day's progress, until it was ready for Christmas.

Finally, the big moment, Christmas Eve, Midnight Mass. We would go as a family. We lived approximately eight blocks from the church. Some years it would snow, adding a sparkle to the evening. For such a festive occasion, the church was always jammed with worshippers, some standing in the foyer. The choir would be singing Christmas carols and when midnight approached, the lights would be turned off, and the procession would begin. Msgr. Lalley, our pastor, carried the infant Jesus in his arms. As he processed down the aisle to the strains of "Silent Night, Holy Night," my Uncle Noche would slowly pull a lighted star along wires that were suspended from the wall in the back of the church to the sanctuary wall in front. Gradually the star was pulled into its place high above the creche in the sanctuary. As Msgr. Lalley arrived with the infant to the creche, Noche would turn a switch, and the whole village scene would instantly light up: cottages, storefronts, poles with lanterns, all neatly tucked in among the folds and Christmas trees. Msgr. Lalley would then bless the creche.

It was a scene to behold! In his own way, it was Noche's yearly gift to the Infant Jesus and to the whole parish.

"The Yule Log"

By: Cindy Watson Pottebaum

Growing up in Marshalltown, Iowa, we lived far away from grandparents, so we usually spent Christmas Eve with our neighbors, the Logans. We had spent a lot of time with them and they became our "second family."

After 7:30 p.m. Christmas Eve services, we would go to the Logan house and have a "Yule Log Hunt." The kids would pair up and get clues as to where our moms had hidden the decorated log. It usually took an hour or more to find it, and the winning team would drag it home to use in the fireplace that night. They also received a special prize for finding it.

As we ate Christmas goodies and warmed up by the fire, we would share our crazy stories about where our Yule Log clues took us. Then Santa would come and pass out gag gifts, selected especially for each person. After having a great time laughing and playing games, we would head back home to sleep and await Christmas Day.

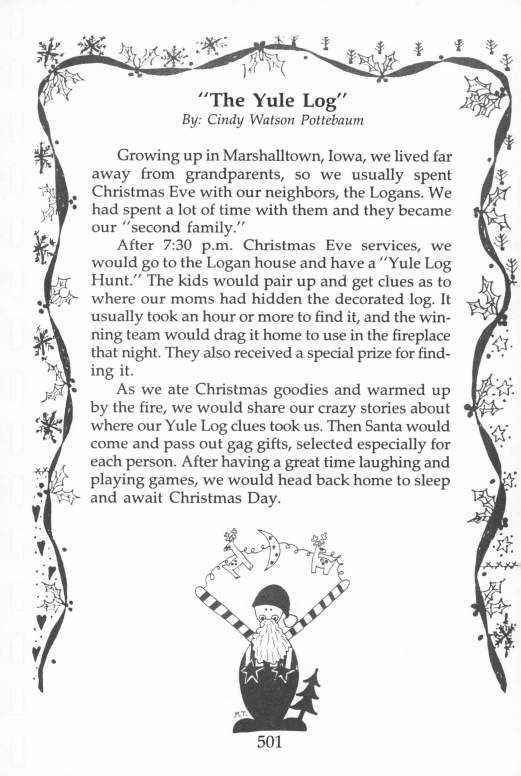

Advent & Christmas

Santa

M.T.

Index

1994

-Index-

MADISON COUNTY

APPETIZERS, DIPS, AND BEVERAGES

BREADS

BRUNCH

CAKES AND FROSTINGS

CANDY

COOKIES AND BARS

DESSERTS

HERBS

MEATS, MAIN DISHES,
AND
MEATLESS MAIN DISHES

509

PIES

SALADS AND DRESSINGS

510

SOUPS AND SANDWICHES

TEA TIME

VEGETABLES

RECOLLECTIONS AND STORIES

ADVENT AND CHRISTMAS